HANDBOOK OF

IS MANAGEMENT

1996–97 YEARBOOK

ROBERT E. UMBAUGH
EDITOR

AUERBACH PUBLICATIONS
A Division of Warren, Gorham & Lamont
Boston and New York

Other books edited by Robert E. Umbaugh:

Productivity Improvement in IS
Quality and Control in IS

Permission to print "A Strategy for Outsourcing" was granted by NDMA Inc.
© 1994 N. Dean Meyer and Associates, Inc.

Printed in the United States of America

Published in the United States in 1996
by Auerbach Publications
RIA Group
31 St. James Avenue
Boston MA 02116 USA

15   14   13   12   11   10   9   8   7   6   5   4   3   2   1

Contributors

ANN SHELTON ANGEL, *President, Technologies Training of the Triad, Inc., Winston-Salem NC*

EILEEN BIRGE, *Director of Information Technology, BSG Alliance/IT, Inc., Houston TX*

CHRISTINE V. BULLEN, *Visiting Assistant Professor, Fordham University Graduate School of Business, New York NY*

ROBERT DEMICHIELL, *Professor, Information Systems, Fairfield University, Fairfield CT*

SEAN D. DOYLE, *Marketing Coordinator, Oracle Corp., Redwood Shores CA*

DONALD R. FOWLER, *Year 2000 R&D Project Manager, IBS Conversions, Largo FL*

PAUL GRAY, *Professor, Programs in Information Science Department, Claremont Graduate School, Claremont CA*

HAL H. GREEN, *Vice-President, Business Development, Aspen Technology, Inc., Houston TX*

RUTH GUTHRIE, *Professor of Information Systems, University of Redlands, Redlands CA*

BARBARA J. HALEY, *Ph.D. candidate, Management Information Systems, University of Georgia, Athens GA*

GILBERT HELD, *Director, 4-Degree Consulting, Macon GA*

WEN-JANG KENNY JIH, *Professor, Management Information Systems, University of Tennessee, Chattanooga TN*

JERRY KANTER, *Director, Center for Information Management Systems (CIMS), Babson College, Babson Park MA*

WILLIAM R. KING, *University Professor, University of Pittsburgh, Pittsburgh PA*

ROBERT MARCUS, *Consultant, Boeing Computer Services, Seattle WA*

N. DEAN MEYER, *President, NDMA, Inc., Ridgefield CT*

NANCY BLUMENSTALK MINGUS, *President, Mingus Associates, Inc., Williamsville NY*

NATHAN J. MULLER, *Consultant, The Oxford Group, Huntsville AL*

JOHN P. MURRAY, *Technical Resource Manager, Compuware, Madison WI*

KATE NASSER, *President, CAS, Inc., Piscataway NJ*

STUART NELSON, *Partner, Government and Financial Services, CSC Consulting, Minneapolis MN*

ED NORRIS, *Senior Security Consultant, Digital Equipment Corp., Littleton MA*

PATRICK OWINGS, *President, GIT, Inc., Chattanooga TN*

JOSEPH PIAZZA, *Certified Disaster Recovery Planner, JAS Technology, Wilmington DE*

JOSEPH J. PRUSKOWSKI, *Vice-President and Chief Technical Officer, Inter-Connections, Inc., Bellevue WA*

STEVEN RABIN, *Chief Technologist, American Software, Inc., Edgartown MA*

HOWARD A. RUBIN, *President, Rubin Systems, Inc., Pound Ridge NY*

DONALD SAELENS, *CIO, Minnesota Department of Revenue, St. Paul MN*

NAVEED SALEEM, *Associate Professor of MIS, University of Houston-Clear Lake, Houston TX*

S. YVONNE SCOTT, *Manager of Business Systems and Planning, GATX Corporation, Chicago IL*

STANLEY H. STAHL, *President, Solution Dynamics, Los Angeles CA*

DJOEN S. TAN, *Director, Tanconsult, Information Management, Hilversum, The Netherlands*

ROBERT E. TYPANSKI, *Manager of Data Access Services, Bayer Corp., Pittsburgh PA*

RAY WALKER, *Senior Consultant, DuPont Engineering, Wilmington DE*

HUGH J. WATSON, *C. Herman and Mary Virginia Terry Chair of Business Administration, University of Georgia, Athens GA*

LEO WROBEL, *President, Premiere Network Services, Inc., Dallas TX*

Contents

Contents

Introduction

DISCUSSIONS WITH TODAY'S IS MANAGERS raise recurring themes: outsourcing, insourcing, client/server computing, process reengineering, data warehousing, downsizing, rightsizing, customer satisfaction—the list goes on and on. It is very much in vogue to talk and write about the strategic use of information systems in business. The idea is for organizations to gain competitive advantage by using information in some way that competitors cannot match quickly enough.

The business press has glorified select information systems that gave (in some cases retrospectively) a competitive advantage to the organizations that developed and used them. As a result of these impressive examples of profiting from the use of information-based systems, the entire information systems industry has been encouraged to search for competitive systems. IS managers trying to heed this advice, however, have found that it is easier said than done.

In many cases, organizations neglect the basics. Most of the organizations that have succeeded in creating information systems of substantial value can attest that the basics remain as important as ever. Successful companies use thorough, practical business planning, treat information as a resource, and integrate the information advantage with other sound business systems.

REDIRECTING IS ORGANIZATIONS

Let's look for a moment at some of the ways change affects most IS departments and, perhaps most important, the IS management team.

For many years, the IS function has been considered a support organization—often one with a minor role in the enterprise. Now, more and more organizations view the IS function in a new light. In some cases (though, admittedly, still relatively few), IS management plays a truly strategic role as part of the organization's policy group. In many other cases, IS management is not involved at the policy level but plays a greater role in strategic enterprise issues than it has in the past.

A second important way that the IS role is changing involves the nature of the assignments given to IS staff. Closer and more frequent ties to user departments are common. The IS department is involved in training and consulting tasks, and users are more likely to involve members of the IS staff in their planning sessions.

HIGHER-QUALITY WORK

IS managers should evaluate what constitutes high-quality work—where perfection is needed and where it is too costly to pursue—and the organizational implications of a quality improvement program. The Ford Motor Co., for example, found that higher quality did not come from adopting a simple slogan. It took years of work and a great many process changes for Ford to realize substantial improvements in the quality of its cars and light trucks. It also took a powerful dose of competition from the Japanese and a drop in market share to shock Ford into recognizing that customers wanted a higher-quality product. At Ford, the program is working—but only after massive effort and organizational growing pains.

Slogans alone will not improve quality, nor will giving the nod to the idea that rewards should be based on quality. The real job for IS managers is to carefully craft and develop an environment that leads to improved quality. More effective control of IS activities must be a part of that environment, as is delegating responsibility for control to the appropriate organizational level.

We live in an era rich in new technology. High-performance PCs with more capabilities seem to be introduced each week. Networking capabilities are expanding. Data base technology is being enhanced rapidly. Almost every aspect of information processing technology is being improved at an ever-increasing pace. In fact, the availability of new technology outstrips most organizations' ability to assess and assimilate that technology. Even research universities have trouble keeping up.

Sometimes our eagerness leads us to institutionalize new technologies before we can properly integrate them. Businesses thus run the risk of once again creating so-called archipelagos—islands of technologies with no bridges in sight—that undermine the goal of having truly integrated, enterprise systems.

MANAGEMENT INVOLVEMENT

Managers who climb the corporate ladder are almost always challenged by complex problems with which they lack familiarity. IS departments face similar challenges in their organizational development.

As the IS function becomes involved at the higher levels of the organization (e.g., through strategic systems, executive information systems, and decision support systems), IS personnel may find that they must keep abreast of rapidly changing technology while learning to understand business issues with which they have less than intimate familiarity. This book aims to help IS professionals meet these challenges.

The *Handbook of IS Management* begins by clarifying the role of the IS management team in information technology (IT) management, strategic planning for IT resources, and business process reengineering. Chapters on the strategic use of client/server technology and how to rein in junk computing provide some easy-to-implement ideas on more effective use of computing resources.

Additional chapters focus on the IS staff's challenges in 4 key areas: supporting internal customers, managing information and data, delivering products and services, and ensuring quality and control. Among the hundreds of topics included in the book, readers will find solutions for implementing data access to corporatewide information, data warehousing, systems development, multimedia applications, operating practices for LANs, benchmarking, auditing, controlling computer viruses, and computer learning.

HOW TO USE THIS HANDBOOK

The *Handbook of IS Management* is an excellent reference for the IS management team—a hands-on source of ideas to improve the effectiveness and productivity of the entire organization.

Many IS managers use the handbook as a training tool. One way to do this is to have members of the team lead discussions of the various chapters. The discussions can be incorporated into regularly scheduled staff meetings or held at a special training session. In this way, IS managers can demonstrate to senior management that the responsibility to train IS staff is taken seriously.

Throughout this handbook, you will find the work of many experts in the field. These authors bring a wealth of experience and education to their writing in an attempt to share with readers some successful techniques for managing IS. I trust you will benefit from the time you spend reading this book.

ROBERT E. UMBAUGH
Carlisle PA
June 1996

Section I
Policy, Planning, and Business Issues

CURRENT TRENDS IN THE IS FIELD make it imperative that IS management rethink IS policy, the strategy that supports the IS function, and planning. The business press reports case after case of IS organizations implementing the most popular approaches to improving service to the enterprise. The problem is that these efforts are failing because they are not integrated with business direction and are not shaped by a comprehensive plan that guides the overall process. Bits and pieces of downsizing, outsourcing, business process reengineering (BPR), critical success factors (CSFs), and other attempts at business redirection will not work if the IS organization lacks a firm understanding of the enterprise's overall direction and a well-stated strategy.

This section of the yearbook helps give meaning to the disjointed efforts that have hindered progress in the past and clarifies the effective use of strategic management techniques in the IS organization.

Companies must modify the way they do business if they are to succeed, and reengineering changes the way they do business forever. Chapter I-1, "Business Redirection and the Role of IT," describes business process reengineering and how IS fits into the overall process. Properly conducted, BPR can have beneficial effects. Because the process cannot occur with the judicious application of information processing technology, IS must play a key role in its success. This chapter provides a comprehensive look at the changes that have occurred in the business environment since the advent of reengineering.

Chapter I-2, "Organizational Architecture for IS," addresses key issues that accompany business reengineering and introduces the concept of IS management plateaus—development stages in the application of information technology. Five management plateaus characterize the development of IT in organizations. On each successive plateau, the costs and risks of the IT investment are higher, but IT's potential to add value to the business and to successfully support business redirection also increases.

Critical success factors were introduced nearly 20 years ago. This management tool helps focus priorities for individual managers, their organizations, and the

IT group. When used properly, the CSF approach can be highly beneficial to productivity and business planning; when poorly applied, the tool is largely disruptive. Chapter I-3, "Reexamining Critical Success Factors," shows IS managers how to use CSFs to think through the complexity that too often surrounds productivity.

Outsourcing brings with it the promise of great reward and regret, depending on how, when, or if it is used. Unfortunately, the risks and costs of outsourcing are sometimes lost amid the rhetoric about outsourcing's benefits. Chapter I-4 presents "A Strategy for Outsourcing" that weighs supposed benefits against realistic outcomes and provides guidelines for cases when outsourcing makes sense. It also clarifies the advantage of retaining the IS function in-house rather than outsourcing this important group to vendors whose agenda is likely to differ from that of the enterprise.

Finally, Chapter I-5 addresses "Strategic Planning for Computer Resources." The management of IT resources is no longer a self-contained operation within IS. From its discussion of problems with user-controlled operations to its development of a collaborative strategy for IS and line managers, the chapter suggests practical strategies for the procurement and management of computer resources.

I-1

Business Redirection and the Role of IT

Wen-Jang Kenny Jih and Patrick Owings

IN 1982, McKinsey & Company consultants Thomas J. Peters and Robert H. Waterman, Jr., co-authored *In Search of Excellence*. The research behind this all-time best-selling business book was conducted at 75 highly regarded companies—about half of which participated in intense, structured interviews during the winter of 1979–1980 and half of which were used for secondary research.

Peters and Waterman found that the companies rated excellent focused on the basics and strived to keep things simple. They identified the eight characteristics of excellent companies as:

- Having a bias for action.
- Being close to the customer.
- Encouraging autonomy and entrepreneurship among employees.
- Achieving productivity through valuing people.
- Having hands-on, value-driven leaders.
- Sticking to the knitting.
- Maintaining a simple organization with a lean staff.
- Maintaining company values while exhibiting tolerance toward individual autonomy.

Peters and Waterman had led a McKinsey task force researching organizational effectiveness. In the course of that project, they found that executives around the world shared McKinsey's own concern that conventional approaches to organizational design were ineffective. Most were particularly suspect of the latest version of the complex matrix form of organizational structure. Still, no other organizational scheme seemed effective either. Through continued research, Peters and Waterman developed the 7-S Framework for organizational structure (see Exhibit I-1-1), which included the usual strategy and structure as well as what came to be known as the organization's software: style, systems, staff (i.e., people), skills, and shared values (i.e., culture).

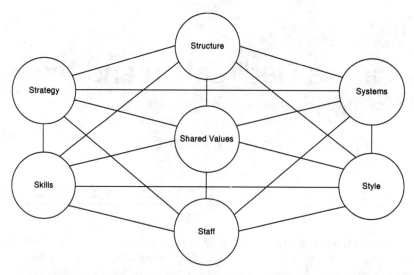

SOURCE: T.J. Peters and R.H. Waterman, *In Search of Excellence: Lessons from America's Best-Run Companies* (New York, 1982).

Exhibit I-1-1. The McKinsey Framework

PUTTING THEORY INTO PRACTICE

What makes all of this so important to a discussion of reengineering and information technology is the fact that much of *In Search of Excellence*'s theory about how successful organizations work was put into practice by many companies throughout the 1980s. During that time, some of the same companies were putting $1 trillion of investment capital into information technology—computers and software—but saw little payback from their huge investments. Profits were flat and annual growth in productivity rose a mere 1% overall, compared with almost 5% annual productivity growth in Japan.

The smallest gains were realized in the service sector despite the fact that 85% of the IT spending took place in that sector of the economy. During the same time period, manufacturing productivity improved 44%. An MIT study of this data concluded that the expenditures on IT capital were less effective in improving productivity than any other type of expenditure considered.

During the decade from 1983 to 1993, the number of PCs in service soared from three million to 23 million and sales volumes for the machines jumped from $1.9 billion to $40.8 billion. During the same time period, mainframe sales rose from $16.5 billion to $35.5 billion, which is significant but sluggish growth. It is better than it appears, because the price/performance ratio improved significantly. The proliferation of PCs in the workplace, however, did not produce white-collar productivity increases.

The reason for the failure of technology to increase productivity in the workplace is painfully obvious. IT professionals and laypersons alike regard IT as a powerful tool to solve existing problems and to improve existing processes and procedures. However, the solution lies in applying several business tools in concert. By using organizational design, human resources policies, and IT, an organization can be strategically reengineered to compete effectively and the benefits of IT can be realized.

MANUFACTURING SUCCESS

Why has the service sector failed to realize productivity gains when manufacturing, through investment in factory automation, including IT, has seen a 44% gain in productivity? The difference is that manufacturers, suffering under international competition, have altered the way people work.

In the automobile industry, restructuring to reduce product development times led to autonomous work groups comprising cross-functional members from design, manufacturing, marketing, and purchasing. Engineers are estimated to spend less than 50% of their time on engineering tasks and the balance of time on coordination of tasks. This waste of engineering expertise on coordination efforts reduces productivity below acceptable levels. What is all this coordination about?

According to Michael Hammer, coauthor of *Reengineering the Corporation: A Manifesto for Business Revolution,* the Adam Smith, Frederick Taylor, and Henry Ford business models are to blame. These models work in a world of stable growth, not in today's world of constant change. Although change of any kind presents substantial challenges, organizational change is far more formidable than technological change. As a result, companies often automate the existing processes they now do manually and see only small, incremental changes in performance. Thus automating simply provides more efficient ways to do the wrong kinds of things. Hammer further believes that the problems facing companies are not the result of their organizational structures but of their process structures. Overlayering a new organization on top of an old process is like pouring soured wine into new bottles.

SO WHAT IS REENGINEERING?

Hammer defines reengineering as the fundamental rethinking and radical redesign of business processes to achieve dramatic improvements in critical, contemporary measures, or performance (e.g., cost, quality, service, and speed). Reengineering is one of the things a company must do when it changes direction. The rate of change today has increased to the point where companies cannot predict what an application will be five years from now. In many instances in the past, it took two to three years to implement a manufacturing IT system. A system could be obsolete by that time, so an entirely different, more dynamic approach is required.

Companies start reengineering by being customer focused, which means asking customers what they want and how they want it. But, even more than that, it means knowing when customers want something and what distribution methods and flexibility are required to meet those needs. This knowledge drives manufacturing processes to meet customer needs better than the competition. This is today's version of Peters and Waterman's staying close to the customer.

Something so obvious should not require books to be written about it or seminars to teach it. But, as Peters and Waterman pointed out, managers—especially American managers—were products of business schools that overemphasized quantitative methods and ignored, for the most part, things (e.g., the quality revolution) that successful practitioners found important. H. Edward Wrapp of the University of Chicago said business schools have done more to ensure the success of the Japanese and West German invasion of America than anything else.

Hammer found that IBM Corp., for instance, had gone through several episodes of attempting to fix a process rather than change it. All had failed. MBA approaches (e.g., queuing theory and linear programming) failed to produce results. What did work was reengineering. In the struggle to bring about change, reengineering provides companies with the means to change work units from functional to process oriented, jobs themselves from simple tasks to multidimensional work, people's roles from controlled to empowered, training to educating, work measurement to results measurement, advancement based on performance to advancement based on ability, values from protective to productive, managers from supervisors to coaches, organizational structures from hierarchical to flat, and executives from scorekeepers to leaders.

FLEXIBILITY IS THE KEY

The business system diamond (see Exhibit I-1-2) shows that process redesign alone is not enough. For reengineering, companies must focus on all four points to achieve results. Information technology plays a vital role in business reengineering; in fact, Hammer calls it an essential enabler of reengineering.

Information technology does not, however, force companies to reengineer. They are forced to reengineer by competition, customers, and change in the market. Without information technology, however, reengineering would be a fantasy. In Hammer's opinion, companies have not even scratched the surface of what information technology is going to do to organizations or businesses. Even today the backbone for reengineering manufacturing processes is going to be an information system that interfaces with the customer and puts all the people who have to make that product, including suppliers, on a single network.

The following example from Japan illustrates perfectly what Hammer is talking about:

> Kao Corporation, Japan's largest soap and cosmetics company, has installed a highly flexible, highly integrated system designed to maximize the flexibility of the whole company's response to demand. One system links sales and shipping,

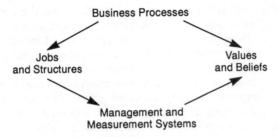

Business Processes

Jobs and Structures

Values and Beliefs

Management and Measurement Systems

Exhibit I-1-2. The Business System Diamond

production and purchasing, marketing, hundreds of customers' cash registers, and thousands of salespersons' hand-held computers in such a completely integrated fashion that Kao claims the year-end closing of the books can be completed by the first day of the new year with a complete financial statement.

At Kao, the split-second linkage extends back to the factories and labs and brand managers can see daily sales, stock, and production figures. Within two weeks of the launch of a new product, information is so complete that any adjustments in packaging or anything affecting sales success can be immediately addressed, long before conventional marketing surveys yield answers. The network is claimed to virtually eliminate the lag between an event in the market and the knowledge of the event within the company. Such rapid information allows Kao to adjust production levels and increase variety without increasing stock levels. In fact, Kao grew to 564 products from 498 while inventory levels decreased.

In this example, flexibility is a key factor. Flexibility means that if a competitor can read the market quicker, manufacture many different products on the same line, switch from one to another instantly and at low cost, make as much profit on short runs as on long ones, and bring out offerings faster—or do most of these things—other companies lose. Current estimates by Aleda Roth, a manufacturing expert at Duke University business school, show that American companies are a generation behind on flexible manufacturing systems.

This should not be a revelation, because historically it has taken a generation or more to master new technology. Electric motors, for example, were used in the 1890s, but substantial productivity gains were not observed until the technology was widely applied in factories almost 30 years later. Information technology is just now penetrating every sector of business, 40 years after IBM sold its first commercial mainframe. Knowing only of mainframe computing, many computing professionals did not foresee the advent of the PC in the workplace and therefore predicted a tightly controlled, hierarchical management structure. Distributed computing redistributes power and breaks down the hierarchy, an unforeseen result of the widespread use of computers in business.

A basic shift in the organization of work with the widespread dismantling of Taylorism, and the concept of an endlessly changing organizational design (i.e., a reconfigurable organization that is small and flexible), have played a significant role in the management revolution that has enabled companies to embrace information technology in radically different ways. The new information-age economy is evolving with its fundamental sources of wealth being knowledge and communication as opposed to natural resources and physical labor. In the future, sustainable competitive advantages will depend more on new process technologies and less on new product technologies. Comparative advantage based on people replaces the comparative advantage of natural resources.

THE NEW REVOLUTION

Today's companies are in the midst of a revolution that compares with the Industrial Revolution in scale and consequence. This revolution is driven by radical changes brought about by the globalization of markets, the spread of information technology and computer networks, the dismantling of organizational hierarchies, and the information-age economy. Each of these four revolutions is happening simultaneously; each causes one another and affects one another.

GLOBALIZATION

Information technology has greatly reduced the importance of a nation's internal market. The Japanese, for instance, have the capacity to produce and sell six times as many video recorders as they themselves can consume. Because of information technology, global market economics of large scale and scope are open to even relatively small countries. The business cycle no longer determines the condition of the overall US economy; global competition does. The net effect is that the chance of the entire economy booming or busting simultaneously is greatly diminished, which means greater economic stability. A negative, however, is that individual companies must react immediately to competitive moves by global rivals. Fortunately, current information technology is creating tools that enable companies to respond competitively.

PARADIGM SHIFT

Thomas Kuhn's book, *The Structure of Scientific Revolutions*, advanced the idea of a paradigm shift in the way people view a set of shared beliefs at any point in time. The sixteenth century supplanting of the Ptolemaic view of the earth as the center of the solar system with the reality of the sun at the center represents a paradigm shift in scientific thinking.

Today's paradigm shift centers around the current trend in business enterprise that demands replacing the bureaucratic, inwardly focused, unresponsive, unproductive, and stifling command and control hierarchy with a dynamic organization that is quick to respond; has a flatter, team-oriented organizational structure based on commitment rather than control; seeks quality and productivity; is focused outward; and is heavily networked with customers and suppliers. The paradigm shift in the information technology that supports business enterprise began in the late 1980s and is driven by the demands of the new, competitive business environment and the monumental changes in the nature of computers. It parallels the new enterprise and works the way people in the new enterprise work—ignoring boundaries in data, text, voice, and image providing the framework for team-oriented business structures.

Information technology enables the open, networked, integrated, client/service business enterprise to become a reality through open, networked, integrated, client/server computing. The excellent company as defined by Peters and Waterman in 1982 is the requirement rather than the exception because organizations that fail to make the paradigm shift will fail or, at best, become insignificant.

Simply throwing computers at business problems does not cause the business enterprise to be reengineered, and the misuse of technology can block reengineering by merely reinforcing the traditional way of doing things. Conventional thinking is the enemy of the paradigm shift, and even Thomas J. Watson, Sr., the founder of IBM, was a victim of his own lack of vision when he proclaimed the worldwide demand for data processing computers to be less than 50 machines! Twenty years later, the minicomputer was seen as a mere toy, and 10 years after that the personal computer was characterized as unnecessary because larger computers were meeting the demands of business.

The application of PCs, of course, was not in duplicating the tasks being performed on large machines, but in entirely new areas of work. Understanding that the conventional, hierarchical ways of thinking about business enterprise severely retard the application of information technology is key to understanding the role of reengineering.

PERFORMANCE RECORDS

To fully grasp the effect of reengineering on an operation, a person has only to look at manufacturing sector performance versus service sector performance. In the 1980s, manufacturing accounted for 15% of IT spending while the service sector accounted for 85%. Productivity in manufacturing, however, rose 44% compared to a mere 1.9% in the service sector. Service industries require 2.5 support personnel for each profession as compared to 0.9 support personnel per manufacturing professional. The performance in manufacturing is superior to the service sector because global competition has become so intense there is no room for poor productivity. Manufacturers have invested in automation, including IT, while also focusing on altering the way people work. Conversely, the service sector has merely automated existing processes without eliminating the causes of poor performance. Manufacturing has reengineered, the service sector has not.

Research involving 300 firms found that the failure to change the organization was the largest obstacle to the efficient application of IT.

The work steps in the service sector were designed in the early 20th century around the mass-production factory using the concepts of scientific management, sometimes referred to as Taylorism, after Frederick Taylor, who advanced the theory. Much of scientific management can be traced back to Adam Smith, the economist who popularized the division of labor concept in *The Wealth of Nations*, published in 1776. But these concepts apply only when there is an expanding market and little competition.

In today's global economy, companies are ruled by the three C's: customers, competitors, and change. Global competitors who can produce goods faster, cheaper, and with better quality while providing better customer service, innovating faster, and producing greater variety have presented a major challenge to the concepts of Taylor and Smith. To meet the challenge of competition, companies must take a flexible, highly integrated, process view of business.

SUCCESS STORIES

The basic differences between the functional view, the information systems view, and the process view of a common task, accounts payable, is shown in Exhibit I-1-3. The significant difference between the process view and the other two views is readily evident. This difference lies at the heart of reengineering because reengineering is about the radical redesign of business processes. Some examples of companies that have successfully used reengineering follow.

Ford Motor Company. Ford has transformed its numerous international design studios into a single, global organization through reengineering enabled by information technology. Using Silicon Graphics workstations and special software, design workgroups at Ford transform design drawings into full-size mock-ups. Changes in the design made manually on the mock-up are fed into the computers using a digitizer. Using global communications costing $35 million annually, Ford links the workgroups of designers, engineers, and marketers interactively for the first time in computer history. Ford expects a 50% return on investment in computer technology, mostly from reducing engineering labor costs. Estimates of the amount of time engineers spend performing essential engineering functions or making technical decisions is less than 50% of the time. Ford relies heavily on improving this ratio to realize dramatic savings. Additional savings are expected from the elimination of mistakes and late changes in designs.

Caterpillar. Caterpillar reengineered its key processes in response to seven quarters of losses in the mid-1980s brought in by Japanese competition, rising manufacturing costs, and declining market share. Caterpillar spent $1.85 billion modernizing 17 factories to increase flexibility and quality while cutting inventories and cycle time. The return on investment is running at a 20% annual rate and inventories have been reduced by almost 40%. The information systems

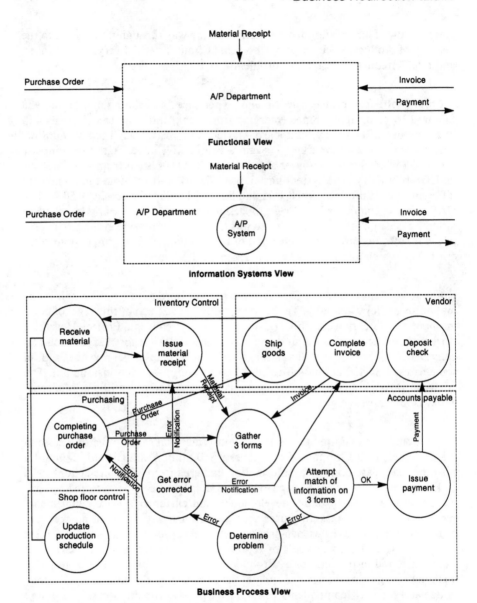

Functional View

Information Systems View

Business Process View

SOURCE: D.L. Schnitt, "Reengineering the Organization Using Information Technology," *Journal of Systems Management* (January 1993).

Exhibit I-1-3. Functional and Information Systems Views

create a flow of information from suppliers all the way through the process to the delivery of products to customers, who benefit from faster delivery, lower prices, and a 50% reduction in quality problems.

Chris-Craft. The pleasure boat maker experienced a declining market in 1988 followed by bankruptcy. Since emerging from bankruptcy under the ownership of a new parent company, Outboard Marine, Chris-Craft has become the low-cost producer in a flat market. To gain a competitive advantage, the company invested $300,000 in a computer-aided design (CAD) system from Unigraphics, an EDS subsidiary. The system has allowed Chris-Craft to triple the number of different designs produced each year and has cut development costs by 50%. The CAD system enabled Chris-Craft to design and build a new model in three months instead of the usual nine months, resulting in market timing that produced a 34% increase in revenues. All of this would have been impossible without CAD, which allowed workgroup design and manufacturing.

American Express. American Express spends more than $1 billion on information technology annually. Taking competitive advantage of this level of commitment to IT, corporate officials launched a new concept, Project Hearth, a work-at-home scheme based on communications links that cost $1,300 each and deliver a 26% increase in call volume, a 46% increase in travel revenue, and, in some cases, a $4,400 annual office rental cost savings for each installation. The potential throughout the communications industry, where millions of people work, is for vast savings.

Dell Computer. Going back to Peters and Waterman's idea of getting close to the customer, Dell Computer Corp. invests $50 million annually to maintain a customer data base that stores information gathered from 35,000 telephone calls or E-mail messages received each day. The data base can be accessed by employees in marketing, product development, and customer service departments across the country. Marketing uses the data to narrowly focus on market segments targeted for greater penetration. The response rate for small-business mailings rose 250% as a result of refining the sales pitch based on customer feedback stored in the data base. Product developers use the data base to guide them in packaging new offerings and purchasing watches the data base for trends in demand for such components as larger hard drives or monitors. The online customer data base gives Dell a competitive advantage in the direct-sales market.

Aetna Life and Casualty. Through reengineering and IT, Aetna Life and Casualty Co. went from 22 business centers, staffed by 3,000 people requiring 15 days to issue a basic insurance policy, to only four business centers, staffed by a reduced work force of 700 issuing the same policy in only five days. This dramatic improvement took place in one year through extensive application of PC networks and reengineering. Aetna's application of information technology and reengineering to sales activities realized savings of $40 million and a 25% increase in sales force productivity.

Federal National Mortgage Association. Fannie Mae saw serious barriers to growth in the early 1990s because its mainframe computer could not keep pace with the growing volume of millions of mortgages to be pooled and sold as securities. Fannie Mae's response to the approaching crisis was a reengineering effort that dismantled the centralized hierarchy of departments and replaced them with cross-functional teams linking financial, marketing, and computer experts at the beginning of each transaction. A network of more than 2,000 PCs and new software makes the system accessible to workers with minimal training. The most astounding part of Fannie Mae's IT-enabled reengineering effort is that the $10 million investment paid for itself in less than one year!

When interest rates dropped and volume nearly doubled to $257 billion, only 100 new employees were added to the existing 3,000-person workforce. The economies realized from reengineering allowed profits to jump 13% to $1.6 billion.

These examples represent only a small portion of the thousands of such cases publicized in articles on information technology and reengineering. The overriding principle is this: the big payoff is in IT enabling companies to create entirely new business processes. Big returns come from reengineering, not computers. This fact is illustrated in the experience of FedEx, which has achieved a highly integrated organization, delivering more than 1.5 million packages each day using real-time tracing and tracking. The integrated computing architecture, which enables accurate measurement of service quality and minute-by-minute information on parcel movements, gives FedEx a competitive edge that most companies have been unable to duplicate. Companies fail to duplicate such success when they fail to remember what reengineering is not: it is not automating, restructuring, downsizing, reorganizing, delayering, bureaucracy busting, quality improvement, TQM, or continuous improvement. Reengineering is starting over with a clean sheet of paper.

FOCUSING ON TOMORROW

According to Tom Peters, there are no excellent companies today. If there are, he says, they believe only in constant improvement and constant change and thrive on chaos. What was nice-to-do in 1979 became must-do in the late 1980s. It is not difficult to see the direct connection between the concepts advanced by Peters and Waterman in 1979 and those of Hammer and Champy in 1993. Some may characterize *In Search of Excellence* as the what and *Reengineering the Corporation* as the how. The how comes from a must-do situation.

Companies must remember that they are never finished with reengineering, it is governed by the strategy of *kaizen*, or continuous improvement. Kaizen is the single most important concept in Japanese management and the key to Japan's competitive success. Tom Peters says that a company should add 10 differentiators every 90 days as a minimum kaizen strategy. The challenge for companies is to be constantly changing in a constantly changing world.

The seven key industries of the next several decades—microelectronics, biotechnology, the new materials industries, civilian aviation, communications, robots plus machine tools, and computers plus software—are all brainpower industries that can be located anywhere on the face of the globe. Where those important industries will be located depends on who can organize the brainpower to capture them. Inventing and perfecting new processes will become the primary advantage for achieving sustainable competitive advantage in the 21st century. People recognize inventing and perfecting new processes as reengineering; therefore reengineering is key to survival in the 21st century.

Improved software is the key to making information technology accessible and business more productive, but the most powerful computer and the integrated network mean little if the average office worker cannot use them. According to the Center for Advanced Technologies (Fairfax VA), workers using a graphical user interface (GUI), such as Windows or Macintosh, are twice as productive as workers operating without GUIs. In addition, workers using software correctly can accomplish in one day what would otherwise require five days, research by CSC Index, Inc. (Cambridge MA) has concluded. Obviously, educated, highly skilled workers, supplied with easy-to-use software are the key to realizing the computer advantage.

LEGAL ISSUES

Other concerns lie in the legal web that threatens to entangle businesses in volumes of restrictive regulations that can rob them of the flexibility needed to remain competitive in the global environment. Other problems center around rights to computerized information maintained in an estimated 10,000 federal government data bases and an unknown number of state and local government data bases. Estimates of the value of the information range from $1.5 billion to $50 billion. A recent confrontation developed between several Ohio newspapers and the Ohio Department of Motor Vehicles, which demanded $21 million for copies of computer tapes holding Ohio's motor vehicle records. The state finally agreed to an amount closer to the records' actual cost: $400. Issues that must be resolved include the following:

- Does the public have the same right to computer data as paper documents and if so, in what form?
- Is the government obligated to provide information stored on tapes or disks in a more readily usable form?
- Are the privacy rights of citizens jeopardized?
- What is the reasonable price of computerized information?
- Does the government have any right or justification in charging the public for such information?

The problems of antiquated communications laws and electronic monitoring of employees also affect the application of information technology.

CONCLUSION

But what about the positive side of information technology and reengineering? What do the visionaries foresee? Hammer says expert systems, for example, will allow companies to replicate the judgment, wisdom, and intelligence of high-capability people through the computer network. The concept of the extended enterprise that would allow customers and suppliers to access information systems is emerging. The new technology of extended reach enables radical changes in enterprise relationships with external organizations.

Major technological changes have historically brought upheaval and disruption to societies and their economies. Improved productivity, driven by this disruptive technology and the accompanying workplace changes it brings, is the only route to productivity gains. Those productivity gains, according to Columbia University economist Frank R. Lichtenberg, are crucial for our long-term economic well-being and are still the only way to boost the nation's standard of living. Reengineering enabled by information technology offers the key to increased productivity. Reengineering is not restructuring, or downsizing, or any of the other business quick fixes tried by many in the past. Says Peter F. Drucker, reengineering is new, and it has to be done.

I-2

Organizational Architecture for IS

Djoen S. Tan

THE ROLE AND IMPACT of information technology in organizations have changed significantly during the past decade. The application of IT has evolved from an administrative support function to a more strategic role. The costs of IT have also evolved from an overhead expense to a business investment. Yet, there is serious concern that the expected value of the investment in IT will not be achieved.

According to the Management in the 1990s research program of the MIT Sloan School of Management (the MIT90s framework), N. Venkatraman noted that the inability to realize value from IT investments is mainly due to the lack of strategic alignment. His strategic alignment model showed that alignment should involve business strategy, business organization, IT strategy, and IT organization. Accordingly, this alignment can be performed on several levels of IT-enabled business reconfiguration.

The above-mentioned research program conceptualizes an organization as consisting of five sets of forces that are in dynamic equilibrium as the organization is subjected to influences from the outside socioeconomic environment and the external technological environment (see Exhibit I-2-1). General management's task is to ensure that all five forces move through time to accomplish the organization's objectives. This MIT90s framework is a so-called consistency model.

The MIT90s framework can be extended to a more complete consistency model of IT management. This chapter defines five IT management plateaus by combining this consistency model with a stage model of the application of IT, based on the levels of IT-enabled business reconfiguration of Venkatraman. The model can also be applied to coalitions of organizations.

CONSISTENCY MODEL OF IT MANAGEMENT

A consistency model of an organization views the organization as an open system with a limited number of basic subsystems (aspect systems) or "forces." To achieve internal and external stability of the organization, these subsystems

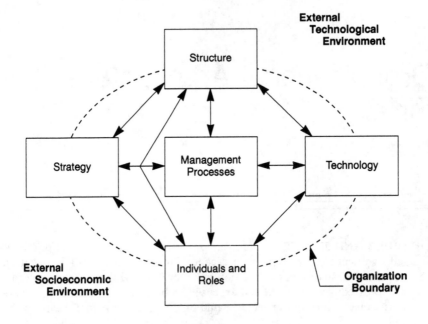

Exhibit I-2-1. The MIT90s Framework

strive for harmony and consistency with each other by mutual adaptation and adjustment.

A consistency model of IT management in organizations is shown in Exhibit I-2-2. The model consists of three domains:

- The environment.
- The organization domain.
- The IT domain.

In accordance with the MIT90s framework, five subsystems are distinguished in the organization domain:

- *Strategy.* The organization's objectives and the ways the organization tries to realize these objectives; the selection of markets and products and the marketing mix (the business plan).
- *Structure.* The organization structure, roles and responsibilities, decision-making procedures, and planning and control systems.
- *Technology.* The technology used for the business processes.
- *People.* The knowledge, skills, ambitions, attitudes, and social relations of the people in the organization (human resources).

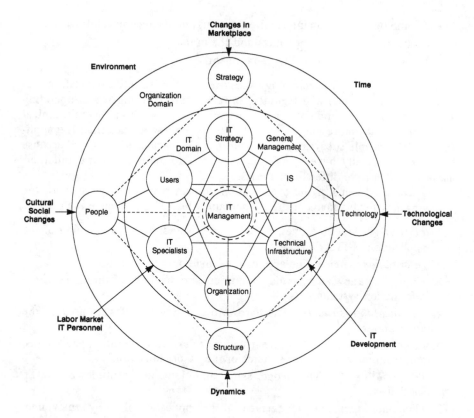

Exhibit I-2-2. Consistency Model of IT Management

- *Management.* General management (senior and line management) responsible for the selection and realization of the business strategy and for adjusting the subsystems in the organization to each other.

All the subsystems influence each other by mutual interaction. The first four subsystems are influenced, respectively, by the changes in the marketplace, the dynamics (the rate of change), the technological developments, and the cultural and social changes in the environment.

The IT domain is a subdomain of the organization domain. In the IT domain, the subsystems of the organization should be focused on the problems concerning the application of IT. For example:

- Strategy focuses on IT strategy.
- Structure focuses on the IT organization structure.

- Technology focuses on information systems and the technical infrastructure.
- People focuses on IT specialists and the users.
- Management focuses on IT management.

In the IT domain, the technology subsystem is divided into information systems (i.e., applications) and technical infrastructure (i.e., hardware, operating systems, and network and data base management systems) because the technical infrastructure has more long-term and common characteristics than the applications. The people subsystem is divided into IT specialists and users because these groups usually have a different view of information systems and their managers often have different priorities.

The five subsystems of the organization domain therefore interact with the following seven subsystems of the IT domain, which also influence each other:

1. *IT strategy.* The objectives, rules, selected standards, and planning of the application of IT.
2. *Information systems.* The applications, including manual procedures.
3. *Users.* The knowledge, skills, ambitions, and attitudes of the users of the information systems.
4. *Technical infrastructure.* The hardware and systems software used by the applications.
5. *IT organization structure.* The structure, roles, responsibilities, procedures, and planning and control systems of the IT organization.
6. *IT specialists.* The knowledge, skills, ambitions, and attitudes of the IT specialists.
7. *IT management.* The management of the application of IT by senior, line, and IT managers, who are responsible for an optimum application of IT by adjusting the aforementioned subsystems to each other.

Subsystems 1 to 3 express the need of the organization for information systems and the knowledge and skills of the users to make use of these systems (the demand side). Subsystems 4 to 6 concern the available IT organization and the capacities of the IT staff and the technical infrastructure (the supply side). IT management should balance the supply and the demand sides at an acceptable cost level.

Environmental forces also directly influence the subsystems of the IT domain within an organization—for example, the impact of IT developments on the technical infrastructure and the labor market for IT personnel on the IT specialists. Finally, in Exhibit I-2-3, time is shown as a third dimension and is dealt with in the following discussion.

IT MANAGEMENT PLATEAUS

Within a continuously changing environment, an organization is continuously searching for new situations in which the subsystems are in equilibrium with each other. Time is a critical factor. The consistency model of the IT organization

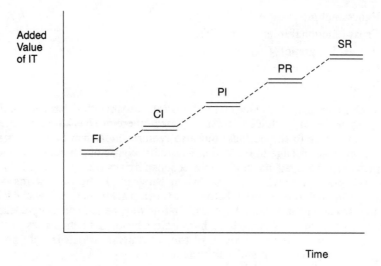

Notes:

FI Functional integration
CI Cross-functional integration
PI Process integration
PR Process redesign
SR Scope redefinition

Exhibit I-2-3. The Five IT Management Plateaus

should therefore be combined with a stage model to take into account time and the changes in the environment and the organization as time passes.

A stage model of an organization assumes that the development of an organization occurs stage by stage, much like human development from childhood through adolescence to maturity. A stage or phase cannot be passed over but can be passed through faster.

A well-known stage model of the development of automation in organizations is Nolan's Stages Theory. Nolan described six stages: initiation, contagion, control, integration, data administration, and maturity. Later on the last two stages were changed to architecture and demassing.

In this chapter, an IT management plateau is defined as a period of time during which the subsystems of an organization and its IT domain are in balance with each other. An IT management plateau is regarded as a development stage of the application of IT. The term "plateau" has previously been used in a framework to plan and control the realization of an IT architecture.

Based on the levels of IT-enabled business reconfiguration of Venkatraman, the following five IT management plateaus are identified:

1. Functional integration (FI).
2. Cross-functional integration (CI).
3. Process integration (PI).
4. Business process redesign (PR).
5. Business scope redefinition (SR).

On each successive IT management plateau the organization is further tailored to the possibilities of IT. Each successive plateau therefore has a higher potential of IT to add value to the business but also requires more complex information systems, more knowledge to build these systems, bigger organizational changes to implement these systems, and higher costs and risks (see Exhibit I-2-3).

On each plateau, a dynamic equilibrium between all the subsystems of the consistency model should exist before the next plateau can be reached by a harmonic development of the subsystems. In this way, periods of relative stability alternate with periods of change. A harmonic development preserves unity by simultaneous and equivalent growth of the subsystems, which is only possible through mutual interaction and adjustment.

The mutual adjustment of the subsystems occurs by means of communication and coordination within and between the organization domain and the IT domain. Each successive plateau requires a higher degree of communication and coordination.

A higher IT management plateau cannot be reached by, for example, merely changing the organization structure and building new information systems. If the IT strategy is not changed, the technical infrastructure not adapted, and management, users, and IT specialists not properly trained, the operation will fail.

Subsystems of the IT Domain on Each IT Management Plateau

Functional Integration. On this first IT management plateau, the information systems support the existing workflow within the business functions (functional departments), such as manufacturing, sales, and finance. Apart from some adjustment of procedures, no organizational changes are needed. Each business function often exploits different technical platforms.

The objective of the application of IT is operational efficiency. The IT plan is an inventory of the users' demands. The IT organization mirrors the business organization and can vary from a completely centralized IT organization for a functional organization to a completely decentralized IT organization for a divisional organization. The information systems are developed and built by the IT specialists according to the functional specifications of the users. Within the IT budget, the IT decisions are made by the IT management.

Until the beginning of the 1980s, most organizations were on this IT management plateau.

Cross-Functional Integration. The information systems integrate the flow of work across several functional departments, such as purchasing, inventory control, and accounting. These systems are more complex to develop and to implement compared to those on the first plateau. Minor organizational adjustments may be required, but the functional structure and the working methods remain largely unchanged. The technical infrastructures of the functional departments concerned must work together. There should at least be some common standards.

The objective of the application of IT is to improve the effectiveness of the business. The IT plan is derived from the business plan. The IT organization cannot be completely decentralized because some form of central coordination is required. The information systems are developed and built by the IT specialists according to the functional specifications of the users. IT decisions are made by a steering committee of line and IT managers.

Most organizations today are situated on this plateau.

Process Integration. The information systems enable the work of a complete business process to be carried out as a single entity. A business process is a set of logically related work activities that achieves a tangible and important business result, such as customer order fulfillment, new product development, or after-sales service. Usually these activities are done by several (functional) departments. The implementation of these information systems requires extensive organizational changes and an integrated technical infrastructure.

The objective of the application of IT is to achieve competitive advantage in existing product-market combinations. The IT plan and the business plan should be adjusted to each other. The IT organization on this plateau cannot be completely decentralized. On the other hand, a centralized organization is not in accordance with the responsibility of the line managers for their information systems. Therefore a selective decentralization (a combination of centralization and decentralization) should be chosen—for example, decentralized systems development and centralized management of the technical infrastructure.

Together with the users, the IT specialists identify and analyze the most important business processes, using for example, the value-chain method of Michael Porter. A project manager (process owner) for each main business process should be appointed. The information systems are built by the IT specialists under the supervision of line management. IT decisions are made by a steering committee of line and IT managers with a member of senior management as chairperson.

Many organizations for which IT is of strategic importance, such as financial institutions and transportation companies, are now situated on this plateau.

Business Process Redesign. Just as on the former plateau, information systems enable the work of the most important business processes to be carried out as single entities. The existing business processes are not taken for granted, however, but are redesigned or reengineered to make use of IT in new ways. So business processes are performed in ways that were previously impractical or impossible. A customer order fulfillment process, for example, can be eliminated by arranging for customers to place their orders electronically. Dramatic organizational changes are necessary to implement these information systems.

This is, of course, only possible with an integrated technical infrastructure. Furthermore, this technical infrastructure should include CASE tools and standard application modules to speed up systems development. A successful business process redesign often depends on the speed of implementation.

The objective of the use of IT is to realize competitive advantage in existing and new product-market combinations. The IT plan and the business plan should be one integrated strategic plan. Because of the consequences of IT for the entire corporation, the IT organization should be selectively decentralized with sufficient involvement of senior management. Users and management consultants of user departments select and redesign the business processes together with the IT specialists. The information systems are developed by the IT specialists together with the users under the supervision of line management. IT decisions are made by senior management after consultation of a steering committee with the same composition as on the former plateau.

Business process redesign or reengineering (BPR) is a hot item. As yet, only a few pioneering companies have experience with BPR. Most companies today face the challenge of reaching this IT management plateau by the end of the 1990s.

Business Scope Redefinition. Here again, information systems enable the most important business processes to be carried out using an integrated technical infrastructure. Optimum use of IT, however, requires more than the redesign of business processes; even the business scope is enlarged or shifted, if necessary. The redefinition of the business scope gives rise to new business processes and redesign of existing processes. This implies radical organizational changes.

The objectives of the application of IT on this plateau is to realize innovative product-market combination. The business plan and the IT plan form one integrated strategic plan. A highly selective decentralization of the IT organization is required. Users and IT specialists develop the new business processes and the corresponding information systems in small teams (fewer than 10 persons). Line management is completely responsible for the new systems. The new systems must be realized quickly by using appropriate tools and standard application modules as part of the integrated technical infrastructure. IT decisions are made by senior management, because of the consequences for the business scope. The strong involvement of senior management and the close cooperation between users and IT specialists require the organization to be a networked organization.

A networked organization is also called an information-based organization. The essence of a networked organization is the integration of thinking and doing. The main characteristics are:

- A diamond-shaped instead of a pyramid-shaped organization.
- Few hierarchical levels and a minimum of lower-level functions (these functions are automated or outsourced).
- Knowledge workers (managers and specialists) as the dominant force in the organization, working together in varying multidisciplinary teams (a highly selective decentralization).
- Intensive use of IT on all levels of the organization (a networked organization cannot exist without IT).
- Self-organizing and self-learning capabilities, because of the integration of thinking and doing.

Corporations will not reach this IT management plateau before the year 2000; for many, it may well take longer.

This highest plateau does not signify that there will be no further developments after this level. The application of IT has, however, become as standard as the use of paper and pencil, and IT processes have become ordinary business processes.

Exhibit I-2-4 summarizes the seven subsystems for each plateau. The first plateau covers Nolan's first three stages. The second plateau corresponds to Nolan's fourth stage (integration). Stage 5 (architecture) and 6 (demassing) of Nolan have characteristics of the third IT plateau.

The IT management plateaus show the natural development of the application of IT in organizations. Owing to the learning processes of managers, users, and IT specialists, different sections of an organization can be situated on different plateaus.

A faster transition to a higher plateau can be achieved by adequate planning and control of the required activities. The higher plateau is then regarded as the goal of the IT strategy. Intermediate plateaus can be defined, if necessary, to realize the transformation in smaller steps and so enlarge the manageability of the migration.

It is not always necessary to reach the highest plateau as soon as possible. This is only true if IT is of strategic importance for the survival of the organization. The conditions for a successful transition to a higher IT management plateau are:

- All subsystems of the organization domain and the IT domain on the present plateau are in balance (i.e., consistent) with each other.
- Senior management has a vision that IT can be used as a lever for competitive advantage.
- A clearly defined IT strategy exists, supported by senior, line, and IT management.
- A climate of change is created within the entire organization.
- The IT strategy is worked out into concrete action plans or projects for each subsystem.
- Adequate control exists for the realization of the projects.
- Senior management provides sufficient commitment and support.

IT MANAGEMENT PLATEAUS IN COALITIONS OF ORGANIZATIONS

Organizations form together with their suppliers, distribution channels, and customers to create a value system. By working together, the value chain of each of the participating organizations can be improved.

Interorganizational information systems enable organizations to extend their reach and capabilities outward to customers and suppliers. They can support or trigger the redesign of business processes across the boundaries of multiple organizations and have the potential to transform a business, a marketplace, or even an entire branch of industry.

The consistency model of IT management shown in Exhibit I-2-2 can also be applied to a group of cooperating organizations or a coalition of organizations. A

IT MANAGEMENT PLATEAUS / SUBSYSTEMS	FI	CI	PI	PR	SR
IT Strategy	Increase efficiency. IT plan based on user demands.	Increase effectiveness. IT plan derived from business plan.	Competitive advantage in existing PMCs. IT and business plan adjusted to each other.	New PMCs. Integrated strategic plan.	Innovative PMCs. Integrated strategic plan.
Information Systems	Support existing workflow in business functions.	Integrate workflow across business functions.	Enable complete business process.	Enable complete business processes after redesign.	Enable complete business processes after scope redefinition.
Technical Infrastructure	Platform for each function	Common standards	Integrated infrastructure	Integrated infrastructure	Integrated infrastructure
IT Organization	From completely centralized to completely decentralized	From completely centralized to federal	Selectively decentralized	Selectively decentralized	Highly selectively decentralized
Users	Functional specifications	Functional specifications	Responsible for IS realization	Redesign business processes and IS	Design new business process and IS
IT Specialists	Realize IS	Realize IS	Design and build IS	Build IS	Build IS
IT Management	IT managers decide within budget	Steering committee of line and IT managers	Steering committee chaired by senior management	Senior management decides after consulting with steering committee	Senior management decides

Notes:

FI	Functional integration	PR	Process redesign
CI	Cross-functional integration	SR	Scope redefinition
PI	Process integration	PMC	Product-market combination

Exhibit I-2-4. Summary of the Subsystems on Each IT Management Plateau in Organizations

coalition or a strategic alliance is defined as a long-term agreement that is more than a usual business transaction but less than a merger or an acquisition.

The organization domain comprises all the participating organizations. The IT domain refers to their joint application of IT. For a coalition of organizations, the same five IT management plateaus in Exhibit I-2-3 can be distinguished as development stages of their joint application of IT.

The subsystems "IT specialists" and "users" comprise all the participating organizations. The interorganizational systems are developed and built by joint project teams of IT specialists and users of the participating organizations. The involvement of users is stronger on each successive plateau. However, close cooperation between IT specialists and users of the different organizations is more difficult to achieve in this case because of differences in culture, among other things. A short description of the other subsystems of the IT domain for each IT management plateau follows.

Functional Integration. Within a coalition of organizations, functional integration implies transaction automation. High-volume, repetitive paper transactions (e.g., orders, receipt notes, invoices) that flow between the participating organizations are replaced by electronic messages (electronic mail or basic EDI transactions).

The objective of the common application of IT is to increase the speed and reliability of the transactions between the organizations. Usually the messages do not link directly into the main applications of the participants. Apart from minor alterations in the working procedures at the boundaries of the organizations, nothing has to be changed.

The IT strategy, the technical infrastructure, the information systems, and the IT organization of the business participants can remain the same. There is no overall IT management. The situation is similar to a completely decentralized IT organization at a single company.

Cross-Functional Integration. On this second IT management plateau, the interorganizational systems enable all transactions of a procedure to take place in the form of electronic messages. A procedure consists of several related transactions often performed by multiple functional departments, such as an invoice payment procedure. Procedure automation requires a direct link into the application systems of the participants, because transactions have to trigger responses.

The objective of the common application of IT is cost reduction. Working methods within the participating organizations are affected by procedural adjustments, but no change of internal organization structure is necessary.

The IT strategies and technical infrastructures of the participating organizations should enable the realization of these systems. This implies at least an agreement on common IT standards. A steering committee of the involved line and IT managers is needed to define these standards and to supervise the realization of these interorganizational systems. The situation is similar to one decentralized IT organization with cooperation on some common systems. Most present-day EDI applications are situated on the first or the second plateau.

Process Integration. The interorganizational systems enable the execution of a main business process between the participants in a value chain—keeping shelves stocked, for example. This is, of course, only possible when process integration has been implemented within the individual organizations and a common technical infrastructure is available. Process integration requires adjustments of the internal structure and the working methods of the participating organizations.

The objective of the common application of IT is competitive advantage in existing product-market combinations. A joint IT plan should exist that is consistent with the individual business plans and IT plans. The definition and the implementation of the joint IT plan is controlled by a steering committee with members of senior management of the participating businesses. Businesses such as department stores and supermarkets are situated on this plateau.

Business Process Redesign. As on the former plateau, the interorganizational systems enable all the transactions of a main process and are fully integrated with the corresponding process-supporting applications of the participating organizations. In addition, however, the potential of IT is exploited to fundamentally alter the way the business process is carried out. This gives rise to radical changes of the internal structure and working methods of the participants. Sometimes even the boundaries between the organizations have to be adjusted.

The objective of the common application of IT is competitive advantage in existing and new product-market combinations. A joint strategic plan, which integrates a business and an IT plan, is necessary to realize the interorganizational systems and the integrated technical infrastructure. The definition and implementation of this plan is controlled by a steering committee with members of senior management of the participating organizations (a federal IT organization). Only a few pioneering companies have reached this fourth IT management plateau.

Business Scope Redefinition. Business scope redefinition can also occur within a coalition of organizations as a next step after the redesign of business processes across the boundaries of the individual organizations. This implies boundary corrections and dramatic organizational changes of the participating organizations.

The objective of the common application of IT is to realize innovative product-market combinations. Entirely new business and market opportunities may be created. This also requires a joint integrated strategic plan. The IT activities are functionally coordinated by senior management. Because of the strong interdependence of the participants, the steering committee on this highest IT management plateau takes the form of a board of directors. The coalition has in fact become a single (networked) organization. It is expected that coalitions of organizations will reach this highest plateau in the twenty-first century.

Exhibit I-2-5 summarizes the seven subsystems of the IT domain on each IT management plateau for a coalition of organizations. Also within a coalition of

IT MANAGEMENT PLATEAUS / SUBSYSTEMS	FI	CI	PI	PR	SR
IT Strategy	Increase speed and reliability of transactions. IT plan based on users demands.	Increase efficiency. IT plan derived from individual business and IT plans.	Competitive advantage in existing PMCs. IT plan adjusted to individual business and IT plans.	New PMCs. Joint integrated strategic plan.	Innovative PMCs. Joint integrated strategic plan.
Information Systems	Transaction automation	Procedure automation	Enable common business process	Enable common business processes after redesign.	Enable common business processes after scope redefinition.
Technical Infrastructure	Different infrastructures	Common standards	Integrated infrastructure	Integrated infrastructure	Integrated infrastructure
IT Organization	Project organization	Project organization	Federal	Federal	Functional coordination
Users	Functional specifications	Functional specifications	Responsible for IS realization	Redesign business processes and IS	Design new business processes and IS
IT Specialists	Realize IS	Realize IS	Design and build IS	Build IS	Build IS
IT Management	IT managers decide within budget	Steering committee of line and IT managers	Steering committee chaired by senior management	Steering committee of senior managers	Steering committee of senior managers

Notes:

FI Functional integration
CI Cross-functional integration
PI Process integration
PR Process redesign
SR Scope redefinition
PMC Product-market combination

Exhibit I-2-5. Summary of the Subsystems on Each IT Management Plateau in Coalitions of Organizations

organizations, all subsystems on each plateau should be in balance with one another. On each successive plateau, the impact of IT on the individual organizations and the relationships between the organizations is more severe, the costs and risks are higher, but the potential competitive advantage generated by IT also increases.

Adequate planning and control of the required activities is necessary for a purposeful migration to a higher plateau. An essential condition for a successful migration is mutual trust within the coalition. Furthermore, the conditions mentioned in process integration also apply to coalitions of organizations.

CONCLUSION

All subsystems of the organization domain and the IT domain should be in balance with each other for the successful application of IT to occur. Good communication between users and IT specialists must exist, as well as adequate coordination by senior, line, and IT management. Each successive IT management plateau requires a higher degree of communication and coordination.

In organizations, as well as in coalitions of organizations, the subsystems of the IT domain on the lower plateaus are adapted to the subsystems of the organization domain. These reactive applications of IT can offer productivity improvements of 10% to 20%. On the higher plateaus, the subsystems of the organization domain are adapted to the subsystems of the IT domain. With these proactive applications of IT, productivity gains of more than 80% are possible.

Depending on the business organization structure, the IT organization on the lower plateaus can vary from a centralized to a decentralized organization. On the higher plateaus, only a selectively decentralized IT organization is appropriate. On the highest plateau, an organization (as well as a coalition of organizations) transforms into a networked organization.

Because a single organization is formed on the highest plateau, the IT management plateaus can also be used as stepping stones to integrate a group of businesses after mergers or acquisitions. This applies especially to organizations with data processing as the primary business process, such as financial institutions. IT is then used as a catalyst for the integration of businesses.

I-3

Reexamining Critical Success Factors

Christine V. Bullen

THE ISSUE AT THE HEART of reengineering failures is not that managers made poor decisions or that consultants were wrong. The issue is that managers need help focusing on what is critical in their environments. Resources and energy applied to the activities that managers can control and improve will result in successes. Corporate life in today's business world is a mix of scarce resources, unrealistic deadlines, instantaneous communication, demanding customers, and fierce competition. It is no wonder that managers may be confused about where to concentrate their attention.

The critical success factors (CSFs) approach helps managers think through corporate complexity and identify the few key areas critical to the survival of their roles and organizations.

HISTORY OF THE CSF METHOD

Since the introduction of the concept of critical success factors in 1979, many organizations have used the approach as a framework for strategic planning. The CSF method directs managers to determine what must go right for successful achievement of goals and objectives. The ultimate value that the CSF method brings is the ability to focus management attention on the tasks and activities that need to be done well to achieve success.

Examples of critical success factors can be found on many levels. Individuals have CSFs relating to their roles and styles. Departments and divisions of organizations identify CSFs resulting from their missions, products or services, customers, and the personal CSFs of their managers. Industry CSFs derive from products or services, customers, and competing organizations. For example, the director of a major urban hospital identified CSFs covering a broad range of topics from "staying on top of the developing technology" to "the support of my spouse and family." In another interview, the vice-president of R&D saw the partnership between R&D and marketing as a CSF for the division. A study of the grocery industry pointed out two CSFs for individual supermarkets: "the right mix of products for the ethnic groups of customers" and "no lost sales due to stock outs." These examples demonstrate the range of activities and ideas that the critical success factor method can reveal.

The method centers on an interview technique in which managers move through three stages: listing their goals and objectives, identifying the critical success factors necessary to achieve the goals and objectives, and suggesting ways in which the CSFs are to be measured. Skilled interviewers take managers through this process in about one and a half hours and have a toolkit of tested questions to elicit a full range of CSFs.

Before the concept of CSFs was introduced, managers tried to use traditional reports based on accounting information to manage their organizations. Although these documents aided in reporting on where a firm stood in terms of generally accepted numerical indicators, they did not tell managers how they were doing regarding factors the managers could actively manage and control. Unfortunately, this accounting-based information was the only form of management report available in organizations. Critical success factors changed that. The method helped initiate a dialogue between line management and technology management that viewed the information provided to managers in a new light: as information that facilitated management tasks. The use of CSFs to determine what should be reported and how it should be measured revolutionized computer-based information reporting systems. As a result, the phrase has become widely used and the concept has been applied in many industries around the globe. To a certain extent, CSFs helped usher in the age of executive information systems by demonstrating that the availability of relevant computer-based information allows managers to improve their decision making.

HELPING INDIVIDUAL MANAGERS

The initial success of CSFs led to their application in other ways. The CSF method helps individual managers accomplish two vital tasks:

- Thinking through the vast number of activities and issues they must perform and reducing that number to a manageable few.
- Setting priorities on the activities so that attention can be focused on the most critical ones.

A study at the MIT Center for Information Systems Research looked at the critical success factors for chief information officers by interviewing numerous CIOs in major corporations. The resulting CSFs paint a picture of the challenges facing the information technology organization in today's firm. They also indicate where the CIO must concentrate effort to be productive and therefore to succeed in carrying out the responsibilities of this role in today's organizational environment.

The following five critical success factors were found in this survey:

1. Building empowering IS/business relationships.
2. Understanding the business.
3. Increasing cost-effectiveness.

4. Challenging the status quo.
5. Building centralized/decentralized organizations.

The example of these five critical success factors for CIOs demonstrates the power of the CSF method to help individual managers focus on critical activities and set priorities for action. This example also demonstrates that it is possible to capture the key strategic concerns of a manager in as few as five CSFs. Even with only five, the manager still has an enormous undertaking to manage these five areas well and realize success in each of them. The following sections discuss the five factors.

Building Empowering IS/Business Relationships

The information systems function must act in partnership with the business function to create the strategic plan for the future of the firm. Business strategy and technology strategy must be aligned to succeed in a highly competitive, global marketplace. Information technology is an integral part of the products and services in many organizations. IT allows organizations to change their strategies and even their basic businesses and succeed. It is no longer a reactive service that supports a business decision after the fact.

For example, American Airlines found that it made more profit through its Sabre reservation system than through its airline business. Top management is thus beginning to view American's primary business as that of a reservation system and not as that of an airline. The computers are more strategic to American Airlines than the airplanes.

In other industries, the capabilities of information systems surfaced as potential competitive weapons. MCI was able to win 10% of the long-distance telephone service market with its Friends and Family program, based on the design of the billing system. Because AT&T traditionally left the billing for long-distance service to the local telephone providers, it does not have the IS capability to directly challenge this customer benefit. Instead, AT&T uses other incentives to meet this competition head on, such as across-the-board discounts on all long-distance calls. A billing process turned out to be a strategic weapon that has helped MCI maintain a competitive position in the market.

Understanding the Business

In the early days of information systems, computer systems were seen as a support service, not too different from heat or air conditioning and electricity. This view was reinforced by the practice of locating many computer rooms in the basements of office buildings. Most IS professionals were also viewed as nonessential, highly specialized technologists who had no need to understand the business. However, as the strategic role of technology became increasingly more clear, the business role of information technology became more critical. The skill set of IT professionals now requires a heavy dose of business acumen. In some organizations, the CIO is chosen based on management skill—technology experience is not required.

Increasing Cost-Effectiveness

While the focus on technology as a strategic weapon was developing, organizations experienced a tight economy, resulting in a parallel focus on cost reduction and improved effectiveness. The introduction of outsourcing to deal with ineffective technology areas fostered a healthy respect for well-honed IT organizations. Today's CIO is expected to captain an organization that is of strategic importance to the survival of the firm and, at the same time, is "lean and mean."

Challenging the Status Quo

The charge of business process reengineering to obliterate old ways of doing things and create efficient, technology-driven, interorganizational processes has been co-led by the chief information officer in many organizations. The CIO has been in a unique position to visualize how information technology can enhance and upgrade new approaches, create communication links between separate organizations, and revolutionize approaches to old problems. With empowered relationships in place, the CIO can challenge and renew the hidebound ways of the firm.

Building Centralized/Decentralized Organizations

The CIO must build a global organization that acts locally, sets universal standards so that local decision making can occur, and manages the communications infrastructure so that distributed processing can succeed. In today's corporation, IT areas must act in both centralized and decentralized ways to support the strategic needs of the firm.

HELPING ORGANIZATIONS AND INDUSTRIES

In the same way that individual managers can think through their personal CSFs, groups of managers can think through their organization's CSFs, and groups of organizations can think through their industry CSFs.

Organization CSFs

Once an organization's top-level managers have identified their personal sets of CSFs, they can compare the sets for overlapping concerns, related issues, and obvious conflicts. This process can be enlightening and often surprising to a group of managers who have worked together for years and assumed that they knew each other extremely well.

For example, in one high-technology engineering company, the CEO and top management were called together to review the critical success factor process. The CEO agreed to initiate the meeting by presenting a personal CSF list for discussion. The top level of managers were in an uproar when they saw the CEO's critical success factors. The CEO's concerns, as reflected in the CSFs, were operational; that is, the CSF's of the CEO were almost identical to those of the management team. What became clear to everyone was that the CEO, who was also the entrepreneur who founded the firm, was reluctant to give up hands-on control of day-to-day activities. The top management team had been hampered by this controlling style without having explicitly recognized it. By focusing on what each person viewed as critical, the CSF process revealed the conflict and made it possible for the management team to move ahead in a productive manner.

Industry CSFs

Determining industry-critical success factors can be a useful process for helping organizations better understand their competition. This information can lead to strategic decisions about product development and marketing. For example, the American automobile industry was producing gas-guzzling luxury car models at the time of the Arab oil embargo in 1973. This accident of history launched Japanese car success in the US The crisis illuminated an unstated (and probably unrecognized) assumption among US car companies that the gasoline supply would never be threatened. Until the oil embargo, two of the CSFs for US car companies were style and engine power, reflecting their firm belief that these features sold their products in America.

Overnight, the oil embargo altered the desires of the car-buying public. Critical success factors were altered radically to support the development of fuel-efficient cars. In the 1990s, fuel efficiency persists as a CSF, but it has been eclipsed by safety concerns for most consumers. While US carmakers could not have anticipated the oil embargo, if they had been looking at what was critical to remain successful, they would have been in a better position to identify some of these important issues and would have built contingency plans.

INFORMATION SYSTEMS PRIORITIES

The critical success factor method also helps organizations determine their IS priorities. This application has grown out of the original report-oriented use of CSFs. As managers identify their critical activities, the information systems required to support those activities can be determined.

Too often the IS plan for systems development is determined by technology-oriented factors such as sophistication of existing systems, desired skill acquisition, and the desire for interesting advanced technology. IS planning can also be affected by politically oriented factors such as the perceived power of the area requesting the project and who has funding available. When information and communications technology are viewed as strategic tools for enhancing the organization's ability to compete and be productive, the focus on systems to support critical success factors determines the priorities. This focus on factors determining what systems will be built is essential to improving organizationwide productivity.

PRODUCTIVITY ISSUES AND KNOWLEDGE WORK

Productivity is one of the traditional measures of an organization's success. It has also been the foremost nemesis of management since organizational work has become more knowledge work-oriented. As early as 1982, it became clear that measuring output in knowledge work was not the right approach. Michael Packer, in the *MIT Report*, proposed a technique using perceptual mapping to measure outcomes. The creativity of this research was that it underscored the importance of defining productivity within the context of the organization trying to measure it. Most organizations are still struggling to understand the notion that productivity is context-specific.

It should be intuitively clear that generalized notions of productivity make little sense in a knowledge work environment. For example, for many years researchers tried to assign measurable factors to secretarial work. Following in the proud tradition of using lines of code as a measure of a programmer's skill, pages typed and typing speed were thought to be appropriate measures of a secretary's value. However, in interviewing managers on the value of their secretaries, these measures are rarely mentioned. Responses are more along the lines of how well the person manages the office, handles telephone inquiries, manipulates the scheduling, and interfaces with the world outside the office door. Although the number of pages typed is easy to see and count as output, the relationship that a secretary creates between the manager and the outside world is an outcome that, although priceless, is difficult to measure.

If organizations have difficulty measuring the productivity of a secretary (one of the first levels of knowledge work), they are hopelessly lost in measuring the productivity of their top management. However, the Packer approach proposed some useful guidelines. Packer suggested that if knowledge workers were interviewed about their activities, they could define what productivity meant for them. For example, if during interviewing product designers listed activities such as "ability to reuse parts of designs" and "quality of the final design," a picture of productivity in their environment could be constructed. More important, ways in which to facilitate or improve that productivity could be investigated. In this example, computer-aided design (CAD) software could be introduced to help improve these factors. An important addition to Packer's approach would be a way to determine from knowledge workers what their critical activities are.

Output in service industries (which is primarily the output of knowledge workers) should be measured by the service transaction unit itself and results of the performance of the service. Changes in quality should comprise two aspects: product innovations and process innovations. An example for illustrating how these aspects work together can be found in the doctor-patient relationship. A patient's successful outcome, when ill, is a cure. The ability of the doctor to bring about this outcome is based on both the process used to diagnose the patient (the process innovation) and the effectiveness of the drug (the product innovation) in curing what ails the patient. Methods for understanding how to bring about process and product innovations contribute to the ultimate goal of improving outcomes and, therefore, productivity in the services sector.

Management expert Peter Drucker asserts that the greatest challenge facing managers in the developed countries of the world is to raise the productivity of knowledge and service workers. Drucker argues that to improve productivity, organizations need to answer one important question: What is the task? Then the organizations must focus management attention on achieving the key task. The example he uses is the nursing shortage. If nurses were not deluged with paperwork for various insurers, hospital administration, Medicare, Medicaid, and malpractice suit prevention, they would be able to carry out the activities of the task they were trained for—caring for patients. Drucker's bottom line is that if organizations concentrated on the key task, then improving knowledge worker productivity would result. Central to Drucker's approach is organizational understanding of what the key tasks are.

INTERSECTION OF CSF METHOD AND PRODUCTIVITY

During the past 15 years, the critical success factor method has forced managers to identify activities that must go well for them to succeed. That is, CSFs are being used to enumerate productivity factors in knowledge work environments. The context-specific nature of productivity requires an understanding of how a knowledge worker achieves goals and objectives. Once the nature of productivity is understood, measuring it becomes a much simpler task. Using the CSF interview approach helps to focus the knowledge worker's thinking on what is essential to improve productivity.

CSF's help managers identify what product and process improvements are necessary. When a manager uses the critical success factor approach, processes can be streamlined to focus on the critical factors. As demonstrated in the US carmaker example, when CSFs are established for an industry, they can contribute to a better understanding of product improvements.

Linking CSFs to Improvement

When the management of an organization pursues the notion of understanding and improving productivity, a clear view of what it takes to achieve goals and objectives can guide the process. For example, in the course of a recent interview, the director of a software development firm identified product quality as a top CSF for the company. Immediately the director followed up with the statement, "Well, that's not exactly true. It is not the quality itself, but rather what customers think of the quality that really counts." Which is a more productive use of this top executive's time: pursuing the improvement of some abstract notion of product quality, or spending time with key customers to build their confidence in the product?

The CEO of a start-up engineering firm identifies the morale of the professional engineers as a critical success factor. This CEO needs uniquely trained and experienced engineers. A great deal of time is spent searching for more professional engineers rather than managing the current staff. The assumption is that the employees are self-starters who do not need hand-holding. Although the turnover rate is somewhat high, the CEO attributes this side effect to competition from other start-ups in the environment. Should more time be spent nurturing current employees?

The executive vice-president of a consulting firm wants to introduce groupware technology to support the sharing of information across departments within the firm. The VP thinks the tasks to get this done include choosing the right technology, getting it installed and fully operational as quickly as possible, and accomplishing all this for the least amount of money. Because the organization is generally computer-illiterate, the best technical people are assigned to review and choose the technology. When asked to consider the critical success factors necessary to make this technology roll-out work, the VP cites the need for employees of the consulting firm who can help the organization use and benefit from this technology. It is actually the organizational aspects, rather than the VP's efforts, that will determine whether the use of groupware is a success. Productivity will only be positive if the technology is accepted by the employees. Time and priorities need to be reallocated to understand the information sharing needs and culture of the organization.

CONCLUSION

In these examples, critical success factors helped focus attention on the areas that need to be managed to increase knowledge worker productivity. It is useless to the overall productivity of the organization to increase work on the wrong activities. Although this approach may create an apparent increase in productivity, it does not truly add value to the bottom line of the organization. The critical success factor method identifies the areas where knowledge worker attention should be focused. It leads directly to both what needs to be done and how to measure progress.

A straightforward approach based on the following steps will increase knowledge worker productivity—the key in a retooled IS organization:

1. Understand the context-specific nature of productivity.
2. Understand the desired tasks.
3. Focus on process improvement.
4. Focus on product improvement.
5. Understand the need to measure outcomes and not outputs.
6. Use critical success factors to help managers throughout the IS organization think through tasks, processes, products, and outcomes.

I-4

A Strategy for Outsourcing

N. Dean Meyer

OUTSOURCING SOME OR ALL of IS activities is an option being considered in many US organizations today. Outsourcing—that is, paying other firms to perform all or part of the IS function—is not new, but there is renewed interest in it. It can be a viable business option when used in the right circumstances and for the right reasons. Outsourcing has been used very effectively in a few cases; it has had disappointing results in many other cases.

In many cases, an IS organization's interest in outsourcing originates with pressure from top executives who use outsourcing as a threat to force change. Outsourcing vendors promise dramatic savings and enhanced flexibility so that line executives have more time to focus on their core businesses. On the surface, these claims seem plausible, but they often do not hold up well under closer scrutiny.

RHETORIC VERSUS REALITY

Each of the claimed benefits of outsourcing has underlying assumptions, each of which must be considered in a decision to outsource.

Cost Savings

Economies of scale seem to reduce costs. The vendor, however, must earn a profit at its customer's expense. Furthermore, external contracting brings added sales and transactions costs.

Most of the savings from outsourcing generally come from data center consolidation. Once a firm has consolidated its data centers on its own, outsourcing is generally more expensive. The only lasting cost savings occur where there are true economies of scale across corporate boundaries—for example, in long-distance communications. In some cases, interorganizational sharing is possible, but such cases must be examined carefully. Hardware no longer presents economies of scale, and many software licenses are corporation specific.

In a few cases, outsourcing has been viewed as a source of near-term cash, because IS assets may be sold to the outsourcing vendor. Selling a strategic resource is an extreme way to save a sinking firm. Furthermore, selling off IS cripples all remaining business units and increases long-term costs.

Better Access to Technology

Equipment vendors suggest they can provide customers with better access to new technologies. In practice, vendor sales representatives are quick to bring new products to the attention of internal IS staff in any case. The firm must judge for itself when to adopt a new vendor offering rather than leave that decision to a vendor that has a vested interest in selling new products. Vendor-owned outsourcing services are also less likely to tap opportunities presented by competitive vendors (e.g., more cost-effective, plug-compatible products).

Increased Flexibility

Some people say that outsourcing converts fixed costs (or such relatively fixed costs as people) into variable costs, giving the firm greater financial flexibility. In fact, most outsourcing vendors require long-term contracts that provide them with stable revenues over time. Renegotiating these contracts may be more expensive than changing internal commitments.

If flexibility is the goal, the contract must be carefully negotiated to allow variability in demand and cost. Flexibility, however, comes at a relatively high price.

Greater Competence

It can be argued that vendors are more experienced than internal staff at running an IS function. This situation can be remedied by hiring competent IS managers as readily as by hiring an outsourcing vendor.

In some cases, outsourcing is simply a matter of paying someone else to experience the pain of managing a dysfunctional IS function, rather than trying to figure out how to make the function healthy again. This costly form of escapism sacrifices a valuable component of business strategy for a short-term convenience.

Downsizing

In organizations that must downsize, it may seem that the outsourcing vendor can move surplus people to other jobs serving other companies. If those other jobs exist, surplus staff can compete for them on the open market with or without the outsourcing deal. When staff members have the qualifications for those other positions, they will get them—regardless of whether the firm pursues outsourcing. If they are not qualified enough to win other jobs on their own merits, it is unlikely that a highly competitive outsourcing vendor will retain them in these positions for long. Ultimately, then, outsourcing does little to change the employment picture for surplus IS professionals.

More Time for Business Issues

Some organizations are attracted to outsourcing because it relieves senior management of having to worry about managing the IS function. The argument is that outsourcing reduces the demand on senior management because a contract is substituted for direct authority. This rarely proves to be the case. In fact, managing an outsourcing vendor is no easier (and is often more difficult) than managing an internal IS executive.

If senior managers become less involved in managing IS, outsourcing may actually be counterproductive. Those who understand the strategic value of IS argue that managers should spend more, not less, time thinking about IS. Without management involvement, the IS function may do no more than it has done in the past. That is, it may continue to invest in administrative systems but fail to find breakthroughs in strategic applications.

Another argument is that when a firm outsources IS, business managers have more time to focus on the corporation's main lines of business. This is only true if IS managers are transferred into other business functions. If the IS managers are fired or transferred to the outsourcing vendor, there are not likely to be more business managers to focus on the organization's business issues than there were before outsourcing. In other words, the business only gets more attention if line management is expanded (and costs are increased). Of course, line managers can be added regardless of whether IS is outsourced.

INSIDERS' ADVANTAGE

There are two key reasons why insiders have an advantage over outsourcing vendors for some key functions within the department: continuity and vested interests. For both of these reasons, insiders are more likely to be invited to clients' key meetings and will be in a better position to play a role in the firm's strategic imperatives.

Continuity

Internal staff members have a history and an expectation of continuity with the organization that may pay off in a better understanding of the business and improved partnerships with clients. By contrast, outsourcing vendors may rotate their staff more easily, because individuals develop loyalties to the outsourcing vendor rather than one customer organization. The insiders' improved partnership advantage pays off in client satisfaction and more meaningful strategic alignment. Long-term employees better understand the clients' culture, strategies, and politics; they also know they will be around to deal with the consequences of their actions.

Vested Interests

Outsourcing vendors may be sincere about partnership, but ultimately they work for different shareholders and ethically must (and will) place their shareholders' interests first. For example, what would happen if, in a needs assessment interview with a client, the IS consultant sees an opportunity for either a $200,000 administrative application that should save clerical time, or a $200 end-user computing tool that could significantly affect the client's personal effectiveness? Although the latter choice may provide a higher payoff and more strategic value, the outsourcing vendor has a strong incentive to recommend the more lucrative administrative system project because it generates more revenues, which are added costs rather than cost savings.

In one extreme case, an automobile rental company wanted to acquire software that would help it make better use of its fleet. An expert in the industry offered to license a state-of-the-art yield management package, but because the company had outsourced its IS function, the outsourcing vendor saw no profit in this arrangement. Instead, the outsourced IS department spent hundreds of thousands of dollars—nearly the price of the package—on a study of alternatives, and then even more money replicating the package to ensure that it had a role in both development and support.

Insourcing

The insiders' advantage may also be used to bring in new revenue. *Insourcing* is a term that refers to sales made by a staff function to clients outside the corporation. A staff function may sell directly to external clients if two conditions are met:

- The staff function has a distinctive competence in a particular area that ensures success in a well-defined niche, in spite of competition.
- Insourcing will improve internal client satisfaction, at a minimum by building a critical mass of specialists in an area that otherwise might not warrant permanent headcount. (Size permits a higher degree of specialization, which in turn reduces costs, improves quality, speeds time to market, and accelerates the pace of innovation.)

Before insourcing is considered, the IS function must be sure that internal clients are completely satisfied with its work. Unless the corporation is pursuing a strategy that takes it into the IS business, it is more important that the IS function help internal clients to succeed than that it makes money on its own.

In general, it is preferable to sell products and services to internal clients, who in turn may add value and sell them outside the corporation. This ensures consistency and coordination with line management's customer-oriented strategies. It also keeps the focus of the staff function on its primary mission—serving internal clients.

WHEN OUTSOURCING MAKES SENSE

Upon scrutiny, outsourcing is usually found to carry with it certain risks. After investigation, many firms have shied away from outsourcing all or major portions of an IS function. Instead, these organizations are pursuing a selective outsourcing strategy.

Outsourcing selected functions can be quite valuable, especially in the case of functions where an insiders' advantage—continuity and appropriate vested interests—are not so important. Indeed, the use of contractors and consultants is hardly new and generally represents a healthy form of outsourcing.

The goals of selective outsourcing include:

- Minimizing fluctuations in staffing that could result from rising and falling demand.
- Maximizing the development of employees by outsourcing less interesting work.
- Minimizing costs by using relatively less expensive employees whenever possible or sharing costs with other corporations.

For this discussion, the term *external consultants* refers to people who are hired to transfer their skills and methods and improve employees' effectiveness. These consultants are distinct from contractors who do work in place of employees.

Generally, consultants may be used by anyone whenever justifiable. Contractors are considered extensions of the staff of employees. Employers should decide when and whom to hire, supervise all contractors, and be accountable for their work.

STRATEGY FOR OUTSOURCING, FUNCTION BY FUNCTION

At a more detailed level, the pros and cons of outsourcing vary by function within the IS department. The five basic functions found in any IS department are:

- Machine-based service bureaus that own and operate systems for use by others (e.g., computer and network operations).
- People-based service bureaus providing routine services that are produced by people (e.g., client support, training, and administration).
- Technologists who design, build, maintain, and support systems (e.g., applications developers, platform experts, information engineers, and end-user computing specialists).
- The architects who coordinate agreements on standards and guidelines that constrain design choices for the sake of integration.
- The consultancy that works with clients to define requirements, set priorities, measure benefits, and coordinate relations with the rest of the IS department.

The issues related to outsourcing can be examined within each of these functional elements.

Machine-Based Service Bureaus

Outsourcing machine-based service bureaus is equivalent to buying computer and network time from vendors. This is a common practice and should be evaluated for each new increment of capacity. It is a form of financing when capital is short and a way to satisfy temporary or otherwise limited needs for specialized platforms. Outsourcing a major portion of the machine-based service bureau may also be useful for a limited period of time during a migration to a new platform.

Permanent outsourcing may be cost-effective when there are economies of scale and multiple corporations can share infrastructure; a common example is in the field of communications, where few companies run their own private long-distance networks. However, this usually does not apply to software licenses, which are generally corporation specific.

Outsourcing should only be used when the same economies of scale cannot be attained internally. If outsourcing the entire function appears to save money, internal consolidation of data centers should also be considered as an alternative.

People-Based Service Bureaus

Some people-based service bureaus can also be outsourced. For example, installation and repair services are commonly outsourced, and training courses can be purchased for many common end-user computing packages.

Vendors offer commercial hot lines that support most of the common end-user computing products, but these are best used in combination with internal support functions. Inside staff should be the first line of support, calling on external resources for a specific class of questions. This approach ensures the required quality of service and handles internally developed packages and configurations. In general, the following guidelines apply:

- Hire enough staff to satisfy the steady demand; outsource to satisfy peak loads.
- Outsource only commodity and end-of-life services; keep new growth opportunities inside.

Technologists

No matter how big the IS organization, it can never afford to hire a specialist in every possible discipline. Contractors are therefore a valuable source of specialized expertise in less frequently used areas.

A preference to buying over making is another variant on outsourcing. Turn-key packages are attractive because they free scarce internal talent from the ongoing burden of maintaining systems, allowing applications technologists to focus on new requirements. Packages should be used whenever the requirements for customization are limited. In most cases, clients appreciate receiving a proposal that offers a choice between custom code and a package—often this amounts to a choice between 100% of what they want for 100% of the cost, versus 80% of what they want for 20% of the cost.

The guidelines here are similar to those for people-based service bureaus: Hire enough staff to satisfy basic demand; outsource to satisfy peak loads. Outsource only commodity and end-of-life skills; keep new growth opportunities inside.

In every case, employees should be used to manage outsourced technologists to ensure quality, systems integration, architectural compliance, and responsiveness to the business.

Architects and Consultancies

The functions of architects and consultancies are highly strategic and require an insider's deep understanding of the corporation. They not only require an intimate knowledge of the business, but success in these functions requires close relations with clients and the rest of the IS function. Although many management consulting firms are willing to sell these two types of planning, such high-leverage functions should never be outsourced.

Architect. Even in the smallest of operations, the architect function is extremely important. Architects facilitate a consensus on standards so the IS function can be responsive to clients' strategic needs—tailoring solutions to their unique missions rather than blindly following a static top-down plan. They are also needed for a firm to successfully evolve toward integrated systems.

Where staff is lacking, the architect function should not be outsourced. It should be part of the responsibility of the chief technologist or perhaps the head of the department.

Consultancy. The consultancy function must not be ignored, however scarce personnel may be. It is essential to ensure a strategic return on IS investments and healthy client relations. (Return on investment is, of course, every bit as important to a small organization as it is to a large one.) Consultants are the primary liaison to clients, diagnosing the client's strategic needs without any bias for particular solutions and setting up contracts with the rest of the IS function. Consultancy requires an insider's understanding of the business and carefully cultivated relationships with key clients—the result of continuity over time. Outside consultants can train and assist internal consultants, but contractors should not be used to do their jobs for them.

Even in the smallest organizations, responsibility for strategic consultancy should be placed somewhere within the IS department. The responsibility may be assigned to one person or, in groups of only a few people, it may be a part-time responsibility of the top IS executive. Because this function depends on relationships with clients and an understanding of the corporation's strategy and politics, the consultancy function should never be left to outsiders.

HOW TO MANAGE OUTSOURCING VENDORS

Any degree of outsourcing necessitates clear designation of responsibility within the organization for acquiring these outside resources. For example, in the case of external technical specialists, the appropriate technologist is expected to know where to find the right people and how to manage them. The internal manager of outsourcing contracts (in any area) is responsible for:

- Shopping for the best deal, negotiating the contract, and managing contractor performance.
- Resolving problems in the relationship and maintaining healthy collaboration between the two parties.

- Generating entrepreneurial ideas within the established charter and domain and deciding whether to make or to buy.
- Establishing clear contracts with internal customers and suppliers and retaining responsibility for fulfilling those contracts (whether outsourcing vendors are involved or not).

For all practical purposes, outside contractors should be considered part of the group that hired them. The fact that their paycheck is written by a different corporation does not change the nature of their work. All outsourcing vendors will automatically live within the bounds of the existing organizational structure, and clients need not worry about who is chosen to staff their projects.

CONCLUSION

In general, outsourcing the entire IS function should only be done in severe cases. Doing so risks higher costs, less flexibility, and a loss of strategic alignment. Instead, each group within an IS department should cultivate contacts with outside contractors and package vendors in its area of expertise and manage them as part of its staff. Each internal entrepreneur should proactively decide whether to make or to buy in the course of every project.

I-5

Strategic Planning for Computer Resources

Robert DeMichiell

IN THE EARLY YEARS OF AUTOMATION, information systems staff were solely responsible for acquisition of information technology. IS professionals identified the basic applications and solicited assistance and bids from selected vendors. IS designed the data base, acquired the computers, developed or bought software, and implemented systems. The process was complex only for those issues directly related to technical feasibility and data base design. Applications priority, the development schedule, user training, processing control, and other project management concerns became more important over the years.

To remain competitive, organizations must acquire and use information technology resources effectively. Numerous options in information systems development have evolved owing mostly to the proliferation of microcomputers and the movement toward object orientation and client/server networks. The introduction of new decision support and systems development tools, including prototyping methods, and users' growing computer literacy and independence necessitate that serious attention be given not only to receiving financial return on investment but also to acquiring quality products from multiple vendors who are reliable. This chapter emphasizes computer resource planning with an integrated procurement process from assessment through allocation—a process that is outlined in Exhibit I-5-1.

THE MASTER PLANNING IMPERATIVE

Some planning framework is needed to place an organization's business objectives in proper perspective and, ultimately, to develop action-oriented solutions for realizing those objectives. Many end users perceive that immediate hardware and software solutions are commercially available. On-the-shelf solutions usually prompt users to ask two questions:

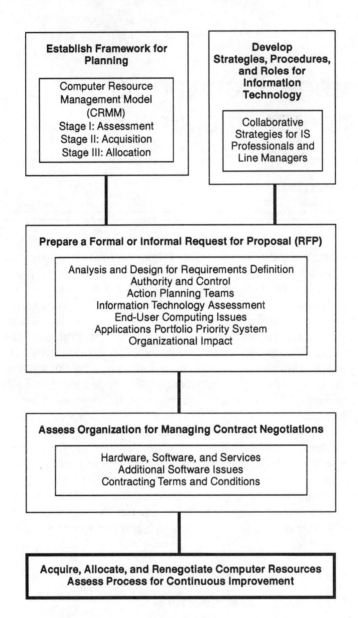

Exhibit I-5-1. Integrating Master Plans with Action

- Why should there be such a long wait for quality results in the organization's applications development cycle and procurement process?
- Can formal applications be purchased, perhaps by end-user departments, rather than developed?

Users may rush to bypass what they perceive to be lengthy procurement and development processes. Small pockets of funds in departmental budgets are available for such independent solutions, and vendors are quick to respond with delivery of hardware and software. Total investment by these independent groups over a long time period is, however, costly and financially unsound. As line managers assume more operating responsibilities in today's information-based organization, IS management will continue to know less about all applications.

Problems with User-Controlled Operations

When IS management is relegated to only monitoring routine data processing activities, information processing capability becomes stagnant. IS management can respond by supporting or ignoring user-developed systems. For IS, the search for a more comprehensive solution is encumbered by the ongoing demands for immediate response, quality enhancement, cost containment, increased productivity, cash liquidity, just-in-time manufacturing and inventory, outplacement alternatives, and organizational downsizing moves.

In user-controlled and independent operations, daily operating procedures often conflict. Departmental data sets are separate entities, and because the data elements may not have unique definitions, data integrity is at risk. In addition, some status reports for senior corporate management require information from several operating functions. Unless the distributed data bases are integrated to a master system with true connectivity to the mainframe, the process requires manipulation of user data files.

When IS and users fail to cooperate, many problems can arise. For example:

- Funding for in-house or outside consultants to help operations run smoothly is often unavailable.
- Neither IS nor the users have the time or expertise to assess requests properly.
- Problem assessments often involve personnel with competing motivations and objectives.
- End users do not provide accurate information concerning application requirements.
- Overeager vendors provide solutions to organizational problems without an implementation plan.
- Insufficient attention is given to vendor contract terms, conditions, and systems deliverables.
- User documentation is either too technical or too simple, and user literacy is not considered.
- Contingency measures for delayed installation or maintenance of new ap-

plications are not identified.

- The roles of IS and end users after implementation of new systems are unclear.
- Access to the computer system by other departments or organizations is undefined.
- Expectations among end users, IS, consultants, and vendors are not delineated.

COMPUTER RESOURCE MANAGEMENT MODEL

To minimize or eliminate some of the conflicts and produce a responsive, manageable operating environment, a long-range master plan with complementary short-term solutions should be established. Traditional organizational models, although applicable for many segments of computer-related management issues, do not address all of these issues. Case data supports a computer resource management model (detailed in Exhibit I-5-2) that encompasses three managerial stages of assessment, acquisition, and allocation of information technology.

Case study data—collected from educational, government, and business environments—uncovered a model for helping organizations implement computer resources that address the concerns of users. Thirty-eight case studies were examined over a decade for attributes relating to managerial issues of information systems planning and implementation. Conclusions were converted into operational action items, including collaborative strategies for IS and line managers, developing a request for proposal, and managing contract negotiations. Later sections of this chapter discuss these conclusions.

Addressing User Expectations

The data revealed that user expectations generally are not addressed. If the organization chooses to examine literacy levels, the review usually occurs after acquisition of computer resources. User activity is a function of computer literacy and computer fluency. Computer fluency levels affect management procedures, responsibilities and accountabilities, resource constraints, priority of applications development, and overall risk-return analyses.

Application of computer resources to the right tasks, computer literacy levels of all personnel, and end-user computing philosophy are all integral parts of the planning and control imperative. For many organizations in which there is frequent change of computer capabilities in hardware, software enhancements, and distribution of computing, a formal declaration of authorities for computer systems procurement does not exist. There is a difference between organizational policy for centralized control and the reality of the situation when users acquire and implement standalone, low-cost PCs. Strategies are needed to develop a master plan. The preferred approach is one in which strategic initiatives and action statements drive the process to integrate information technology into business practice.

Stage I: Assessment
Management of the Organization
 Structure and Modification Mechanisms for Change
 Philosophy, Goals, Decision-Making and Managerial Styles
 Operating Procedures and Work Flow (Formal and Informal)
  Organization Charts: Hierarchy, Project, or Matrix
 Levels of Authority: Responsiveness and Control
Perception of Automation
 Strategic and Operational Feasibility: Definition of Feasibility
 Business Function Operations
 End-User Information Systems Literacy, Fluency; Power Users
 IS Professionals: Education, Expertise, Interests
 Current and Future Requirements; Untapped Opportunities
Planning
 Organizing for Automation or Automation Changes
 Master Computer Resource Plan
  Control Issues: IS and End-User Applications Development
  *Task Forces: TQM System and Authority
  Impact on Organization (Local, National, International)
Request for Proposal Guidelines
  Development, Production, and Implementation
  Technical, Economic, Legal, Contractual, Administrative Issues
  Level of Specificity, Scope, Constraints

Stage II: Acquisition
Contents of Selection Plan
 Authority, Review, and Control of Process
 Organization, Scope, Timing, Constraints
 Communication and Ethical Issues (Internal and External Reporting)
 Validation and Confidentiality
 Continuity and Continuance of Selection Committee
Implementation of Selection Plan
 Master Plan Conformance: Business Plan and IS Plan
  Application Priorities and Schedule, Organizational Impact
  Computer System Redesign, Resource Changes, and
   Constraints
Make-or-Buy Decisions
 Hardware, Peripherals, Data Communications, Software
 Support Services (Consultants On-site, Off-site), Modification,
  Maintenance
Contract Negotiation
 Solicitation of Bids
 Terms and Conditions of Contract: Mandatory and Desirable
  Requirements
 Data Collection, Evaluation System, and Analysis
 Clarification of Bids, Contract Award, Installation, and Acceptance

Stage III: Allocation
 Master Plan Conformance and Continuous Evaluation System
  Renegotiation
 Organizational Assessment, Annual RFP Modification
 The Three Stages Revisited: Assessment, Acquisition, and
  Allocation

  *The underlying concept for the total quality management (TQM)
  approach is to have cross-functional task forces with authority.

Exhibit I-5-2. Computer Resource Management Model (CRMM)

COLLABORATION BETWEEN IS PROFESSIONALS AND LINE MANAGERS

Several design and acquisition issues demonstrate the large scope of the process. The planning effort is a tremendous undertaking, and the frequent change of key personnel can discourage systematic approaches. However, if the organization is willing to commit time to the project at the outset and focus on creating an adaptable long-term solution, then this approach is beneficial to the organization. The financial portion of the contract focuses on cash flow and tax breaks. A phased-in approach with documented milestones and prioritized applications can be implemented. In this way, some results can be realized while the process unfolds.

Vendor relationships should be developed for the long-term with negotiations based on predetermined issues. Procedures establish not only the impact of business programmatic changes, but also the opportunities afforded by technology updates on computing resources. As hardware and software products proliferate and their costs decrease, other extensive systems studies and procurement groups do not have to be reestablished. Historical records are helpful in preventing duplication of effort.

The proposed computer resource management model (CRMM) uses committees and task forces to focus on design of the best system for the whole organization. A committee should assess technology in all facets of the organization before any procurement action is taken.

All facets of end-user computing become planned activity. Software development by users becomes part of the total effort and should not produce any independent data bases or file incompatibilities. Overall benefits of this approach are reduced costs, minimized risks, appropriate use of available resources, and improved management. The key concept is to quickly develop the master plan, appoint the right people to a loosely coupled network structure of task forces, and produce results on a timely schedule.

Forums

Senior-level managers, including corporate information officers, must provide forums where ideas can be introduced and emerging strategies can be converted into action. Because information technology must be mobilized to support these strategies, the specific responsibilities of the task force must be identified at the outset.

Line managers and IS professionals must reach a detailed formal agreement addressing the use of information technology for making gains in personal productivity, adding business value to the organization, enhancing the image of the firm, and improving the quality of products or services. Forums should not be complaint centers for current operating problems; these comments are better handled by a separate action team concentrating on those issues.

Forum activity should be visionary. Forums should assess corporate strengths and use them to grasp both near- and long-term opportunities. Other collaborative strategies are outlined in Exhibit I-5-3.

1. Securing top-level support for managing information technology in these key areas:

Authorities to control ongoing process by collaborative task forces.
Task force makeup: cross-functional teams of IS and line management.
Dissemination of information formally to all organizational elements.
Implementation plan with flexibility for new users and applications.
Strategies with vision and integration of information technology into business plan.
Decision-making criteria and impact on information technology procurement.
Requirement for planned implementation for migration to new technologies.
Creation of new reward systems commensurate with project oriented work.
Support of an educational program for new organizational structures.
Encouragement to design and implement self-directed teams (task forces).
Discouragement of independent information technology activity.
Integration of information technology in financial planning process.
Requirement that IS, line managers, and vendors meet business objectives.
Requirement that IS, line managers, and vendors communicate for effectiveness.
Emphasizing strategies with action plans are more effective than crisis reaction.

2. Developing a specific set of objectives for management, including:

Scope, constraints, milestones, membership roles, and responsibilities of task forces.
Critical success factors and actions needed to exploit them.
Identification of corporate strengths and application opportunities.
Identification of corporate weaknesses and conversion to strengths.
View of future (5 to 10 years) technological advances in hardware, software, services.

3. Creating a forum for ideas, including:

Discussion of process and criteria for justification of resources.
End-user involvement, including in applications development.
Impact of process on organizational philosophy and business practices.
Establishment of a communications system using groupware and other mechanisms.
Several task forces loosely structured to address issues, problems, and opportunities.
Allowance for immediate and long-term timely solutions.
Authority clearly established for planning, control, and implementation.

4. Resolving the issues through:

Emergence of the most effective and practicable solution for the business.
Consideration of technical, economic, operational, political, and human factors.
Focus on productivity and total quality management issues.
Schedule of activity consistent with task force recommendations.
Resolution of application portfolio problems, priorities, and conflicts.
Resolution of charging scheme; budget planning and expenditures.

5. Assessing solutions in terms of:

Programmatic or staffing changes for alternative solutions.
Internal and external impact on organizational structure and workforce.
Technology and management advances and their impact on alternative solutions.
Focus on business value and less on information technology development.

Exhibit 1-5-3. Collaborative Strategies for IS Professionals and Line Managers

6. Planning the information technology selection process, including:
Schedule for procurement process and evaluation.
Immediate, short-term, and long-range acquisitions.
Procedures for all phases and all participant roles and responsibilities.
Full consideration of, and accountability to, task force recommendations.

7. Establishing RFP process and working RFP, including:
Comprehensive framework used as continuous reference document.
Flexibility on scope and constraints for standard and fast-track processing.
Historical record for justified changes to RFP as new information emerges.
Continuous dialogue back to task forces for additional information.
Focus on the need for long-term relationships with vendors.

8. Addressing design issues, such as:
Total systems solution with integrated segments, or phases of migration to
     new information technology.
Inclusion of all computer-related operations in systems design plan.
Exploration of standalones, networks, and connectivity concerns.
Outsourcing possibilities as integral part of solution.
Specific criteria for vendor evaluation and establish evaluation system.
Provision for a secure, easily accessible, and comprehensive data base.
Requirements-driven architecture, not just current computer system adaptation.
System for creating and implementing system standards for hardware and
     software.
Provision for physical standards (e.g., optic fibers, equipment, services).
Pathways for expansion of internal computing to external electronic highways.
Data base entry, access, and change authorities: who, why, what conditions, how.
All levels of management participation: cross-functional task forces.

9. Executing the selection plan by establishing:
Time frame for developing evaluated costs for vendor comparisons.
Formal procedures for solicitation, contract negotiation, and bids.
Definitions of terms used in contract to resolve semantic differences.
Clarification of mandatory and desirable requirements.
User-driven, business oriented standards and specifications.
Product modules, phased-in approaches, application priorities, and schedule.
Nontechnical evaluation: training, openness for future change, flexibility.
Vendor procedures, constraints, responsiveness consistent with client objectives.
Confirmation of vendor, line managers, and IS working relationships afterward.

**10. Negotiating and renegotiating the contract annually, according to these
criteria:**
Acceptance of systems or services by all key participants.
Evaluation standards, procedures, and timing.
Insurance that vendors communicate only with authorized team.
Product criteria: product quality, performance, reliability.
Vendor criteria: trustworthiness, long-term relationship, financial stability.
Feedback to appropriate task forces on status of process and any new
     developments.
Development modification procedures, conditions, limitations, and costs.
Continuance of this concept of shared participation and ownership of automation.
Communications of the process to senior-level management: costs, benefits,
     trade-offs.
Consistency with corporate philosophy for integration of information technology.
Commitment to service line management: immediate and long-term plans.

Exhibit I-5-3. (continued)

DEVELOPING THE REQUEST FOR PROPOSAL

The request for proposal (RFP) document provides specific deliverables. The effort spent developing a solicitation document should equal the expected return from the information processing capability.

Strategies incorporated in this document should emerge from task force discussions, findings, conclusions, and recommendations. The selection team for information technology concentrates on procurement, but it will have the benefit of the wisdom, experience, and cross-functional perspective of task force activity to justify its request for proposal.

Actions to Consider in RFP Development

The Race for Installation. Analysis and design activities are costly and usually do not show any immediate return for the expenditure. Frequently, these phases are accelerated for purchase of hardware and software. Guidelines include:

- Conducting an assessment to make a deliberate decision of the level of detail to be undertaken for analysis and design. Somewhere between the very general specifications and the very specific terms and conditions lies a balanced portrayal of information for the RFP.
- Ensuring that the effort is commensurate with return-investment and risk-return ratios. Intangible benefits, hidden costs, and expected productivity gains for new opportunities should be identified.
- Ensuring consistency between the desired level of detail required of vendors and the RFP.

Authority and Control of Selection Procedures. Procedures may be documented but not implemented. IS management may not be situated high enough in the organization to provide objective leadership to control computer resources. IS should act to:

- Place IS management at a level high enough to form an action team with authority and responsiveness.
- Establish formal authorities for computer resource allocation with input from end users.

Task Forces or Advisory Planning Groups. The process of managing information technology does not end with advisory group recommendations; it must be a continuous process if it is to affect the organization. Activities center around:

- Creating advisory groups to design, implement, and oversee all aspects of the process.
- Developing operational mechanisms that will not impede progress and that allow for new users, new applications, and new priorities consistent with changing business requirements.

Information Technology Evaluation Team. Because the evaluation process is multidisciplinary (involving end users, technical experts, contracting and purchasing personnel, and legal and financial personnel), the makeup and size of the group depend on the current and intended scope of computing in the organization. Guidelines in this area include:

- Selecting a team with expertise for proper evaluation of the product or services sought.
- Assigning as chairperson an experienced business operating manager with leadership abilities.

End-User Computing. End users must be an integral part of the procurement process to achieve success in using information technology effectively. Issues of applications development and other related user activity must be addressed at the outset by:

- Formalizing end-user and IS relationships for each aspect of procurement.
- Documenting specific objectives that exploit strengths and reduce weaknesses.
- Capitalizing on new business opportunities made possible by technology and people.
- Ensuring that the management of information technology is consistent with business planning.
- Providing for mainframe connectivity and hardware and software compatibility.

Administrative versus Other Types of Computing. This issue is philosophical, power-based, and political. Computing resources are, after all, an expensive budget item. Policy guidance should be established. Examples are: administrative versus instructional use of computers in higher education; administrative versus research and development for business. This activity involves:

- Tapping members of the computer selection group to examine and suggest solutions for conflicts (total fund allocations and schedule for implementation).
- Creating a system for measuring the computer literacy level of all administrators, staff, and computer professionals.
- Establishing organizational standards and incorporating these capabilities in RFP requirements.

New Technology's Impact on the Organization. Although it is not always possible to anticipate the full impact that computer systems will have on an organization, some assessment of how new technology will affect the organization should be a goal at the outset of the process. The RFP represents not only technical and financial specifications for computing, but also indicates future areas to be supported by technology.

Hardware, Software, and Services
   Strategic and operational cost/performance data, support services, and training.
   Requirement for vendors to respond to predetermined format.
   Individual component costs, depreciation factor, and discounts.
   Data communications issues: definitions of system responsibilities.
   Phase-in methods: annual modifications and business disruptiveness.
   Purchase, lease, or other payment plans, with proper comparison of bids.
   Maintenance specifications: end-user standards and requirements.
   Operational capability demonstration and references.
   User-friendly systems and applications software.
   Concurrent usage of system: response peak loading and priorities.
   Processing throughput measurement.
   System expandability: memory, communications channel, and user stations.
   Connectivity and compatibility issues for internal and external systems.

Additional Software Issues
   Ownership, site licensing, maintenance; intellectual property issues.
   Ethical and leadership issues with all aspects of use of software.
   Conversion terms and conditions: data entry, programming, and testing.
   Memory requirements and compatibility with system upgrades.
   Levels of priority: utilization, recovery, debugging, and file management.
   File protect options for updating and enhancements.
   Customizing features: buyer allowances and prohibitions.
   Control of processing schedule: end-user options.
   Acceptance criteria and time frame for trial period.
   Termination clauses.

Other Contracting Terms and Conditions
   Backup system: procedures, costs, and responsibilities.
   Training requirements: computer literacy assessment and location of users.
   Documentation of all phases of management of information technology.
   Implementation planning: schedules and actions.
   Technical assistance from vendor: constraints, costs, and accessibility.
   Multivendor systems: authorities and responsibility tree.
   Cost guarantees and time period for which applicable.
   Replacement of hardware, software, peripherals: cost for upgrades.
   Confidentiality issues of contract negotiation and implementation.
   Formal negotiation procedures: time frame and conditions.
   Account management: personal contacts afterward and for implementation.
   Cancellation provisions and payment schedule for changed arrangements.
   Protection against natural disasters.
   Provisions for major organizational changes (including mergers and acquisitions).
   End-user involvement through all phases of contracting.
   Noncompliance penalties: timeliness, completeness, and opportunities lost.
   Site preparation: physical conditions, remote sites, and cable installations.

Exhibit I-5-4. Self-Assessment Guide for Managing Contract Negotiations

NEGOTIATING THE CONTRACT

It is important to promote an atmosphere in which philosophy, discussion, and action merge to produce the best solution for each unique party. Contract negotiation suggests a lengthy process. Because arbitration and debate are encouraged by these guidelines, terms and conditions are examined extensively. Conclusions resulting from a discussion of issues form the basis of a written document that is then enforceable should disputes arise. A self-assessment guide for managing contract negotiations is presented in Exhibit I-5-4.

The purpose of a written agreement is to ensure that all parties understand the terms of the requested service. To deflect lengthy and costly litigation, legal staff should review the document prepared by the client for computing capability acquisition.

CONCLUSION

Organizations need a concrete strategy when procuring computer resources. The computer resource management model discussed in this chapter can be used by the average nontechnical administrator and the IS professional. This model, derived from case data collected over a decade from a variety of organizations, is based on universal concepts that apply to information technology assessment, acquisition, and allocation.

An organization need not apply the entire process (selection plan, RFP, negotiation) to realize the benefit of automation. The CRMM approach applies to any type of organization at any staff level (division, department, or individual end users).

Some people may wonder if a formal plan is really necessary and practical in terms of the effort needed to draft it. The answer is yes. Response is critical to competitive ability. Similarly, accurate, complete, and reliable information is critical to success. Organizations that have operational objectives, make creative use of the right information getting to the right people at the right time, and employ structured, documented approaches to computer resource management are competitive.

Some form of plan, even if it addresses only a few carefully selected and important issues, is necessary. The questions it asks of users and IS professionals in justifying a purchase and relating it to business operations is invaluable and practical.

It is especially important that organizations adopt some form of master plan for computer resources now that solutions proliferate and more informed users engage directly in information technology. The new tools must be used for the right applications. End-user computing and user-developed applications require formal agreements with IS staff. The plan, or some similar document, together with the selection plan and contract, can help avoid costly mistakes and serve as the basis for progress.

Section II
Managing Information Technology

ALIGNMENT OF INFORMATION TECHNOLOGY and business is crucial in today's information-intense environment. For that alignment to occur, IT and business executives must work together and have mutual respect for and understanding of each other's role and objectives.

Chapter II-1, "Aligning IT and Business Through Computer-Information Literacy," guides IS executives in two tasks that help achieve this alignment: developing a program that raises business executives' level of technology understanding, and taking a leadership position in fostering a better working relationship with business executives. The pervasiveness of information technology in today's competitive environment necessitates that senior management be properly trained to take full advantage of the vital information resource.

Today's technology environment is characterized by a rush to implement client/server computing, which is still an immature technology. As with any major change in technology, an organization must carefully plan the move to client/server computing. Chapter II-2 helps IS managers create "A Strategic Approach to Client/Server." By looking at the business case for client/server computing, its fit with the organization, and its potential for facilitating organizational change, the approach fosters understanding of whether client/server technology is right for an organization and of the need for a go-slow strategy to its adoption.

Organizational change is the primary driving force behind client/server computing. IS managers have felt the brunt of organizational change, especially that caused by technology. Chapter II-3, "Client/Server as an Enabler of Change," is a case study in organizational change at the Minnesota Department of Revenue. The chapter shows IS managers how strategic change was fueled by the need to serve customers better and improve revenue—the very objectives that drive desired change in the business world—and how it was implemented through the use of client/server technology and business process redesign.

IS managers have been troubled over the years by the inappropriate use of technology, but until now little has been written about this misuse, known today as junk computing, and how to manage it. Chapter II-4 warns against the use of information systems in a way that does not directly advance organizational goals and offers IS managers advice on "Managing Junk Computing."

Today's IS environment can be a bit demoralizing, even to the most gifted of IS managers and staff. Chapter II-5, "Morale Management in Today's IS Environment," discusses declining morale amid downsizing, rightsizing, and budget cutting. Managers should view the management of morale as an ongoing formal activity that requires planning and phased implementation. The chapter provides examples of proven management activities that improve employee morale and form the basis for organizational success.

Lastly, Chapter II-6, "Leveraging Developed Software," describes an approach to making an investment in software even more valuable to the enterprise. Leveraging is the reusability or portability of application software across multiple business units. The chapter uses an example from the manufacturing sector to show how leveraging software works and the conditions necessary for its success. Leveragability is the extent that the application can remain unchanged as it is installed and made operational at each location. Because leveraging can reduce the cost of acquiring and maintaining software, IS managers should make it an important part of their IS strategy.

II-1

Aligning IT and Business Through Computer-Information Literacy

Jerry Kanter

THE PRESIDENT OF A MEDIUM-SIZE manufacturing company feels that executive use of computers is highly overrated. Rather than send an E-mail message to someone, why not go down the hall and talk to them? Computers can become a crutch, causing people to spend too much time in the office and worrying about details that should be handled by managers. The true barometers are talking to key customers and key managers while maintaining a personal feel of what is happening in the marketplace. The senior executive is responsible for year-end results, not necessarily for what happens each of the 365 days.

The chairperson of an insurance company feels that computers and the information they provide are the all-pervasive strategic weapons of an organization and the major vehicle for competitive advantage. This chief executive officer (CEO) feels obliged to lead the rest of the organization in harnessing the power of information. The presence of a computer on the CEO's desk and the executive's championing position on key IT issues send the proper message to the rest of the organization.

These two scenarios reflect the positions of a significant proportion of executives as reported in surveys and news stories. Although the scenarios at first may paint diametrically opposed management styles, there is logic behind each of the viewpoints. This chapter defines the terms *computer literacy* and *information literacy* and points out why the attainment of each is important to senior business executives, senior IT executives, and the business as a whole. Finally, a six-step education program is suggested as a vehicle for imparting computer-information literacy to senior management.

COMPUTER LITERACY

Computer literacy is a popular term, but its use is a bit vague. Most often it refers to a familiarity with the use of personal computers, including the employment of word processing, spreadsheets, data bases, and the other popular software tools. In addition, executives with computer literacy are regular users of E-Mail and also may access outside news and financial data bases for business use. Executives with computer literacy are thought of as keyboard-facile and comfortable in front of a PC, where they may spend as much as an hour a day or more. By this definition, the insurance chairman is computer literate. The manufacturing president is not.

A survey conducted in 1993 asked 100 senior executives to estimate the degree of computer illiteracy among senior executives in large companies. The average reply was that 55% of the executives were computer illiterate, for the following reasons:

- Computer skills are low priority at most companies.
- Executives feel intimidated by the computer.
- Too much of time already is needed to learn how to use the computer.
- There is general resistance to change.

Exhibit II-1-1 lists the range of personal computing applications that many executives use regularly during their business day. A subjective judgment is that the threshold of computer literacy is a score of three or more on six of the items, totaling one hour of use a day. Although use depends on the particular industry and type of business as well as company culture, computer familiarity and use are generally considered highly advantageous to a senior executive. Personal computer use may not be not critical per se, but it is a positive facilitator for attaining information literacy. Discussion in this chapter will return to focus on the statement of the manufacturing executive that computers can get in the way of meaningful dialog on key business issues.

INFORMATION LITERACY

Information literacy, often confused with computer literacy, is a much broader and more encompassing term. Information literacy implies an understanding of the general concepts of information processing, how information systems shape and support a person's job function, a department or operating unit, or an enterprisewide application that may be linked with the company's customers as well as its suppliers. It is an awareness of the growing role of the technological enablers that allow a company to reengineer entire business processes. It implies a perspective that appreciates the need, for example, of an overall information architecture or the role of a communications network that provides connectivity, both within the company and throughout the world. Executive information literacy also implies an active commitment and involvement in relevant information technology projects.

	Skill Level			
	Poor	Average	Good	Minutes/Day
E-Mail	1	2	3	4	5	____
Voice Mail	1	2	3	4	5	____
Word Processing	1	2	3	4	5	____
Spreadsheets	1	2	3	4	5	____
Data Base	1	2	3	4	5	____
Presentation Graphics	1	2	3	4	5	____
Groupware	1	2	3	4	5	____
Corporate Data Base Access	1	2	3	4	5	____
Executive Information System	1	2	3	4	5	____
Statistics	1	2	3	4	5	____
Job-Specific Application	1	2	3	4	5	____
Department Application	1	2	3	4	5	____

Exhibit II-1-1. Computer Literacy Assessment

Exhibit II-1-2 lists suggested measures of information literacy. Again, a subjective threshold is a score of three or higher on six of the items listed. Although degrees are implied in the term *knowledge level*, the general thinking is that the senior executive should be able to carry on a meaningful conversation and discussion of the subject listed with someone from a more technical background. He or she should also have an understanding of the importance and scope of the items listed in relation to their business significance to the organization. In addition, the executive should have a sense of the effort in time, talent, and investment necessary to introduce and maintain an effective, business-oriented IT organization.

As a starting point, information literacy involves an understanding that competitive business performance is based on an appreciation of the critical nature of information, regardless of whether the information is computer based. However, relatively more information will inevitably be computer stored and generated.

Information technology must be aligned with the business. This is a repeated statement heard at all levels of management. Many elements support the alignment concept, but the starting point would seem to be an alignment between the senior executives of an organization, starting with the CEO and the chief information officer (CIO) of the company. Without collaboration and understanding at the top, it is almost impossible to gain the collaboration that is needed throughout the organization.

It has been stressed that the CIO must have a solid understanding of the business to align IT with the business. Does it not follow that the CEO must have an overall understanding of IT to be an effective partner in the alignment? This side of the alignment is not heard as much. Yet, a successful alignment depends on a true partnership. A shared understanding of these issues is a necessary starting point for executive information literacy, and the CIO has the opportunity to see that it happens.

	Degree of Involvement-Knowledge		
	Low	Average	High
• Involvement in IT projects in the last year	1 2	3	4 5
• Role in application development in department	1 2	3	4 5
• Participation on steering/advisory committees	1 2	3	4 5
• Knowledge level of the following subjects:			
— Business process reengineering	1 2	3	4 5
— Information architecture	1 2	3	4 5
— Communications networking	1 2	3	4 5
— Relational data bases	1 2	3	4 5
— Local area networks	1 2	3	4 5
— Client/server computing	1 2	3	4 5
— Executive information systems	1 2	3	4 5

Exhibit II-1-2. Information Literary Assessment

CAN COMPUTER LITERACY GET IN THE WAY?

Computer literacy presents a challenge to many senior managers. Most CEOs and senior managers, now in their late 40s or 50s, had scant (if any) contact with information systems during their college years and, according to the survey of senior executives, many of these managers feel the computer is still intimidating. The use of such graphical user interfaces as icons and pointers is, however, having an affect on even dyed-in-the-wool cynics.

Some executives, however, who are computer literate, still feel that computer literacy gets in the way. Consider the case of one CEO who is both computer and information literate, having been an executive at two high-tech companies, both of which placed high value on personal computer use and information literacy by their executives. In this new job, however, the CEO sees the office PC getting in the way. He sees the CEO role as being out of the office, meeting and talking to people and personally motivating the workforce. At least in the beginning of a new job, this CEO sees where the PC can be a lure, a trap. He knows from experience that once an individual gets started with a PC, the pressure builds to solve the particular problem at hand regardless of its importance.

For example, if someone is having difficulty with a spreadsheet, the tendency is to look for assistance from the IT help desk or from the local expert. A typical 10-minute job can develop into an hour-long exercise. Adding several of these events together can take valuable time away from important direct contact with key managers. Why not delegate those tasks involving computer use, thereby saving time for projects involving information literacy? An interesting study conducted by Nolan, Norton & Company in 1992 showed that peer support, the time spent by local experts in helping their colleagues, if measured, amounts to two and a half times the cost of the visible hardware, software, and training costs of a PC workstation. This is a bit frightening; however, experience supports the Nolan, Norton findings.

There is a great deal of difference in the decision not to use a PC by an executive who is computer literate and one who is not. Many executives, who could benefit greatly by using computers, do not use them because they lack the necessary literacy and are embarrassed about launching a program to attain it. Most would agree that information literacy is the more significant knowledge, but more are coming around to the belief that computer literacy is an important vehicle in attaining it.

An office PC is a microcosm of the enterprise use of IT in the company. Employing E-Mail and spreadsheets and accessing data bases for both internal and external information gives people an understanding and sense of the importance of data bases and communication networks to business effectiveness. There may be valid reasons for the executive's use of a PC system that only is realized by experience. The general conclusion is that there is a rationale in imparting computer literacy to that portion of the 50% of senior executives who do not have a computer in their office, and who are not computer literate.

COMPUTER-INFORMATION LITERACY: THE MENTORING PROCESS

Providing computer-information literacy offers a significant opportunity for the CIO to further the link of IT and the business, because it begins the process of building mutual credibility at the senior management level. The following six-step approach helps impart that literacy. The steps are not the total prescription for literacy; rather, they constitute a starter set, a motivation for continued executive awareness and involvement in information systems matters.

Identifying Major IT Champions

It is generally easy to identify the half dozen or fewer senior executives who make the major decisions that drive the corporation. The organization chart may not be the best starting point because some of the thought and action leaders are not found high on the chart but rather in key strategic areas of the company. Particular attention should be given to identify those who are or will be the IT champions who will sponsor major programs. These people will benefit from a more complete understanding of the new IT concepts that are emerging (e.g., business process reengineering) and the technology that drives these new initiatives.

Assigning IT Mentors to Senior IT Executives

The next step is to review the senior IT managers who have the potential to become mentors to the senior business managers. Although these managers will have a solid technical perspective, they will be primarily business oriented and well respected by the company for placing business needs above the technical solution. These people avoid acronyms and technical jargon. In addition, they have an interest in education and are able to convey ideas and complex thoughts to others.

Assessing Individual Executive Cognitive Styles

Each executive's computer-information literacy should be assessed using the measures presented in Exhibits II-1-1 and II-1-2, and then reviewed with the individual. The assessment serves as the starting point for developing the individual training programs.

It is important to understand the cognitive style of the senior executives selected as candidates for the IT mentoring program. Left-brain managers are more intuitive in nature and tend to rely more on the feel and overall sense of a situation, whereas right-brain managers are more analytical and rely more on numbers and statistics in reaching decisions. The latter tend to be more comfortable with using PCs and usually have a high degree of computer literacy. Many have come from the engineering ranks. The left-brain managers often have marketing or sales support backgrounds and rely heavily on their perspective concerning people.

One school of thought suggests that humans have different types of intelligences, with different parts of the brain controlling different abilities. For example, people are so constituted that some learn better from doing as opposed to reading. Well-known psychologist Howard Gardner indicates the existence of six intelligences: linguistic, musical, logical-mathematical, spatial, bodily kinesthetic, and personal.

Ted Reid, a psychologist and computer consultant, builds on Gardner's work, correlating types of intelligence and effective computer-learning techniques. Reid posits that the logical-mathematical and the musical do best with programmed instruction; the linguistic with written documentation; the spatial where the overall picture is shared first and the various tasks overviewed; and the bodily kinesthetic with a hands-on, do-it-yourself, trial-and-error approach. Those with personal intelligence, probably the majority of senior executives, will learn more effectively with personal, individual, one-on-one instruction. Although this is an oversimplification and it is apparent that many people have more than one intelligence, business people have generally been observed to fall into one of these six categories.

Although the colleges and business schools of this country may be turning out progressively more graduates with enhanced logical-mathematical skills, experience finds that executives with strong personal skills continue to be the predominant model. Nonetheless, the first step is to establish the management style and intelligence characteristic of the executives in question. It is useful to consider these differences in structuring learning techniques. Because most senior executives are predicted to be high in personal skills, a one-on-one, highly interactive mode of learning will be most effective.

Reviewing Pending Major IT Initiatives

The essence of the mentor educational approach is that the best education may not look like education at all. It is based on an existing problem to be solved and is definitely just-in-time (JIT) learning. The important thing is that the executive applies what he or she learns immediately to the problem at hand, and that the problem is a vital one to his or her area of responsibility. The project may be the development of an executive information system (EIS) that provides key operating and financial indicators to the senior executives of the company or it could be a major business process reengineering effort being launched in a key area of the business. The education program developed should focus on the elements necessary to gain a better understanding of the role of technology in the specific area of change.

Aligning Mentors and Business Champions to IT Initiatives

The mentors should be assigned based on the fit between the personalities and perspectives of the mentor and the executive. A high degree of compatibility must exist. In addition, the mentor must have a real understanding of the actual project selected and the technology options.

Developing Training Plans and Scheduling for Selected Initiatives

Cyrus Gibson, who is responsible for designing and delivering executive IT learning to a wide range of companies, has stated that just-in-time, needs-based learning is the most effective way of reaching executives. In times of economic tightness and heightened competitive pressures, executives do not want to be away from the action. Formal classroom instruction will not suffice. The education must be in real time and relevant to what is happening today.

The session logistics should be tailored to the executive's schedule and mode of operation. Most executives have 12-hour workdays of wall-to-wall meetings, with phone and individual inquiries punctuating the day. The information system executive must break into this agenda, to obtain an hour or two every week or so. Optimally, the session should be held first thing in the morning. The IS executive should make effective use of visual aids, state session objectives clearly, and use as illustrations real-life situations with which the business executive is familiar. The more customary two- or three-day, one-shot seminar must give way to the continued one- to two-hour modules that stress learning as a process, not an event.

Similarly, to develop computer literacy, the one-on-one approach and the one-to two-hour slots should be employed. A friendly introduction to E-Mail or the Internet should serve the purpose. Selecting a reasonable learning tool is crucial, because the executive will quickly lose interest if he has to grasp several dozen command or function codes. Again, the emphasis should be on the real world using actual company statistics or financial data. For example, data on product movement for the past two years can be accumulated by branch office, sales territory, key customer, or product line. Then, with simple icon pointing, the data can be manipulated for reporting historical information or used to project future product or customer activity. This exposure is more meaningful after the relevant issues have been discussed because the personal computer world is really a subset of the bigger corporate computer world. In other words, individuals are dealing with data bases, communications, and end-user computing.

CONCLUSION

Information literacy is undoubtedly more important than computer literacy. However, it is becoming clear that in many instances computer literacy forms the educational base for information literacy. For the crucial alignment between IT and business to occur, IT and senior business executives must work together and have a mutual respect for what the other is trying to accomplish. The personalized education program suggested here is an excellent vehicle for initiating the necessary respect.

The suggested approach predicates simple checklists to begin the assessment of the two literacies. Based on the results, a learning program focusing on training key executives by programs personally tailored to the individual executive's cognitive style is suggested. This approach runs counter to the standard process that is commonly used in many companies, where classes are held for any interested attendees. Although this may satisfy some, it is ineffective for senior managers. With information so pervasively important to companies, it is time to ensure that senior management is trained to make competitive use of this vital resource. The solution is to employ the IT-senior executive mentor approach, and personalize training rather than generalize it.

II-2

A Strategic Approach to Client/Server

William R. King

AN INCREASING STREAM of evidence attests to the beneficial impact of computers on organizations. That conclusion is hotly contested by some who require indisputable evidence of cause and effect, most of which cannot be measured.

There is indisputable and significant anecdotal evidence of productivity and profit gains tied to computing in firms in such industries as banking, insurance, and retailing, and in such applications as computer-aided design and customer service.

As many companies now face a round of budget requests to finance client/server computing, one thing is clear: there are organizations that have reaped great benefits from major new applications and new generations of computing systems, and there are also those that have not—or at least there are those that have taken many years to achieve significant rewards.

Just as the early mainframes and PCs offered the prospect of vast increases in computational power at relatively low cost, client/server technology offers new varieties of opportunities for significant computing benefits at low unit costs. It also holds the potential for enhancing enterprisewide communications efficiency and effectiveness. Some vendors of client/server products claim 50% reductions in IS costs and faster transaction throughput by an order of magnitude. However, these potential benefits will not automatically be realized by all firms that adopt client/server, any more than significant instantaneous benefits were realized by all those who installed mainframes in the early computer era. Those that fit client/server computing into their organizations are likely to reap significant benefits, but those that merely add on client/server systems probably will not, at least in the short run.

Today's near-compulsion to install client/server systems is illustrated by the CIO of a large Paris-based company, who said, almost apologetically, that the firm had not yet embarked on client/server on a widespread basis because it had too many other important things to do. The CIO's resignation to the conventional wisdom, that when the organization finished these important things it would naturally progress to implement a client/server approach, is somewhat surprising. It did not occur to this CIO that the client/server model might not be a good fit with this firm and its plans and culture.

It seems that in some organizations, IS professionals are in for another round of computer system investments motivated by "keeping up with the Joneses" and based on flimsy projections of benefits that may never be realized. Anyone who desires to avoid the possibility of a pell-mell rush to the next generation of computing should probably adopt the mantra: the pioneers are those who get killed on the frontier.

THE CASE FOR DEVELOPING A CLIENT/SERVER STRATEGY

As businesses have downsized, it is natural to consider the downsizing of computing. The current economics of computing—in which the power of a mainframe can now be had on a desktop—lead naturally to the consideration of a client/server approach.

IS Definition of Rightsizing. When the number of employees in a business firm is being reduced, the term *rightsizing* is often used as a mere euphemism for downsizing. However, in the IS world, rightsizing has a specific meaning: adopting the right computer platform for each business application.

Client/server computing thus enables rightsizing because it permits everything from front-ending graphical user interfaces (GUIs) for existing mainframe applications, to upsizing desktop departmental-level applications to servers with more robust operating systems, to offloading mainframe applications to extend the useful life of mainframes, to peer-to-peer client/server computing in which processes are dynamically distributed among clients and servers.

Client/server computing holds the prospect of giving everyone in an organization access to the right information at the right time. The old bugaboo of mainframe systems, in which people often waited or pleaded for the information they needed, is potentially overcome. With client/server computing, another specter of the 1980s—an inexperienced MBA armed with a PC spreadsheet and some questionable data making a serious recommendation to management and not being countered with valid corporate data—may become only a distant memory.

So, there is a strong case for many organizations to move to client/server computing, especially when the leading vendors advocate open systems and the inclusion of existing hardware and software into an enterprisewide client/server network.

THE CASE AGAINST CLIENT/SERVER

No single best computing system architecture exists for all organizations. Some firms that do vast amounts of number-crunching and transactions processing will be best served by existing mainframe-based systems for years to come. Firms in which security is critical will find that client/server computing does not yet offer the necessary level of protection against natural disasters or unauthorized access. Other organizations that have been ill-served by mainframes, free-standing PCs, and LANs will find the client/server architecture is the one that finally meets their needs.

However, client/server technology is as yet immature. Despite the conventional wisdom that it is the wave of the future, this immaturity makes it a high-risk venture if it is embarked on in a big way.

The classic "invest now or wait until the technology improves" conundrum is most serious when the technology under consideration is quite immature, because the decision to invest in an early generation of technology carries with it the risk of early obsolescence and of significant implementation difficulty. With a more mature technology, obsolescence is the only major issue.

Firms that determine that client/server computing is important to their business success may benefit from a major enterprisewide conversion. For others, a go-slow approach is more desirable.

As with any major new technology, the adoption of client/server computing is likely to be fraught with mishaps, cost overruns, and failures to meet schedules. If it were not so, many IS professionals would not recognize that they are operating in the computer arena.

In any case, a client/server strategy and implementation plan are needed.

ELEMENTS OF A CLIENT/SERVER STRATEGY

Several major strategic questions accompany decisions about implementing client/server computing. They are:

- How potentially important is it to the business?
- How well does client/server computing fit with the organization?
- What are the alternatives?
- What is the company's vision concerning the ultimate role of client/server computing in the enterprise?
- Can client/server computing be used as a facilitator of organizational change?

Related tactical (i.e., implementation) issues are:

- The selection of an organization unit in which client/server computing might best be piloted.
- The development of a plan to implement client/server computing in an orderly, phased manner.

Importance to the Business

If a strong business case can be made for client/server computing, there may well be justification for pioneering it. In several firms, client/server computing has already produced (or is expected to produce) a competitive advantage (e.g., greatly speeding up claims processing in an insurance company or loan approvals in a lending institution).

A good way to assess this business case is through a value-chain analysis. Such an analysis assesses what value enhancements client/server computing may provide in each link in the chain—inbound logistics, operations, outbound logistics, and after-sale service.

Organizational Fit

It is increasingly clear that the success of a managerial system depends on its fit with an organization. To be effective, organization systems must fit in many dimensions—structure, practices, culture, strategy. A basic question is, does the client/server architecture facilitate or inhibit the way in which the organization operates? Client/server computing is likely to be facilitative, for example, in organizations with a great deal of collaborative work, such as in teams, task forces, and projects. If the organizational culture has fostered communications outside the chain of command, client/server is likely to help; if the organization has been hierarchical and the culture has not allowed such communications, client/server may be disruptive.

What Are the Alternatives?

Because client/server computing is a major strategic choice, a range of alternatives should be clearly defined and evaluated. Outsourcing and a major program to stretch out the useful life of mainframes will often be among those alternatives.

Outsourcing. Outsourcing can be a way of getting rid of headaches, turning fixed costs into variable costs, and ensuring that competent technologists will manage the firm's networks and computers. Of course, if the business highly depends on information systems, outsourcing may lead to a "hollowing" of the enterprise, so it needs to be carefully thought through for its long-run implications.

Extending the Life of Mainframes. Extending the useful life of existing mainframe systems can be embarked on in a major way through a program of rescheduling runs to off-hours, cleaning out and archiving data that is not likely to be needed instantly, and moving applications to workstations. In addition, the simplest varieties of client/server computing may be used, such as front-ending the mainframe with GUIs and using minicomputers armed with appropriate software to search data bases and to translate mainframe messages.

A Vision

Whether there is currently a good fit, a vision of the ideal practical role of client/server computing in the enterprise should be created. This may be done by the CIO as an adjunct to a business vision that has already been created, or jointly by the CEO and CIO in the form of a business vision that incorporates the technology architecture.

For example, some organizations have adopted the learning organization concept as a vision or goal. Although the learning organization is not precisely defined, it is clear that communications and memory capabilities such as those currently provided by Lotus Notes software is potentially important to extending learning beyond individuals to teams and organizations. Any company that has the creation of a learning organization as a part of its vision must plan for an information infrastructure that facilitates organizational learning.

Organizational Change

One example of client/server computing as a facilitator of change concerns employee empowerment. Indeed, empowerment without adequate systems support and monitoring is a recipe for disaster. So, if empowerment is an element of the business vision, client/server computing may be one element of a strategy to pursue that vision, even if it is not currently a good fit with the organization.

Client/server computing also can go hand-in-hand with business process re-engineering, because it has the potential to enable the streamlined structures, integrated processes, and shorter cycle times that are often the objectives of process redesign.

IMPLEMENTING THE STRATEGY

Whether an organization takes a massive or modular approach to the adoption of client/server computing, it needs an implementation plan. In those many cases in which a massive approach is undesirable, a planned evolutionary path is needed.

Experimenting

One useful implementation strategy is to select an organizational subunit or application that appears to offer significant potential for client/server computing and to develop a system there. This system can serve as a pilot for the entire organization and, if it is successful, as a model for other subunits to emulate.

In making such a selection, consideration must be made of the long-term impact of a potential failure of the pilot system. If the implementation of a client/server system in the subunit or application is fraught with missteps and unexpected problems and costs, the guinea pig unit may be traumatized (even though a great deal of learning may occur that will help in other areas). In the worst-case scenario, a mission-critical application or unit will be fouled up through experimentation with client/server computing.

This scenario suggests that an organization should not experiment on its most critical subunit—the one that is the key to business success or is the keeper of a core business technology. Often, a unit or application that is currently functioning badly can make a good target for a pilot system, assuming that the quality of the current computer support is believed to be part of the cause for poor performance. Such a choice has the added advantage of providing visible, timely benefit if the pilot is successful.

Developing an Enterprisewide Implementation Plan

After experimentation is complete, the initial general plan for application-by-application or unit-by-unit implementation of client/server systems will probably need to be revised. Pilot testing provides a much better assessment of the practical benefits that can be expected, as well as of their timing. The difficulties encountered in the pilot can also be extrapolated to various units. This data provides a basis for identifying a growth path for client/server computing in the organization.

Clearly, such a plan must involve standards—not just for platforms, protocols, and data bases, but also for how new applications and units are to be brought online. For example, appropriate standards might specify processes for end-user involvement in developing applications, the use of prototyping, and the parameters for training the people on whom the success of client/server computing ultimately depends.

CONCLUSION

Client/server computing offers great potential for an organization. However, for many, a go-slow approach will produce the greatest benefits.

A client/server strategy must rest on a business case and give consideration to the fit with the organization. The strategy must be the best of a set of carefully considered alternatives, be based on an integrated business and technology vision, and consider whether client/server computing can be a facilitator and enabler of change.

An implementation approach that involves pilot testing the technology in a non-mission critical application or unit, and then using the results of the pilot project to develop a step-by-step growth path, will be useful for many firms.

II-3

Client/Server as an Enabler of Change

Donald Saelens and Stuart Nelson

THE BUSINESS PRESS is full of talk of reinventing business to be more responsive to customers. The Minnesota Department of Revenue (DOR) has put words
into action. For Minnesota businesses, a redesigned sales tax system will mean
less heartburn at tax time and fewer dollars spent on lawyers and accountants to
help them comply with the state's sales and use tax laws. For the state, the project
is expected to enable the DOR to resolve delinquent accounts in less than 90 days
(instead of up to two years) and reduce the number of paper tax returns it
receives.

This chapter describes the reengineering project and its targeted changes in the
department's mainframe-based systems and in the DOR's functional orientation.
The IS principles guiding the client/server development effort are also shared.

FAILINGS OF A RIGID SYSTEM

As the state's tax- and revenue-collecting arm, the DOR has frequent and
direct contact with Minnesota businesses and citizens. Under the old system,
DOR employees operated within a compliance process that offered no systematic
capability for accommodating exceptions or being responsive to changing business practices and demographics.

Continuous changes in the state's complex sales and use-tax laws often left
businesses confused about how to comply with the law. They simply received
their tax forms in the mail with directions to file and pay. When they called the
DOR for help, they found employees there hard to reach or unable to answer
their questions because employees did not have the appropriate information
readily available. As a result, businesses ended up sending in the wrong returns,
the incorrect payment, or nothing at all.

The state sales tax system is one of three major tax systems under the DOR's
jurisdiction (the others are income and property) serving 151,000 businesses and
administering more than $2 billion in sales and use taxes annually. The sales tax
was originally created in the late 1960s as a temporary measure. Over the years,
the tax became permanent; businesses also sprang up in the state and many
companies evolved into new lines of business. The tax system and the DOR fell

out of sync with the times and with business growth, reaching the breaking point in the late 1980s. Employees could no longer trust the taxpayer data because maintaining updated information on all businesses was virtually impossible. In addition, it took months to properly process returns. The agency had trouble effectively dealing with problems and questions taxpayers had about their returns and payment.

The chief contributor to these problems was the DOR's outdated computer system built 25 years ago. Although the business environment changed over the years, the agency was constrained by the computer. Employees could not apply common sense to case management because the computer set the parameters. As a result, many good suggestions from employees on how to improve the process could not be accommodated because all cases had to be made to conform to the computer.

Another problem that hamstrung the agency was its functional orientation. Employees were charged with narrowly focused tasks—auditing, data entry, and payment processing, for example. This job design, which contributed to employees' inability to address taxpayer concerns outside of their area of expertise, was reinforced by the DOR's criteria for judging and rewarding employees. Instead of measuring employee performance with an eye toward the entire sales tax process, the agency emphasized the accomplishment of individual tasks and activities.

These inefficiencies took a toll on the state's bank account. Because the DOR could not swiftly identify taxpayer problems, many businesses—more than 13,000 in 1992—paid either less than they should have or nothing at all. Problems in collecting this revenue were further compounded because more than half of the delinquent companies were no longer in business. Inaccurate information in the agency's computer made it difficult for employees to know who was in business and who was not. Because every delinquent case represents potentially lost revenue to the state, the DOR needed to make it easier for companies to file (and file correctly), and it had to give employees the tools and means to reduce the time it takes to track down and collect taxes from nonfilers.

THE REENGINEERING PLAN

The agency began by redefining its mission and its image among taxpayers. In addition to holding regular meetings of top officials, the DOR solicited input from employees and taxpayers. The result of the two-year strategic planning process, the agency's first, was a comprehensive business plan and a succinct mission statement: to win compliance with Minnesota's revenue system.

What is unique about this mission statement is how it positions the agency in relation to taxpayers. Embodied in the new mission statement is a philosophical shift from demanding compliance to winning it. This new philosophy places equal emphasis on making it easy for people to file and pay the right amount of taxes, helping them understand what is expected of them, and enabling them to choose the right option for compliance that best fits their needs.

To reach this goal, changes were targeted in the department's mainframe-based systems and the DOR's functional orientation. Among the other constraints the agency faced were increasing workload, a declining cost/benefit ratio, and the end of several years of budget growth.

The agency had already received funding to replace the 1960s computer system, and DOR executives wanted to ensure that it was invested intelligently. After reviewing the challenges, the agency decided that rather than reautomating the current inefficient work processes, it should apply its funding to a complete reengineering of the sales tax system.

The overall reengineering project involved three phases:

- *Phase 1: Vision and strategy.* The DOR reviewed the sales tax system business processes and established targets that would bring significant improvements in performance.
- *Phase 2: Business process redesign.* Ten months later, teams used the targets established during phase 1 as the basis for creating and developing redesigned business processes.
- *Phase 3: Development and implementation.* Another 10 months later, the final phase began involving the development, testing, and implementation of appropriate information systems, job designs, and management systems.

PROCESS REDESIGN FOR CUSTOMER SERVICE

With the support of the highest levels of DOR leadership, the project team—which comprised representatives from all areas of the agency, as well as several external consultants—redesigned the sales tax system's six key processes:

- Taxpayer registration and profiling.
- Sales and use tax filing.
- Filing processing.
- Ensuring compliance accuracy.
- Ensuring payment.
- Performance information dissemination. The IT support for each of the redesigned processes will be discussed later.

All processes cross divisional lines within the organization.

The result of this process redesign effort is a significantly streamlined sales tax system, the heart of which is the taxpayer registration and profiling process.

A New Registration and Profiling Process

Because many of the problems the DOR experienced in the past stemmed from its lack of timely and accurate taxpayer information, the new process was designed to handle greatly expanded registration options available to taxpayers and more detailed information about companies' operations.

Today, when a taxpayer registers, a unique, customized profile is created in the system's data base. This profile—which can be updated by any DOR employee or even by the taxpayer—collects and stores pertinent company information, including the type of business the company is involved in, how long it has been operating, its location, and its relationship with the DOR. In addition, taxpayers can register in several different ways (e.g., phone, fax, or mail) and can be accommodated easily regardless of whether they are filing permanently, seasonally, or just once.

DOR employees are now able to send customized return forms to taxpayers instead of generic forms. Another advantage of the customized taxpayer profile is that it allows the agency to be proactive in supplying businesses with tailored education and service options. Using information from the profile, the DOR can inform taxpayers of industry-specific educational offerings or potential law changes.

Process Improvements

Before the process redesign, a taxpayer with payment problems was continually handed off to different employees, each of whom handled a small portion of the case. Now, most delinquent taxpayers can be assigned to one DOR employee who follows the case through to completion or resolution. Employees are empowered to make decisions throughout the process to resolve cases more quickly and to take accelerated enforcement action to ensure that every case is resolved within 90 days. The future work load of cases for businesses still operating is expected to improve significantly. Today's volume is 5,700 cases with an average age of 20 months and a balance of $3,500. By interceding early, DOR employees will be able to ensure that the state receives the revenue due more quickly and that the process does not become a burden on the taxpayer.

The greatest opportunity for improved efficiency is in the area of filing processing. Each year, the agency receives approximately 900,000 paper returns filed by Minnesota businesses. Every one of these returns must be received in the mailroom, opened, sorted, and routed. The information on the returns is entered manually into the computer by a team of employees, after which the team microfilms the returns for future reference. The DOR expects to reduce the number of paper returns it receives to 600,000 because many more taxpayers will qualify for quarterly or annual filing, and state and local option tax returns have been combined. Initially, high-dollar businesses will be required to file and pay electronically; the agency plans to further trim the number of paper returns it handles because 95% of businesses, regardless of dollar volume, will have the option to file electronically.

INFORMATION SYSTEMS DECISIONS

Crucial to the success of the redesigned processes is the information technology developed to support them. The agency's 25-year-old mainframe system, patched numerous times throughout the years, could no longer deliver the performance necessary for DOR employees to be effective. Therefore, the team designed and built a completely new system, based on a client/server architecture that would be flexible enough to meet the needs of the redesigned environment.

Technological underpinnings of the system are Macintoshes and Windows-based PCs that are linked by local area networks to both a miniserver and the agency's existing legacy mainframe. This technology provides users with a much more friendly environment in which to operate. The client/server architecture brings processing power and critical information to employees' desktops. It can also easily accommodate the multitude of exceptions and differences that DOR employees encounter from taxpayers as large as Northwest Airlines to those as small as traditional mom-and-pop businesses.

In addition to the technology, several other factors contributed to the project's success. First was the fact that the agency's IS department was involved from the beginning of the project, not brought in at the tail end to build supporting systems in a vacuum. IS was also represented on the executive steering committee. This provided the opportunity for a better understanding among the IS staff of what the users needed to do their jobs more effectively.

Another factor was the set of IS management principles relating to, among other things, technology infrastructure, applications development, and data that the project team devised to guide itself through the project. These principles helped to keep team members focused on their mission. They are:

- Infrastructure:
  - Networked intelligent workstations will be available on every knowledge worker's desk.
  - Cooperative processing will be implemented in a client/server architecture, with each platform handling what it does best.
  - An open systems architecture is favored over closed proprietary architectures.
  - Mainframe systems will not be modified beyond what is necessary to support existing data.
- Applications development:
  - Pilots and prototyping are to be used to help us learn and apply new ways to deliver information products.
  - The underlying information technologies will be transparent to the user.
  - Applications will be written to operate on or as close to the workstation as possible.
  - Development will occur on IBM and compatible equipment, not on Macintoshes.
- Data:
  - Information will be located at the level that will best facilitate its shared access.
  - Existing data will continue to be stored and maintained on the mainframe. New data will be stored and maintained on the client/server platform.
  - Data redundancy will be avoided except in cases of performance.
  - Data will be transmitted electronically whenever feasible.

Finally, the team selected a proprietary Accelerated Applications Development (X/AD) methodology that makes extensive use of pilots and prototyping. The team thus avoided spending two years defining requirements and then pushing the system onto users all at once. The resulting system more closely reflects users' true requirements (and was more readily accepted by employees). The methodology promotes the use of time-boxing, which limits the amount of time available for a task, a design iteration, a work session, or even an entire development project. The project team was able to define, design, and implement applications in 12 months.

THE INFORMATION TECHNOLOGY CHANGES

The redesign effort resulted in significant changes to the way the DOR conducts business. Without the appropriate enabling technology, however, the improved operations would exist only on paper. The following sections discuss the major changes enacted in the agency's six key processes and how information technology was applied to make these changes a reality.

Taxpayer Registration and Profiling. The redesigned registration and profiling process expands the registration options available to taxpayers as well as the information about their operations. To support this new process, the project team developed the following:

- New registration screens, expanded taxpayer profile data base structure, and follow-up structure.
- A process to synchronize the new taxpayer data base with existing mainframe systems.
- A system to distribute and manage the disbursement of available taxpayer identification numbers.
- A system to accommodate taxpayers' electronic access to and update capability of their profile information.

Sales and Use-Tax Filing. New filing cycles have been established; returns can be customized; and taxpayers can have options concerning the method they use to file and remit sales and use taxes. To address these changes, the team developed:

- A new flexible sales tax system to create customized, computer-readable sales tax returns based on a taxpayer's profile.
- A 24-hour touchtone computer response and personal computer bulletin.
- Software for customers' use in filing, paying, and requesting information on sales and use taxes.

In addition, the team upgraded the existing workstations to accommodate responses to and interactions with taxpayers, and it modified the core tax system on the mainframe to handle individual use-tax reporting.

Filing Processing. The actual processing of the tax returns received by the agency presented several challenges to the project team. To satisfy new mandates—for example, that critical tax return information be available online on the day of arrival (with the balance of that information being available within seven calendar days), that filing information must be 98% accurate, and that tax remittances be deposited immediately—the team implemented an imaging and scanning system to capture filing and payment information and developed interfaces between the core sales tax system and other existing systems.

Ensuring Compliance Accuracy. The profile information obtained during the registration process is used by the agency to customize its services to taxpayers on the basis of their needs and compliance history. To provide access to such information, the team developed.

- Software for electronic links to taxpayers.
- A compliance screening data base with an automatic update from transaction data bases.
- Statistical applications and expert systems to identify candidates for specific compliance actions.
- A work flow management and case preparation system to automatically assign and track compliance activities.

Ensuring Payment. This process is divided into accounts receivable resolution and registered nonfiler resolution. In the new process, delinquent taxpayers are to be assigned to one DOR employee who has discretion in choosing how to deal with them. The goal is to resolve all cases within 90 days of identification. The process is supported by PC-LANs that provide access to the work flow management system as well as other information systems and offer a place to record case activity for future reference in assistance with case resolution.

Performance Information Dissemination. As part of the process redesign, new measures have been instituted to monitor the department's progress in winning compliance. To help management in applying these measures, the project team developed automated performance measurement capabilities and links in all new information systems. The team also created and installed a technological infrastructure to support the development and operation of the online systems containing the sales tax performance measures.

EFFECTS ON THE ORGANIZATION

An effort of this magnitude has profound implications for the organization. The project generated uneasiness among the IS staff, especially certain technology specialists who were faced with a completely new technological environment and new job responsibilities.

One of the biggest challenges the project team faced was approaching the redesign of jobs with the same openness of mind used in redesigning the processes. When it comes to the human perspective, friends and colleagues are involved. It does not help the organization or its employees to adapt to the changes if these human issues are avoided.

Project leaders initially thought they could gain employee acceptance of the new system if they just communicated to employees what was happening. But the team quickly discovered that communication is not enough; people actually have to start doing the new work and using the new technology as soon as possible.

This was accomplished in part by instituting a technology lab in which employees could feel safe to experiment and make mistakes. Although communication about what the organization is trying to accomplish alleviates some concerns employees have about new technology, there's no substitute for hands-on experience.

All DOR employees experienced firsthand how IT could be used to break down organizational barriers and draw people together. One of the earliest deliverables of the project was an integrated infrastructure of 500 workstations equipped with groupware products. Within four to five days of installing the application, employees who were formerly not allowed to communicate with each other were in touch by electronic mail, and DOR leadership could communicate directly and immediately with all employees.

Lotus Notes was installed as a departmentwide tool for team members in the sales tax reengineering project. Discussion data bases were established for the individual teams that focused on the separate business processes that made up the overall sales tax system. These data bases were used to share ideas and concepts and to coordinate information across teams. In addition, data bases were established to track project issues and their resolution, as well as to document decisions that could be referred to as needed by any member of the project.

CONCLUSION

The project demanded a lot of energy, time, and brainpower from the entire DOR staff. The outcome, however, benefits both taxpayers and the agency.

For taxpayers, the new system not only makes it easier to comply with the tax laws, but it will also reduce their cost of compliance. (The Minnesota Retail Merchants Association has estimated that Minnesota businesses spend $55 million a year to comply, most of which is spent on professional expertise to help them navigate through changes in tax law.) If they have questions about taxes, businesses now know where to go for help, and they can get that help much more quickly and completely. In addition to being given instructions on what they must do to comply, they are asked what changes would help them comply more easily. Businesses are encouraged to participate in the policy-making process to ensure that sound, realistic policies are created.

For DOR employees, the reengineered environment and new technology give them the flexibility to be creative in how they approach their work. Instead of single-function jobs, employees have multifunctional responsibilities. Rather than focusing inward on information flow, employees emphasize an external customer view. They are no longer handcuffed to a rigid method of dealing with taxpayers, largely because the new client/server system supports the new processes and provides everyone with instant access to important information.

II-4

Managing Junk Computing

Ruth Guthrie and Paul Gray

JUNK COMPUTING. The words evoke a variety of images of deeds most computer users are familiar with or guilty of:

- Sending copies of status memos to an entire organization rather than to the people who need them.
- Endlessly revising a document or a presentation to make it super perfect.
- Running meaningless what-if cases on spreadsheets.
- Playing computer games.

The phenomenon is real, although its cost probably does not reach the $2 billion estimated in the popular press.

This chapter presents the findings of a year-long study of the performance gains (and losses) of junk computing. It also offers managers recommendations on how to reduce performance losses without stifling their employees' creativity.

WHAT IS JUNK COMPUTING?

Junk computing is the use of information systems in a way that does not directly advance organizational goals.

This definition attaches a stigma to any computing that is not work related or goal oriented. Indeed, the word *junk* itself has an immediate negative connotation.

It is important to recognize that junk computing does not always diminish productivity; rather, it has the potential for adding value to a work environment. Social aspects of computing, unrelated to organizational goals, contribute to team building and facilitate communication. Junk computing can also satisfy individual curiosity and the desire to explore.

Junk computing can be measured in terms of time, cost, use, or personal behavior, but determining whether a particular instance of computing is junk is often subjective. Junk computing can have both positive and negative effects on an organization. It is caused by excessiveness, environmental conditions, social or cultural pressures, individual behavior styles, and miscommunication and mismanagement.

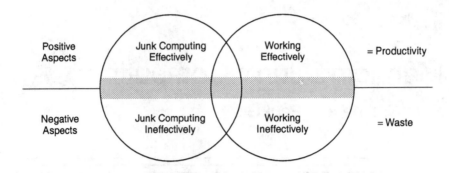

Exhibit II-4-1. Positive and Negative Aspects of Junk Computing

Exhibit II-4-1 depicts the positive and negative aspects of junk computing. At work, people who perform tasks highly effectively are judged productive, whereas the efforts of others who perform less effectively are judged wasteful. This judgment is, of course, subjective. The gray area in the exhibit represents the cases for which the difference between productivity and waste is unclear. Similarly, as the exhibit also shows, junk computing can be effective or ineffective.

Exhibit II-4-2 lists the performance gains and losses resulting from junk computing. Pure junk computing, such as compulsive game playing, adds no value to organizational goals and is perceived as such. However, cost can determine whether an activity is junk. If high-wage earners can produce a product, such as graphics, using lower-wage staff, then performing the task themselves becomes junk even though no coordination time is involved. Time, quality, and satisfaction also determine whether an activity is junk.

TYPES OF JUNK COMPUTING

Extended interviews with 22 users at various levels in a manufacturing organization identified 19 types of junk computing activities (see Exhibit II-4-3).

Seven types of junk computing were most frequently mentioned in the interviews: games, personal work, junk reporting, excessive computerization, excessive detail, excessive attention to form, and E-mail.

Games and Personal Work. Games and personal work are examples of non-work-related computing. Most individuals saw these activities as negative. A mid-level line manager said she played solitaire sometimes because she needed to take a break from the many documents she was required to read. She also had an employee who was found on several occasions playing computer games in his office instead of performing expected tasks in an engineering lab. The manager

Gains	Losses
Ability to Produce Finished Product	Corporate Record/Memory
Computer Composition	Creativity
Control	Department Obsolescence
Coordination	Excessive Attention to Form
Enhanced Self-Confidence	Games
Fewer Secretaries	Hardware Mismatch
Increased Spatial Ability	Loss of Sight of Real Goal
Learning	Manipulation for Manipulation's Sake
Paperless Office	Needless Applications
Playing	Needless Reporting
Reduced Coordination Time	Needless Storage of Old Data
Relaxation	Overcoordination
Speed	Overiteration
Streamlined Processes	Playing
	Personal Work
	Skills
	Software Mismatch
	Standardization and Control
	Time Away from Work
	Too Much Data

Exhibit II-4-2. Performance Gains and Losses from Junk Computing

---

felt the problem with this particular worker went much deeper than game playing.

Junk Reporting. Organizations create reports that are never read, distribute them to endlessly growing lists, and populate them with erroneous or meaningless data. Typically, people stack such unused reports on the bookshelf or throw them away.

Computerization, Detail, and Attention to Form. Computerization, detail, and attention to form are all necessary in a computerized world. These abilities give workers information, organizational skills, and quality that could not be attained before the advent of computers. However, when carried to extremes, these characteristics become junk computing.

Examples of such excesses abound. A director of human resources questioned the use of an elaborate electronic class-scheduling system. And a manger of operations automation found he was required to schedule every minor activity he was involved in, instead of focusing on goals and major milestones. Yet, in interviews, program managers indicated that they did not require these levels of updates. Estimates of the time required to achieve quality of form often exceeded the time to do the work. In each case, people did excess computing not because

Junk Computing Activities

Junk Computing Activities	E	P	C	B	M
Most Frequently Identified Types					
Games		X		X	X
Personal Work		X		X	
Junk Reporting	X			X	
Excessive Computerization	X			X	X
Excessive Detail	X		X	X	X
Excessive Attention to Form	X		X	X	X
E-Mail					
Frequently Identified Types					
Inappropriate Tools		X		X	
Inappropriate Skill Level				X	
Perfectionism	X	X		X	
Learning and Experimentation					
Duplication of Effort	X				
Infrequently Identified Types					
Having Too Much Data		X		X	
Using a Computer for Status		X	X		
Other Identified Types					
Finding Data or Diskettes					
Lack of Systems Integration					
System Changes Causing Problems					
Not Asking for Help		X	X	X	
Loss of Standardization					

Key:
E—Excessiveness
P—Physical environment
C—Cultural and social environment
B—Individual behavior
M—Miscommunication and mismanagement

Exhibit II-4-3. Junk Computing Activities and Their Causes

it was needed but because it could be done. A large part of this phenomenon is a technical form of keeping up with the Joneses. If one person computerizes a report and adds a few tables and a logo, others feel inadequate and follow suit.

E-Mail. People send a single message to a large distribution list. Almost all the people who receive such messages view them as junk E-mail. Some miss meetings and information because they don't check messages often enough. Others dedicate large amounts of time to reading and responding to mail of no value. Conversely, one project engineer got so many E-mail messages that he simply ignored them all. A line manager received E-mail status reports she had not asked for.

E-mail accounts for 18% of Internet use. Users learn quickly that subscribing to list servers can result in hundreds of E-mail messages daily, many of them inappropriate to the server's topic. Another popular temptation is net surfing, an enjoyable, aimless browsing of the Internet with questionable business value.

Exhibit II-4-4 briefly explains each of the remaining 12 types of junk computing.

WHY DOES JUNK COMPUTING EXIST?

As shown in Exhibit II-4-3, the main causes of junk computing are:

- Excessiveness.
- The physical environment.
- Cultural or social pressures.
- Individual behavior styles.
- Miscommunication and mismanagement.

Excessiveness. An activity in and of itself does not constitute junk computing. Rather, when a person spends an inordinate amount of time doing it, it becomes junk. For example, we found people who spent days creating a magnificent presentation for a short, low-level meeting. Excessiveness, together with individual behavior styles, was the most prominent cause of junk computing.

The Physical Environment. A physical facility that is inadequately or improperly configured to support productive work encourages junk computing. If games exist on a system, people will play them. Incompatible systems (e.g., a PC printer and a Macintosh computer) result in high transaction costs for transferring, reentering, and finding information, and for training. At a higher level, not integrating MRP2 with the corporate financial package causes workers to perform junk computing to put these packages together. These incompatibilities are not new. Junk processes existed before the computer. Now, automation has made them simply faster and more frequent.

Cultural or Social Pressures. If rewards are given for creating elaborate computerized presentations or producing massive documentation, employees will

Inappropriate Tools. Either not having access to the right tool (a resource problem) or using a tool that was not optimal for the task (a training problem). Examples: Using a spreadsheet as a word processor; "machine hopping" because needed tools are not available on a single machine; creating color charts when a color printer is unavailable.

Inappropriate Skill Level. Not knowing enough about what software can do (a training problem). Example: Repeatedly typing or drawing rather than using the copy feature.

Perfectionism. Numerous repetition of a task in slightly different ways in the expectation of higher quality.

Learning and Experimentation. A positive form of junk computing that can also be excessive or unjustified. Example: Learning C++ when a project requires Ada. Taking time away from other work to learn the intricacies of a departmental LAN.

Duplication of Effort. Creating personal data bases when the information readily exists elsewhere, or rekeying data that is available electronically. Example: Making a personal spreadsheet of program cost data rather than accessing the corporate record.

Having Too Much Data. Producing and storing vast amounts of data that cannot possibly be processed for information.

Using a Computer for Status. Having a PC in one's office to appear computer literate, or having a high-powered system that exceeds the needs of the job. Example: Having a Sun Workstation to do word processing.

Finding Data. Time invested looking for lost information in the form of files, file names, and lost diskettes.

Lack of Systems Integration. Not being able to readily merge data from differing systems to gain insight and knowledge, causing wasted time when managers perform manual merges.

System Changes. Changes to one computing system that negatively affect other existing systems. Example: Old programs that will not run under a new operating system.

Not Asking for Help. Searching for a solution on the computer to a computing problem when experts are readily available to help.

Lack of Standardization. Time lost because individuals keep reinventing formats and aesthetics.

Exhibit II-4-4. Additional Examples of Junk Computing

---

produce these items. A copycat phenomenon exists as well. For example, if one person produces a fancy presentation for a manager, other people will do the same.

Individual Behavior Styles. Junk computing is also the result of individual behavior styles. It is often said to occur among people characterized as enamored with technology, or as a natural course of work. In any office, some people stand out as experimenters with technology (be they good or bad at it); others are seen as not prone to use technology at all.

Some employees prefer to control every aspect of work rather than delegate tasks to subordinates or peers. By producing their own work, these individuals gain control over how the final product looks. However, they wind up overproducing the actual product, which is paper.

Furthermore, when high-level people, such as managers, create their own viewgraphs instead of allowing professional artists to do the job at a much lower cost (and with attention to standards and quality), they raise more than the expense of the task. A behavior style that causes managers to not do the managerial work for which they are hired leads to significant and more serious opportunity costs.

Miscommunication and Mismanagement. Miscommunication and mismanagement between management and employees run along a two-way street. Managers ask for things that they don't really want or need, and employees try to win favor by embellishing their work. For example, management requires updated spreadsheets, reports, and presentation materials too frequently. In the case of presentations, employees spend so much time creating glitzy presentation materials that real work suffers. Such presentations do not even yield helpful or insightful feedback. Because of vague task descriptions, excess dry runs and revisions are required. Many of these excesses are the result of bad management; computing simply increases the amount of time and money spent on them.

Mid-level managers indicated that when senior managers see a glitzy, computerized chart or schedule, they instantly praise the work. In recognizing people with compliments, they indirectly ask people to spend time making things pretty.

Operations-level employees believe that management uses technology to avoid working with people. However, many operations-level employees do not clearly understand what program management does. Whereas they perceived team leaders' updating of schedules and reports as waste, from a management perspective, such updating during slow times is a great time saver when time is at a premium.

Mid-level program managers also believe that managers use technology, particularly computing, to avoid people. Unlike the operations-level people, who see this practice as a status issue, mid-level managers believe the impersonality of computing offers a way of avoiding confrontation. Often we observed that when things went wrong on a program, it was emotionally easier to propose a technological solution even though the problem was procedural or human in origin. Purchasing new, improved, user friendly information systems, leading to more junk computing, was easier than confronting employees and rearranging work flows.

WHAT CAN MANAGERS DO ABOUT JUNK COMPUTING?

Faced with junk computing, most managers (such as the project engineer who simply ignored his E-mail) apply bandages. An account manager hired only people already competent with technology. Other managers assign more work.

We believe that several more global control tactics can help manage junk computing. Although these tactics can be effective, their excessive application carries risks. The wise manager will trade off the gains from these tight control mechanisms with the losses from a more laissez-faire attitude.

Controlling Excessiveness Through Awareness

Once sensitized to the topic of junk computing, people begin to apply more critical standards. But awareness is a subjective control mechanism. People will still produce outputs they feel are priceless even though recipients consider them junk. Nonetheless, heightened awareness produces a form of control through self-regulation.

Controlling Environmental Factors

Eliminating the Potential for Junk Computing. Managers can take a strict approach to controlling junk computing. A rule stating no games, no personal work, strictly enforced, eliminates computing that is clearly not work related. Simply not installing games and deleting existing games from hard drives can deter their use.

Similarly, a manager can eliminate applications that do not add value. For example, a design group may be given CAD/CAM systems but no E-mail based on the premise that design professionals should spend less time corresponding and more time designing.

Although easy in theory, deleting software is difficult to enforce in practice.

Standardizing. When no rules exist, employees spend extraordinary amounts of time inventing. For example, time is wasted selecting fonts, formats, and presentation graphics templates. Dictating that all documents be prepared with the same font or that standard formats be used for viewgraphs saves time. Employees no longer try to gain recognition through glitzy paper products and they create less chart junk.

Applying End-User Computing Policy Uniformly. Five strategies for managing end-user computing are laissez faire, monopolist, acceleration, marketing, and operations-based. These strategies can be used as business policies to control the level of junk computing. A firm can adopt a policy toward junk computing that best reflects its approach to the regulation of technology.

The most relaxed strategy, laissez faire, would not require standardization and allows users freedom to experiment and play. The strictest strategy, operations-based, creates an environment in which computing systems and processes are highly regulated and highly similar. Whichever of these policies is applied to end-user computing should be applied to junk computing.

Controlling Behavior

Training. Sensitivity to junk computing can be introduced during training. In addition to learning what computer applications do, employees can learn how the applications add value and how to use them appropriately and effectively. Such training helps people realize that they need not always use a computer to be productive.

Economic Control. Creating a situation in which users are charged for their computing resources may eliminate some junk computing. The danger in doing this is that it may also eliminate potentially useful computing. For example, a user charged for E-mail usage may log on to a computer system less frequently or may cease to use E-mail altogether.

Controlling Mismanagement: Fostering Sound Management and Communication

Avoiding Management-Created Problems. Managers can bring junk computing onto themselves through lack of direction, rewarding aesthetics not thought, and being unable to deal with people. By examining how the messages they send and the requirements they impose affect people, managers can learn to send messages that foster the right behavior.

Creating an Environment that Recognizes Junk for What It Is. Good managers cultivate environments in which thought is valued and rewarded. Instead of becoming the quality police for their department, managers should foster employee monitoring of quality. Peer pressure to produce high-quality work in content and form is highly effective. It creates a working environment that is challenging and satisfying.

Controlling Technology

Some technologies offer solutions for minimizing junk and maximizing productivity. For some users, E-mail can be a highly time-consuming application with low value and redundant messages. Software filters screen and rank messages by priority, saving the user valuable time. For example, a user may want to answer messages from superiors first, take more time to answer questions from subordinates, and ignore seminar announcements.

An information filter is also capable of actively seeking information on topics of interest to a user based on a user-defined profile. This approach eliminates the time-consuming, low-skill task of sifting through data. Filters can also eliminate the temptation for people to become sidetracked on other topics when faced with too much information.

Technological devices can actively seek games and resumes on a network and eliminate them. However, users can store games on a diskette or disguise them as work-related files. This countermeasure is an example of the dictum that all systems are competitive. In other words, no matter what you do, someone will try to beat it. It is also possible to monitor network activity and investigate anomalous use patterns. Technological spying on employees' computer work can discourage positive investigation and experimentation. In this case, the manager faces a paradox: although frivolous computer activity is undesirable, a good manager wants clever people to try new things.

GOOD JUNK COMPUTING AND THE PROBLEM OF CONTROL

Control is a difficult issue in junk computing because it can stifle creativity. A manager does not want employees to spend hours creating computer output that does not directly advance organizational goals. Yet the same manager wants people to explore new technology and new possibilities. In deciding how to control computing activity, a manager must decide whether the waste associated with a free environment is so great as to warrant strict control. In our experience, junk computing is not always harmful, just as work is not always productive.

We know that the use of a wide range of tools and integrated rather than isolated information systems is more productive for knowledge workers. Furthermore, in computing, people perceive that the quality of what they produce is strongly linked to their ability to deal with aesthetics.

An organizational policy of strict control may cause resentment, particularly among knowledge workers. Too often, a control policy is applied throughout an organization when it is only appropriate for specific groups, such as production units.

In summary, even though our study yielded many examples of junk computing, the learning from them should be encouraged. As Exhibit II-4-2 shows, junk computing results in performance gains as well as losses.

CONCLUSION

Junk computing exists. It occurs, often as not, because people do the right things; they just do them to excess. It occurs because management does not recognize it, or gives signals that encourage it. It occurs because people feel empowered by the computer but do not realize that they are neither the most efficient nor the most effective person to do a job. And finally, it occurs because people are not trained properly.

Junk computing may be one explanation for the much-discussed productivity paradox—the idea popular in the late 1980s that office productivity was not improving despite massive investments in desktop computing. The cost of junk computing eats away at productivity benefits. Management that is sensitized to junk computing can use the methods recommended here to reduce the performance losses resulting from junk computing.

II-5

Morale Management in Today's IS Environment

Donald R. Fowler

A STRAW POLL of computer professionals at a national meeting surveyed factors, either positive or negative, that affected morale. The responses, which came mostly from mainframe technical professionals, indicated that morale was being negatively affected by four key issues (see Exhibit II-5-1). Respondents gave almost no examples of positive reinforcement within the business organization.

The most pressing morale issue was concern for both long-term future careers in information systems and in maintaining job positions within the current business organization. The next most prevalent issue was lack of trust in senior management, experienced as a lack of confidence in management to lead, properly communicate, and properly enable personnel. The third issue involved the sense that the business or IS organization was adrift and going in different directions. No goal or direction was apparent, and employees fear that no one is in charge. The last issue concerned resistance to change within the organization or business. Other responses included personal conflicts, monetary issues, and job evaluation disagreements.

CAREER CONCERNS

Concerns over career had multiple causes. Respondents indicated that their companies were no longer investing in education. Instead of developing skills in the current staff in such new areas as client/server computing, local area networks (LANs), object-oriented technology, or data base management systems, businesses are buying new skills through contractors or hiring new employees.

Eroding Skills. When mainframe professionals do not acquire new skills, they are left with quickly eroding skills that become less marketable. The value of these employees within an existing business structure also immediately decreases.

The respondents said that they felt unable to perform some new job requirements because of their lack of professional skills, interpersonal communications, negotiation, writing and public speaking, and decision making. They feel trapped,

Category	Percentage of Responses
Career concerns	42
Lack of trust in management	22
Lack of direction	14
Change resistance	12
Other	10

Note:
Results are based on 44 responses. Data was obtained
and compiled by Washington Systems Consulting, Inc.

Exhibit II-5-1. Straw Poll Results of IS Professionals' Concerns

because they were required to carry out new responsibilities regarding team
management, employee enablement, and interaction with user groups with no
idea of how to do them. They felt that senior management was setting them up
for failure.

Fear of Client/Server. Respondents were equally concerned with unrelenting
trade press reports on the demise of the mainframe. Although a client/server
environment is beneficial and extremely open in nature, client/server technology
is still in its infancy. Lack of overall systems management tools and processes,
burdening of user departments with administration functions, and many software
vendors' slowness in correcting problems are some of the hidden costs currently
being exposed. Some organizations are reverting to mainframe solutions because
of these hidden costs.

These computer professionals said that their companies were racing to
client/server solutions and that the mainframe would be dead within a couple of
years. In most cases, this impression was not founded on a stated company
objective but on what they read in the trade press.

Disappearing Voice. The respondents also believed that the company decision makers were no longer relying on technical professionals to implement
technology business solutions. Instead, decision makers are following a solution "du jour," based on what products are deemed the hottest in the trade
publications.

DEFINING AND MEASURING EMPLOYEE VALUE

All these factors leave IS professionals with low self-esteem and even lower
company value. Even professionals who are considered important company resources are concerned over their current and future value to the business. But
what is the definition of value?

Defining Value

Can most employees state in 25 words or less how their skills support the business? Does the business have a clear definition of value? Is value stated in terms of a business's bottom line, customer support, continuous improvement, or IS client satisfaction? Does each employee clearly understand the value statement? Have discussions occurred between management and employees on how current skills and job duties provide value and what future skills are required to increase value? Of equal importance, can management state what value it brings to the business?

Value frequently can be equated with the basic competence required by a business. As information systems change, the basic competency of today is antiquated tomorrow. An example might be a mainframe organization that has developed COBOL applications for the last 20 years. As time went on, this organization learned more about systems analysis and design, structured code, reusable code, and defect elimination before production. The cost of coding declined and the quality of the code improved. This is a current basic competency made up of many different skills (e.g., in-depth knowledge of COBOL, analysis, and testing).

However, if this mainframe COBOL shop looks at the application of technology required by the business in the next two or three years, the need for COBOL skills fades. Object-oriented languages and prototyping design approaches, along with the skills required for these new competencies, may be needed.

Measuring Value

Exhibit II-5-2 shows how employee and organizational value can be defined and identified in terms of basic competence. This method is a combination of function point, critical success factor, competency, skills, and valuation approaches. Purists find fault with this method, because it lacks detail for each of the previously mentioned approaches. However, it has been successfully applied, serves the purpose at sufficient depth, and can be done as a unit.

The upper blocks of the exhibit show activities to determine current basic competence and value at the organizational level. Employee value in relation to this competence should be stated in realistic and reasonable terms that are consistent across the business.

The lower blocks of the figure show activities for figuring out future basic competence, which is based on the future business direction, and how to acquire it. Should or can this new competence be filled from inside the organization? Does a current competence provide any starting point for new ones? Does a current basic competency disappear or slowly diminish as a new basic competency evolves?

Each basic competency is broken down to specific technical and professional skills. Performing this breakdown is laborious because no single source provides all of the possible permutations. A fairly quick and successful approach is given in the following paragraphs.

First, the competency and value should be identified in a short sentence or paragraph. An example is, "We achieve a consistent 99.999% availability and

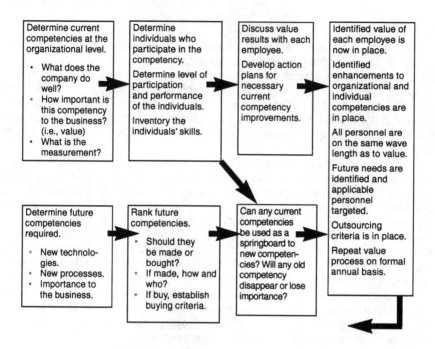

Exhibit II-5-2. **Measuring Employee Value**

subsecond response time for mainframe (host) customer support applications, thus enhancing our external business customers' satisfaction through same-day order entry and confirmation, and order query and fulfillment information." This statement means that the IS organization has proven and successful systems management processes in availability, performance, and capacity management. The statement also provides a general value measurement, which is customer satisfaction.

How does a manager determine which skills make up each of these disciplines? For performance management, for example, the manager should list the skills needed to do this function. Technical skills for performance management include in-depth knowledge of operating systems, network protocols, transaction processors, data and storage management, performance tools, and performance methodologies. Professional skills include written and oral communications, negotiation, and time management.

Once the skills have been identified, an inventory is made of employee skills. Important to list are the strengths and weaknesses within a skills set that affect an individual's value within a particular competency. Training, mentoring, or formal education should be planned to address weaknesses. Strong areas should be used to mentor others. The findings should be discussed and the plan presented to the employees in one-on-one sessions. At the end of a session, an employee should have the following:

- A clear understanding of current and future areas of basic competence.
- A clear understanding of valued skills.
- A clear understanding of skills that need to be improved.
- An agreement with management as to attaining needed improvements.

Benefits of Knowing Value

Using this or a similar approach helps address many career concerns. It shows employees their value in terms of the skills that they possess and that are important to the business. It provides a map for increasing their value and helps to show the company's direction. However, this activity by itself does not answer all of an employee's concerns about lack of direction.

The first iteration of this value method is usually lengthy and at times frustrating, but the immediate effects on employees' self-esteem and feelings of worth are worth the effort. Subsequent iterations become much easier.

SKILLS PLANNING

The process of identifying basic competence can be used as a springboard for skills planning. Skills fall into two main classifications:

- Technical skills, which are hardware, software, and protocol oriented.
- Professional skills, which involve communication, project management, personal interaction, and decision making.

Improving Technical Skills

Technical skills are cultivated through formal classes, self study, hands-on experience, and certification by specific vendors. Mainframe support personnel can further be designated as operations and technical support. Operations personnel should focus on such new skills as LAN administration, workstation support, and automation tools. Technical support personnel should focus on PC operating systems, network operating systems, and high-level development languages. Many vendors offer certification testing and training. Many mainframe professionals are entering these certification programs on their own and obtaining a solid working knowledge of desktop environments. Their value to the business increases dramatically when they become conversant in PCs.

Management must consider the appropriate company support for these individuals. Should the company provide education funding for these certifications? Will these certifications add to the individual's value within the business? Do these certifications help the business achieve organizational competencies?

Most training and consulting companies offer formal training courses at client sites. Recommended are training programs structured to immerse prior mainframe personnel into the PC, LAN, and client/server environment. Courses should provide hands-on experience or use case studies. Both types of activities aid in reinforcing formal lecture materials.

Many management teams overlook the Internet as an inexpensive source of subject matter expertise for employees. The volume of information available on such services as CompuServe and Internet nodes and bulletin boards is astounding. Authorization of subscription and connect charges for all staff pursuing new skills should be part of the skills-development plan. Management should place a cap on connect time charges, and any access charges belong to the individual. Subscribers should operate in the workstation environment they are attempting to learn. Also, employees should install any software themselves, customize it to their own requirements, and read the support documentation. Knowing where to find answers is a key objective of any training program.

LACK OF TRUST IN MANAGEMENT

Trust is neither inherited nor given; it is earned. In today's downsized business world, many management teams have tried to apply traditional management techniques. With downsizing comes such new necessities as empowered employees and work teams. Each of these concepts can fail miserably if certain old-style management techniques continue to be used. Both empowerment and teams are critical to a functional and productive downsized organization.

If empowerment or work teams fail, morale spirals downward and management trust diminishes. The causes of such a failure are straightforward. As shown in Exhibit II-5-3, employee empowerment should be considered the foundation for organizational success. There is a clear-cut and proven path for success. It is called *planned implementation*.

Employee Empowerment

Failure starts with a management team that fails to properly enable staff, plan the rollout, and define measurable objectives.

Empowerment has been attempted by simply announcing to employees "You are empowered; go forth and multiply." This approach fails for the following reasons:

- Everyone has a different definition of empowerment.
- Success requires skills many employees have never acquired.
- Management's actions often run counter to empowerment.

The implementation strategy shown in Exhibit II-5-4 shows how an organization can avoid these mistakes. First, an organization defines empowerment. One IS organization defined it as the offer and acceptance of authority and responsibility showing a trust and confidence in the ability of individuals to act on their own initiative in support of customer service. The key words in this definition are offer and acceptance. Not all employees should be offered an empowered status nor will all employees accept such a status. Many employees

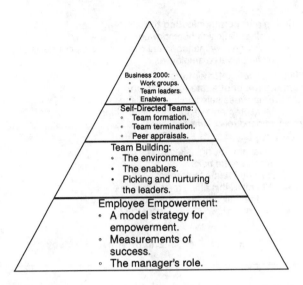

Exhibit II-5-3. Components of a Successful Downsizing Effort

are task-oriented people that no amount of enablement training can change. Empowerment of the masses leads to chaos.

Enablement Training. Some employees thought to be capable of being empowered refuse to accept the status. This refusal can usually be overcome by providing enablement training (e.g., negotiation and communications skills courses). A large computer company attempted to empower a group of highly regarded technical experts at one of its main sites. Management became involved resolving conflicts in the company's various development labs caused by these experts. The cause for these problems turned out to be the experts' lack of ability to negotiate. They would stake a position and refuse to move from it. By providing these experts effective training in how to negotiate and build consensus, the conflicts ceased.

Permission to Make Mistakes. Some employees refuse empowerment because they do not know what the result of erroneous decisions will be. Management should make it clear that everyone makes mistakes and should learn from these mistakes. A pattern of making the same mistake should be recognized and addressed. A possible course of action is having management act as the coach. An employee should know why a decision was faulty and how and why management would have made a different decision. This is a critical preimplementation activity that management must do.

Building and communicating the strategy
- A clear definition of empowerment.
- Policy on how management responds to a poor decision made by empowered employees.

Planning the implementation
Forming the pilot management team
- Employees selected by established criteria.
- Measurements of success determined.
- Phased rollout implemented.

Morale issues
- What am I being asked to do?
- What are the risks?
- How do I relate to others?
- When will this affect me?
- Do I perceive management buying into this?
- How do I know if I am successful?

Exhibit II-5-4. An Empowerment Strategy

Senior managers must buy into this stated approach to assisting empowered employees in improving decision-making skills. An empowerment plan implodes if an employee makes a decision and is attacked by upper management. All levels of senior management must be willing to accept the risk of a bad decision and assist in coaching and mentoring for improving people's decision-making skills. Obviously, management may have to correct a bad decision, but it should be done constructively.

Having senior management state how incorrect decisions will be handled shows employees that careful thought went into the empowerment plan and eases their fear of the unknown.

Avoiding Chaos. Empowerment of the masses leads to chaos. The initial implementation should include a pilot program for empowering select employees. A set of established criteria determines which people to empower. Such criteria include:

- Professional skills (e.g., negotiation and communication).
- Technical skills.
- Personnel skills (e.g., leadership).

Once these employees are functioning well within the empowerment role, they should help select the next employee empowerment group.

Measures of Success. The final activity that should be considered before any rollout is how to measure success. Without a stated approach to measuring success, many employees feel that management is setting them up for failure.

Management must create and communicate measurements of success, which can include:

- Thank-you letters from clients or customers.
- A peer-voted award.
- Baseline and delta surveys of customers for such specific metrics as:
  — Organizational response-time reductions.
  — Customer satisfaction.
- Baseline and delta surveys of such employee perceptions as:
  — Job satisfaction.
  — Productivity.
  — Communication.

Staged Implementation. A phased rollout is necessary to avoid major problems. One functional area at a time should be carried out. This allows both the employees and management to become comfortable with the empowerment approach. Some managers will not relinquish control and will block empowerment. By phasing the rollout, these managers can be more easily detected and appropriately dealt with. Peer managers and upper-level managers should be prepared to have open and frank discussions with recalcitrant managers and suggest areas of immediate improvement.

WORK TEAMS

Once empowerment has been sufficiently achieved, the implementation of work teams can be seriously considered. Why are work teams so important? Because of the emphasis on reducing costs and improving service, an organization must enter the world of teams for any chance of success. There are two forms of teams:

- *Project teams.* These accomplish a specific project or mission and are of finite duration. They are also known as *departmental workgroups.*
- *Self-directed teams.* These address ongoing business processes or functions. They are formed across departments and may involve personnel from all aspects of a business.

The focus of this chapter is on project teams because their implementation is the first step in developing work teams.

A Team Is Composed of Individuals

A team consists of individuals motivated to seek ways to complete the team's mission. The individuals making up a team are by definition, just that, individuals. All team members must provide a conducive atmosphere for accomplishing the team's mission. Each member must be able and willing to accept specific roles, duties, and responsibilities within the team.

The glue that holds a team together is the team leader. This individual must possess skills in consensus building and personnel management. Some organizations require their team leaders to have proven strong project management backgrounds. Most successful project managers have such people skills.

A team goes through phases as it goes on its mission. These phases are categorized as:

- *Excited and motivated.* Early in the team's life, every member is enthusiastic and highly motivated.
- *Confused.* As the team proceeds, roles and duties become clouded and overlapped. Energy is wasted and time is lost.
- *Doldrums.* There comes a point when every member becomes frustrated, tired, and generally fed up with the team and other team members.
- *Renewal.* The team finds some key answers and activities are leading to progress. Most everyone is happier.
- *Hysteria.* The team is running out of time. Everyone is swamped with work, and the mission is in doubt.
- *Success.* The team completed the mission with excellent results. Everyone is tired and glad the project is over.

The Team Manager's Role

Managers should consider their role during each of a team's phases. Most important, is the team's manager considered a member of the team? Do the team members introduce the manager as a teammate or as a manager? If the manager is introduced as a teammate, he or she has successfully made the transition to the team mode.

The manager should be viewed as the arbiter, mentor, and coach for the team. Occasionally, disputes arise within a team that cannot be settled, and the manager should listen to the dispute, make a decision, and inform all the team members why and how the decision was arrived at.

Mentioning is an extremely important function for a team manager. Many teams become frustrated when they cannot weave their way through the corporate maze. The manager should point team members in the right direction and possibly first contact the other corporate entity for the team. The manager should ensure that the other party realizes the team represents the manager's functional area and is regarded as speaking for that functional area.

The initial contact is important. People form their perceptions of others in the first few minutes of contact. If the manager knows that a specific person in another department has particular traits that might affect the initial contact, the team should be briefed on these traits and how to handle the initial contact. The manager should review the team's mission frequently with all team members to ensure they stay bounded by what has to be done. Teams will frequently try to go beyond their bounds.

The manager should also ensure that the team methodology is being followed. A standard methodology ensures teams are formed, given a mission, and dissolved at appropriate times and in appropriate ways.

Determine the Team Charter:
- Mission.
- Members.
- Tasks.
- Completion.

Determine How Teams Are Formed:
- Avoid uncontrolled growth of teams.
- Start small with a few teams.
- Establish scope and authority.

Determine How Teams Are Chosen:
- Team member criteria:
  - Subject matter expertise.
  - Knowledge of company history.
  - Growth experience.
- Inter-and intradepartment.

Determine How Teams Are Dissolved:
- Team completion criteria.
- Documentation.
- Thank you.

Exhibit II-5-5. A Strategy for Teams

Team Methodology

The methodology (see Exhibit II-5-5) provides three key activities needed for improving the chances of team success. The first key activity is to decide how teams are formed. For example, one organization wrote a document that defined how to create mission statements, choose necessary team members, and write team rules of order. What the document lacked, however, were any controls on when and why teams should be formed. The number of teams mushroomed. In a department of 38 people, there were, at one point, more than 40 teams. Nobody was getting anything done because all employees did was hold team meetings. Each team's mission appeared important, but no general control existed. Team A needed deliverables from Team B; Team C required information from Teams A and B; Team B could not get anything done because Team D was not scheduled to complete its necessary activities for three months. Another team was formed to look into why the teams were in gridlock.

Controlling the Number of Teams. To avoid this situation, an organization must start small and with few teams. The established teams must be essential to organizational success. Any list of success items should be ranked, and the first team should be formed to address the important item.

Importance of Mission Statements. A team must be given a concise mission statement that establishes its objective. The mission statement should bound the scope of the project, establish the authority level, and be frequently reviewed by the team to avoid creeping outside the original project scope.

Composing a Team. The next piece of the team methodology is a consistent approach to team content (i.e., the players). This involves answering such questions as:

- What types of subject matter experts are needed? What level of subject matter expert is needed?
- What is the availability of such experts?
- Will excessive assistance be needed from other functional areas?
- If so, should people from other functional areas be considered members of the team?
- Can team members with less experience be used and given an opportunity for growth?
- Does the expertise level of people available to fill the team cause unavoidable delays in the target completion date?
- How long does the team have to identify the tasks that must be accomplished?
- Are all tasks assigned to team members?
- Are they correctly assigned?
- How will tasks be tracked?

Disbanding the Team. The team must answer the following questions to know when the team mission is deemed complete.

- What are the final deliverables that mark the end of the team's mission?
- What is the form of the final team documentation?
- How is the team recognized or thanked for the completed mission?

CONCLUSION

This chapter presented suggestions for sustaining employee morale and satisfying the needs of the business. Planned implementation of an empowerment strategy and work teams and well-thought-out measurements of success remove much of employees' fear of the unknown. Keeping employees in the dark or giving them minimal information negatively affects morale. Managers must be forthright, open, and candid about the needs of the business, employee careers, and implementing empowerment and work teams.

II-6

Leveraging Developed Software

Hal H. Green and Ray Walker

THE RESULT OF LEVERAGING, successfully done, is a continual reduction of both the upfront costs associated with acquiring and installing software applications as well as the long-term support costs. These cost reductions are achieved through economies of scale realized as common elements of a software application are repetitively applied and costs are prorated across a larger set of installations.

This chapter examines the issues of leveraging application software in a manufacturing context. Leveraging, or the reduction in application life cycle costs (illustrated in Exhibit II-6-1), can be discussed in either a context of spanning multiple locations within a single business unit or spanning multiple businesses within a single product type.

Although the example used comes from the manufacturing sector, the principles can be applied to nearly any IS environment.

MAINTENANCE AND SUPPORT COSTS

The process of acquiring automation, process control, and plant information systems has traditionally involved one-of-a-kind development projects. The needs of each site were individually assessed, software was selected and purchased, and local resources (often in the form of system integrators) were contracted to provide services. This business paradigm is easily executed, but it has resulted in a profusion of unique, site-specific systems. By multiplying atypical applications, manufacturers discovered that the costs of supporting these unique sets of applications increased because of the lack of commonality or no economy of scale. Compounding the problem is the plethora of applications serving different needs or functions of the manufacturing user communities.

Business structure and organization are also issues to consider. Manufacturing sites are usually autonomous, with at least cost-center responsibility if not profit-and-loss responsibility. A large manufacturing site may make multiple products or product grades. Production areas within a single site are usually product defined. A single product may be made at multiple sites for sourcing, distribution, and marketing reasons. Business units are formed around one or more

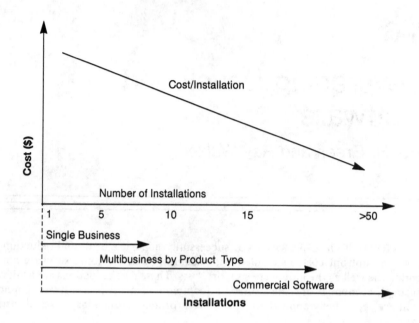

Exhibit II-6-1. Application Life Cycle Cost and Leverage Opportunity

product lines. A business unit may span multiple products on multiple sites. Hence, any given site may support many business units.

Information and control systems (e.g., process control, product control, and quality control) are usually required to be in-plant systems. Enterprise systems (e.g., material requirements planning or MRP, warehousing and distribution, and order management) are most often shared across multiple sites as supply-chain functions.

Manufacturing applications that directly affect the manufacturing process have historically been contained on site. This situation has resulted in a physical architecture different from a central mainframe with dumb terminals at remote sites. Whereas manufacturing applications are often computer-intensive, few simultaneous users are served.

Unique site manufacturing applications crowd the IS landscape, owing their existence to differences in product or area requirements. Factors that have contributed to this condition include:

- The need to exchange process control data with other manufacturing systems.
- The autonomy of manufacturing sites to make IT investment decisions.
- The lack of a vision for future integration of direct manufacturing systems with other plant IS applications and systems.

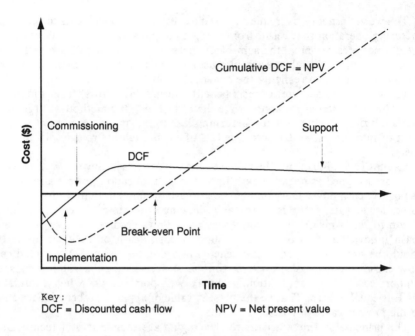

Exhibit II-6-2. Application Software Investment Performance

Historically, manufacturing applications were constructed in a purely vertical sense with automation, not integration, in mind. Shared applications, while functionally isolated, were often interfaced with other applications through a variety of means. The resulting set of disparate and unique legacy systems has driven support costs higher, even as support resources are shrinking.

One textile fibers manufacturing business estimates that for every dollar invested in development, $0.25 per year is incurred for maintenance and support, including both direct and indirect costs. Taken over a 10-year anticipated life of an application, this amounts to a present value for support of about 2.5 times the total costs of the initial development.

ECONOMICS OF LEVERAGING

Because leveraging is foremost a business objective, it is important to note the economic effects of leveraging as a capital decision process. As leveraging occurs, the costs of application software go down per site. Assuming benefits from the software are constant, the net present value (NPV) of the per-site investment increases. Exhibit II-6-2 shows a sample discounted cash flow (DCF) curve from an initial investment in an application.

The word "benefits" is frequently used to describe enhancements to the manufacturing operation that result from using an application. For an investment to yield a net present value, the sum of the present value of the future cash flows resulting from the initial investment must be greater than the present value of the costs associated with realizing the benefits.

The investor (plant site) expects benefits (future cash flows) from the investment (initial costs) at an appropriate discount rate. One method of organizing and analyzing benefits in manufacturing seeks to maximize net present value of a set of information system projects identified through a strategic planning activity.

Exhibit II-6-2 illustrates the shape of the curve of cash flows over time when costs are assigned as negative cash flows for an application project and benefits as positive cash flows. Development costs (cash outflow) initially cause the curve to go down. After commissioning and allowing some time for use of the application to reach maximum effectiveness, cash flows become positive as benefits (cash inflow) begin to be realized. Support costs (cash outflow) continue but should be small compared to the benefits accruing per period. Discounted cash flow causes the net cash flow over time to steadily decline, assuming constant support cost for the application. A break-even point occurs when cumulative DCF is equal to zero. That is, the present value of application benefits are equal to the present value of costs.

The principal business drivers for leveraging are economic, not technical. A successfully applied program of leveraging an application or capability across multiple manufacturing sites reduces the installed costs per site while minimizing the ongoing support and maintenance costs of the delivered applications. Assuming manufacturing benefits result from the application, the result of leveraging is a maximum net present value of the investment across one or more manufacturing sites.

Exhibit II-6-3 illustrates the economy-of-scale effect as a measure of the resources required per installation. Leveraging has the effect of driving the total costs per site to some base level that is set by the costs of off-the-shelf components plus resources required to install the system at each respective site and make it operational.

Leveragability, then, can be economically measured as a function of the costs associated with planning and implementing each site's respective requirements. Exhibit II-6-4 demonstrates the effect of leveraging as the number of sites to receive the application increases. Leveraging is therefore an economy-of-scale effect. The greater number of sites in the leveraged effort, the greater the net present value of the investment across the collection of target sites or installations.

CONSISTENT DATA

Because the business drivers for leveraging are clear, it is reasonable to ask why leveraging is not a pervasive business practice. Some of the barriers to achieving leveragable software include:

- Misperceptions of leveraging.

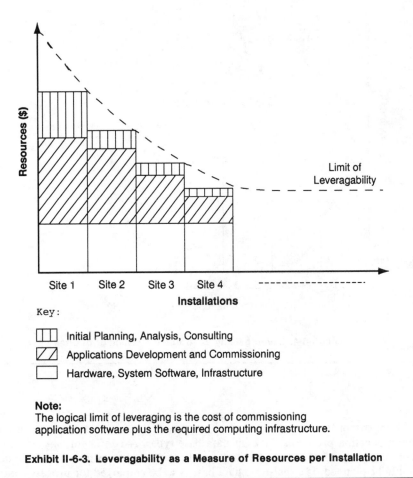

Exhibit II-6-3. Leveragability as a Measure of Resources per Installation

---

- Absence of a long-term manufacturing applications migration plan.
- Lack of a consistent architectural framework.
- Corporate culture ("not invented here" thinking).
- Ad hoc approaches to applications development.
- Conflict between corporate IS/engineering and the manufacturing sites' objectives.

Whereas application leveraging does not have to mean "one size fits all," some consistent framework for applications must exist. Although the data content of applications varies between businesses or sites, applications should fit into a common architecture across the domain of sites or businesses over which the application is implemented. Without such a common framework, leveraging does not occur.

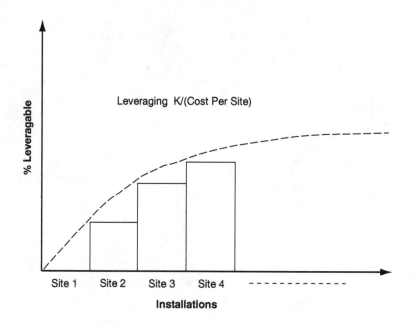

Exhibit II-6-4. Leveragability as Affected by Number of Sites

The common architecture must not stop at the point of defining hardware, communication protocols, or even data base types. A consistent way of understanding the types of data to be stored and the type of repository for those data should be planned. If a real-time data base is to be employed for process control and monitoring, for example, what are the valid types of data to be managed by this portion of the plant manufacturing application architecture? What are the valid functions to be addressed by this part of the architecture?

Often, the answers to these questions are blurred by misconceptions. Sometimes companies select a particular data base vendor and perceive they have accomplished leveraging. On the contrary, the applications must be able to use the target data base existing at the sites if they are to be leveragable. This degree of leveraging implies that ideally, standards for the development of applications that use the selected data base are determined before development and acquisition of applications.

Data Standards. Data standards go beyond a textual specification of functionality, however. Textual specifications usually emphasize desired functionality of the application and fall short of defining a model of the data to be employed. Information engineering, which is now rapidly becoming a standard for data base design, is an improvement over narrative specifications. This methodology incorporates data modeling and functional modeling using the entity-relationship diagram (ERD) and activity hierarchy diagram (AHD), respectively.

To prepare for leveraging applications, IS management must answer several questions:

- What are the standards of technology to support applications?
- What are the standard tools for building and maintaining manufacturing applications?
- What are the standards for modeling and describing requirements?
- What types of data will be stored and operated on by these systems?
- What are the standards for screen design and user interaction?

TECHNICAL ARCHITECTURE ISSUES

It is often impractical to know every aspect of each plant's or site's technical IS architecture before commencing development. It is important, however, to have a common way of viewing existing and proposed systems in the context of the types of data they are to manage.

A data-centered architectural framework can be used for information and control systems in manufacturing. Exhibits II-6-5, II-6-6, and II-6-7 provide an overview of the framework. Data is viewed in three distinctive categories: "in-area" for process control, "manufacturing operations and control" for plantwide product control, and "production history" for plantwide and businesswide decision support.

This architecture places such functions as MRP, order management, and inventory management as business-level or supply-chain functions. Exhibit II-6-6 decomposes these three categories of data stores into further detail. Exhibit II-6-7 maps a specific example set of data concerning the subject of quality to the architecture of Exhibit II-6-6.

These diagrams portray a topological way of viewing manufacturing data. They also reveal a fundamental obstacle to leveraging. Without some type of agreed-on taxonomy of data, leveraging becomes difficult. An application framework should recognize and position the desired suite of application software during the planning or analysis phase of the project.

Many workable approaches can be applied for modeling manufacturing applications, but both data types and functions must be central to any discussion of modern plant IS architecture. In the end, it is the types of data to be managed that must be understood between applications if cost-effective integration is to be obtained.

Given optimum conditions of similar or like plant logical and physical architectures, the ability to leverage an application is, nevertheless, still influenced by a variety of factors. First, it is important to note that the closer the application is to the manufacturing process equipment, the less the application will lend itself to leveraging. Process control applications are inherently tied to the site process control systems, which often vary greatly. It is rare for a process control application to be totally independent from the field/equipment instrumentation that is measuring and controlling the process.

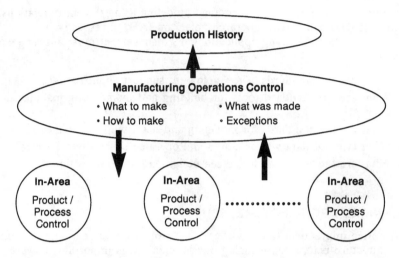

Exhibit II-6-5. Typical Manufacturing Information Processing Requirements

A valid approach to designing leveragable applications is to place only real-time applications at the process control level of the architecture. These applications must, by the nature of the data they manage, be positioned such that they can access the real-time process control data base.

In contrast, applications that can be logically positioned farther from the front-end process control data base tend to offer greater leveragability. Such applications are usually data base applications related to the product rather than to the manufacturing process. The integrated operations or manufacturing execution level of type 3 applications in Exhibit II-6-6 lists some of these product or subject-based applications.

Leveragability, then, is limited to the extent that it is specific to the site's manufacturing processes. It is therefore incumbent on the applications designer or purchaser that applications be properly positioned within an IS architecture and, further, be constructed to be as generic as practical with respect to the process control system.

MEASURING LEVERAGABILITY

The ultimate measure of leveraging is the resulting business benefit—the reduced cost of delivering a working capability from site-to-site across an enterprise. Can leveraging be quantitatively analyzed before commencing a rollout to forecast the required resources/costs per incremental site? The following paragraphs illustrate one approach.

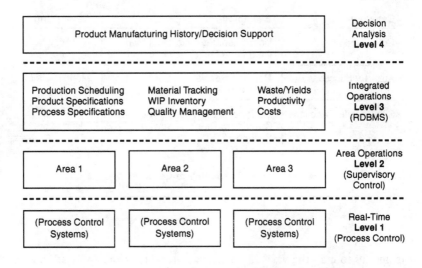

Exhibit II-6-6. Direct Manufacturing Application Framework

	Example Data	Typical Orientation	Typical Usage	Integration Scope	Typical Volume
Multisite Decision Support	Lot/Batch Quality Summary	Subject / Table	Multisite Read Only	Business	Low
Cross-Area Integrated Operations	Lot/Batch Quality Detail	Subject/ Table	Transaction Driven	Site	Medium
In-Area Operations	In-Area Quality Result	File/Field	Event Driven	Area	Medium
Process/ Machine Control	Process/ Quality Parameter	Tag or I/O	Real-Time	Machine/ Process Step	High

Exhibit II-6-7. Manufacturing Data Types and Usage

Category	Examples	Leveraging
Core Capability	User/Client Screens, Data Model, Data Base Implementation	High
Auxiliary Functions	Reports, Specialized Functions, Particular Screens	Medium-High
Site-Specific Functions	I/O Processing, Data Occurrences, Quantity of Users, Hardware, System	None-Low

Exhibit II-6-8. Taxonomy of Leveraging

It is helpful to map the various functional elements of the application against an expected quantity of its leveragability. A spreadsheet can be used to view the various components according to three categories:

- Core functionality.
- Auxiliary functions.
- Site-specific functions.

The data types and functions that constitute the application set can be decomposed into these three categories. Exhibit II-6-8 depicts such a decomposition.

Because the data model underpinning the application is foundational and can be understood independently of user screens and reports, it is likely the purest representation of core capability. Functions of one or more applications can be separated by some rationale into independent subfunctions. Subfunctions can be assigned to one of the three leveraging categories.

Site-specific functions are those that must be customized to a particular site and therefore offer the least leveragability. Auxiliary functions may be items like reports, specialized functions, or perhaps particular user screens. Such functional items may be leveragable across a subset of sites but perhaps not across the whole of the target domain. Core functions are those that can be leveraged across every site in the target domain without modification.

Analysis of Target Domain. There are two possible sources for meaningful information on which to base estimates for assessing leveraging. The best information source results from an exhaustive analysis across the target domain. An analysis of the subject areas across multiple sites is able to calibrate the data/functional model according to the extent of changes likely as the application is moved from one site to the other.

Pilots and Prototypes. Another valid source of information comes from completed projects, pilots, or prototypes. These assets are excellent, because they provide a test bed for quantifying leveragability. In any case, usually more than two sites must be sampled to have a meaningful representation of the whole.

Weighting Factors. Assuming one of these two possible sources of information, it is possible to assign leveraging weighting factors to each function or process of the application. Weighting factors should reflect, more or less, the extent of variability in each subfunction or capability of the application with respect to target sites. Weighting factors can also be used to assess resource requirements as measured in development resources or costs. This discipline reinforces an effort to maintain as much of the application as practical within what may be called the core, thus driving greater leveragability.

Breakpoint values for leveragability can be defined, quantitatively, by what is in the core, auxiliary, or site-specific categories. One hundred percent leveraging means that no modification is required in the application to make the application operational across all sites in the target domain. Zero percent leveragability implies unique tailoring of the applications to each site. The end state of the leveraging analysis should portray the incremental costs of moving the complete application across all sites in the target domain.

CONCLUSION

Leveraging is driven by management's recognition of the inherent costs of unique site-specific solutions. An effective business practice explicitly declares leveraging to be part of the IS strategy. The goal of leveraging is to maximize the net present value of the IS investment.

As companies continue to invest in information technology, significant assets are being created. The management of these assets should be performed with the same decision process that is applied to other important capital assets.

Section III
Supporting Internal Customers

SUPPORTING INTERNAL CUSTOMERS has always been the primary function of the information services organization, but this role has taken on new meaning as customers have become more independent in their use of information technology. Called end-user computing during the 1980s, client-based computing is now the focus of information processing in many companies, and in those where it is not, it soon will be.

To manage an increasing work load, hold costs down, and keep services levels high, IS departments must adopt a consultative approach to supporting internal customers. This means shifting the primary focus of internal client support from happy clients to productive clients. Chapter III-1, "The Consultative Approach to Client Support," provides guidelines for moving to such a customer-focused approach, which allows support groups to explore alternative ways of providing service to internal customers. The chapter discusses steps for conducting client feedback sessions and outlines the skills needed to implement a successful consultative approach to client-based computing. This is a workable solution to otherwise unmanageable increases in technology support requests.

"User Involvement in Project Success," Chapter III-2, offers ideas on how to improve user involvement in projects designed for more effective and productive use of information technology. Often a systems project is never given the chance to succeed, because the expectations placed on it conflict and can never be met. The chapter describes an approach to project leadership called Theory W, which is designed to prevent such a situation. This theory is used to manage expectations and risk by having all parties involved in a project—users, systems developers, and senior management—negotiate a set of win-win conditions that guide the project throughout. A case study is used to illustrate win-win conditions and show why they are necessary for a successful project of any size.

Following the establishment of a set of win-win conditions to guide the implementation project, user participation in IS projects is considered the key to systems success in most organizations. Typically, this participation is implemented through user participation in a design team. Practical considerations, however, require representative, rather than universal, participation.

Unfortunately, there are few standardized guidelines for selecting user participants to serve on a design team. Chapter III-3, "Selecting User Members of an IS Development Team," examines the design team concept to derive the relevant selection criteria. Contrary to the commonly held view, this examination reveals that users' functional expertise is the most critical criterion.

The issues surrounding access to computer-resident data are among the most pervasive computer-related problems in most large corporations. These issues affect all users and all application areas. Chapter III-4, "Implementing Corporate Data Access," points out the critical capabilities needed to make large improvements in the business application of information processing technology. The underlying requirements are identified and a phased deployment strategy is described. The intent is to ensure that the data is available when required, easily and quickly, and that data is part of a logically integrated management system.

One way to deliver this data is through an executive information system (EIS). The growth in the number of companies developing EISs, as well as in the systems' popularity once implemented, leads many to say that the acronym EIS now stands for "everyone's information system." These systems deliver information about marketing, finance, and other business topics to business management in easily used form.

One delivery vehicle being adopted by many companies is Lotus Notes. Notes is attracting attention for potential use with EISs because it offers functions and strengths that compensate for weaknesses in traditional EIS software. Chapter III-5 describes "Using Lotus Notes in Client Support Systems" and discusses the results of a survey conducted among early users of Notes in the development of EISs.

III-1

The Consultative Approach to Client Support

Kate Nasser

IN THIS AGE of technology cost containment, fluid information-based organizations, and cuts in training budgets, productivity is key; embracing a productive customer philosophy is well worth the effort. The IS department's biggest hurdle in implementing this philosophy is a lack of customer trust. To earn it, support staff members must understand their end-user customers' business needs and expectations and, just as important, exhibit that understanding. Awareness is not enough; trust is built first by listening and then by visibly and audibly illustrating understanding. Without first building a base of trust, end-user computing (EUC) support groups cannot implement a productive customer philosophy.

This philosophy does not sanction discourteous or patronizing behavior that is sure to make the customer unhappy. The manner in which the problem is solved or the request is filled remains important with the productive customer philosophy. The difference is that the problem solvers using a happy-customer philosophy do not always use their expertise to find the solution that will make the customer productive. Instead, they yield to the customers' definition of what will make the customer happy. The staff members using a productive-customer philosophy start with the customers' trust in them and their respect for the customers' business needs. From there, customers and staff work in partnership to find the best solution.

To bring customer service excellence to end-user computing, the IS manager must exemplify to the support staff the customer service philosophy they need to communicate to and use with end users. Defining a customer service philosophy is the first essential move toward service excellence. If technology support groups overlook this phase, miscommunication with end users is likely to follow, resulting in an antagonistic and uncooperative working relationship.

Defining the philosophy involves knowing whether the support group's primary customer service goal is to have happy end-user customers or productive end-user customers. Although having both would certainly be ideal, it is not always feasible. For example, an end user might call and request a word processor that is different from the standard everyone else in the organization is using. The happy-customer philosophy that says the customer is always right would lead the support group to automatically submit a purchase order for a new word processor. The productive-customer philosophy would lead the support staff manager to ask the customer a series of questions about his or her technology needs. (In requesting a new word processor, the customer has not articulated a need but has described his or her proposed solution to it.) This needs analysis must be done in a timely, action-oriented manner so the end-user customer knows that the questions are not just another IS bureaucratic stall.

HISTORY OF CLIENT SUPPORT

The prevalence of a happy-customer philosophy has its roots in the history of end-user computing. The introduction of microcomputers came at a time when non-IS staff (i.e., end users) had reached their limit on long IS backlogs and slow responses to requests. IS at that point was focusing neither on happiness nor on productivity.

Even as IS and end-user customers were both approving large numbers of microcomputer purchases, IS did not analyze the total support needs and infrastructure demands of using those computers. IS allowed end users to do whatever they wanted until they had a problem. The stage was set for a reactive troubleshooting approach to end-user computing and a happy-customer philosophy.

Because IS did not take microcomputers seriously or see the financial and business impact of computing without standards, procedures, or expert input, it established a precedent of nonpartnership with end users. In fact, end-user computing support groups were not even part of IS in the early years. The EUC philosophy was to be responsive by giving customers what they wanted—as quickly as possible. Their goal was to distinguish themselves from the slow-moving, unresponsive IS departments by focusing primarily on customer happiness.

MAKING THE TRANSITION

Organizations have changed dramatically since the introduction of personal computing. Networks alone have brought legitimacy to standards for the desktop. Client servers now hold and run critical applications. Access to information highways is becoming a strong factor to competitive advantage. Compatibility and accessibility among applications, functions, and departments are tacit if not explicit end-user customer expectations. Customers expect their end-user support groups to provide expert guidance—even though these same customers may complain if the answer is not what they initially wanted to hear. The stage is now set for a consultative approach to end-user computing, a shift from the historically reactive setup.

Making the transition to a consultative approach to client support requires the IS manager to learn and understand the differences among needs, expectations, problems, and solutions and then train the support staff to make the same distinctions. The following case study illustrates these differences.

An end-user customer, Pat, is a marketing manager with responsibility for key product launches. Her department is a fast-moving unit that needs a lot of support. Pat is dissatisfied with IS service and is meeting with senior IS staff members who support marketing. She complains, "My department has problems using the company's systems and technology. When a crunch hits, the technology seems either to break down or my department cannot make it do what is needed."

IS responds that its training courses explain how to use the technology and systems. Pat answers that her department does not always have time to refer to the training manuals and follow them step by step, especially right before a product launch, and these launches are central to the company's business. IS replies that it is understaffed and cannot always respond immediately to Pat's department's requests. The discussion continues with no resolution, and the marketing department eventually goes outside the company for technical guidance and support.

This case study did not have to have an unhappy ending, however. IS could have adopted a consultative approach. If, during discussions with Pat, IS managers had asked themselves the following questions, the encounter would have gone much differently:

- What are Pat's needs?
- What are the marketing department's needs regarding technology?
- What problems is marketing facing?
- What are marketing's expectations, and how can IS best address those expectations?
- What are the solutions to marketing's needs and problems?

In the previous case study, the managers were looking for the end user to define the problem and maybe even the solution. Because IS was exploring very little and listening even less, customer service during this discussion was very poor. Without effective questioning and objective listening, IS cannot solve Pat's problems, nor will Pat feel that the department has provided excellent customer service.

By using a productive-customer philosophy, the IS staff could be much more consultative in discussions with end users. A consultative dialogue would enable support people to determine needs, problems, expectations, and solutions. In the previous case study, IS established a position based on what it thought marketing was requesting. If the staff had listened effectively, the conversation would have gone something like this. Pat would have said, "We have problems in using the systems and technology we already have. When the crunch hits, the technology either breaks down or we cannot figure out how to get it to do what we need."

IS would have responded, "We have some logs with us from the calls your group has made for help. Could we discuss a few of these calls?"

Pat might have replied, "Good. This first one noted here was two days before our launch. We were gearing up and producing slides for our key customer campaign. The graphics package would not let us change style backgrounds from one slide to the next. The technology would not do what we needed, and we could not stop at that point to take a training course."

IS might have answered, "We understand your frustration. Certainly, a training course at that point is not appropriate. One of your people did take the training course last year. Evidently you are still experiencing some difficulties?"

At this point, Pat would probably say, "Yes, but can't your staff give us help when we need it?" IS would reply that it certainly wants to help marketing and it has a few ideas. Does marketing have a schedule for its launches—those crunch periods? If IS could plan for these periods, it might be able to put a staff member on call for marketing's after-hours requests.

In addition, IS might offer to meet with marketing before the launch to understand the functions it would be trying on the system. A staff member could coach marketing staff on how to perform those functions. If marketing needs hands-on support, IS could explain these needs to a contractor and provide figures on how much a contractor would cost.

The differences between the two versions of this meeting are striking. Both happen every day in organizations throughout the country. The first scenario is plagued with assumptions, disclaimers, and traditional claims about being too busy to provide the service requested. The second version is exploratory and searches to define needs and expectations before deciding on solutions. The IS group neither refuses Pat's solution to just send someone down when they need help nor accedes to it without comment. The IS manager negotiates for a proactive solution to gain information about launch support needs. In addition, the manager mentions that if hands-on support is essential, the support group can coordinate and oversee contract help. The staff members are providing value because they understand the marketing department's real need.

The answer to the first question (What are Pat's needs during the discussion?) is simple. Pat needs to see the technical staff involved and committed to making things better. Furthermore, Pat will be more likely to explore solution alternatives if IS shows more interest in finding workable outcomes.

The answer to the second question (What are marketing's needs regarding technology?) is that they need technology that helps them have a successful launch or at the very least does not hinder a successful launch. The problem marketing is facing is using the technology during crunch times—when it is critical that they be able to use the technology. Marketing's expectations are that the IS support group will help them use the technology they procured for them.

The best way for the IS department to address marketing's expectations and find a solution to marketing's problems and needs is to realize that help does not have to be hands-on during a crisis. In fact, the most effective help prevents the crisis in the first place. The IS manager can offer a proactive solution during a tense meeting in which Pat, the customer, is focusing on the next expected crisis. The happy-customer philosophy would give Pat whatever Pat suggested. The productive-customer philosophy allows the experts to offer other solutions to meet the customer's needs and prevent crises. Knowing the difference between a need, a problem, an expectation, and a solution is key to excellence in customer service.

Addressing all aspects of marketing's needs is another key factor in service excellence. The meeting just outlined could have lasted much longer and investigated issues of business challenges, technology training, and other outside solutions. In this case, IS will bring focus to marketing's business challenges during the next meeting and beyond.

IS will build rapport, credibility, and trust by using a consultative approach in such meetings and by delivering expert, timely solutions.

To achieve a consistent reputation of customer service excellence, IS must address other business units in the same manner. At no time should IS act as if its purpose for existence is technology. Customer-focused end-user support, the productive-customer philosophy, is the future of IS.

MARKETING AND IMPLEMENTING CUSTOMER-FOCUSED SUPPORT

Step 1: Understanding Customer Needs and Expectations

Customer-focused support begins with IS working to understand customer needs and expectations. End-user feedback sessions, which are a special type of focus group, help do this in two ways. First, by their very design, these in-person sessions focus on customers and communicate the IS manager's interest in providing excellent service. Second, the sessions allow for much clearer understanding of end-user customers' needs and expectations than paper or electronic surveys. For example, an end-user customer statement such as "We need immediate support for all the in-house application systems" is vague. What does the term *immediate* mean? Does the word *all* mean all the ones they use, all the ones ever coded, or all the ones they see as critical to the business? In-person feedback sessions allow for immediate clarification of end-user requests. Such clarifying questions eventually help dispel the myths that end-user customers are unreasonable and want the moon for no cost. Consultation, partnership, influence, and negotiation seem real and feasible during and after successful feedback sessions. Planning, structure, and expert facilitation are critical to the success of these sessions.

The planning starts with the IS manager and key staff brainstorming about how they believe end-user customer departments view current service and support. This step generates possible caution signs to consider in running the sessions. It also allows the IS manager and staff to sense which end-user customer departments are their allies and which oppose them.

At this point in the planning, the IS manager should formulate three open-ended questions to pose in every feedback session. Standard questions from which to work include:

- What support services does the end user find valuable?
- What services are not valuable?
- What services does the department need that IS is not providing or procuring?

The important components of the session are timing, notetaking, and communication. A 75-minute session with 25 participants usually works well, and assigning two scribes to take notes on the proceedings ensures more accurate capture of the feedback. One notetaker should work from a flip chart to make the notetaking visible to the participants so they will know IS is listening. The IS support group can review these flip charts later. The second notetaker should be typing directly into a computer. Flip charts are for summarizing an idea, and word processing is good for noting details IS can use after the sessions for developing its new customer-focused support processes.

The session needs rules about communication; otherwise it can deteriorate into an endless voicing of complaints that serves only as a therapy session for venting dissatisfactions. The meeting leader, which may be a specialized facilitator or the IS manager, opens the meeting with purpose, goals, exit outcomes, and suggested communication formats. A wish-list format requires participants to pose their opinions in action-oriented suggestions for IS rather than in broad accusations.

IS support staff members should attend the session to listen and to understand end-user customers, and they must follow these guidelines. The guidelines should be covered in a separate preparation session held for IS members before the feedback sessions. The main rule is that IS support group members should not participate verbally except to ask clarifying questions or respond to nonrhetorical questions from participants.

These guidelines prevent IS staff from becoming defensive during the feedback sessions and taking time with attempts to explain why they cannot fulfill individual requests.

When running multiple feedback sessions, the IS manager and support staff—as well as the outside facilitator if one is used—should debrief each other between sessions. Staff need a chance to vent any frustrations they felt but did not voice during the previous session. Having done this, they are more prepared to listen during the next session. In such feedback sessions, IS support staff who are used to hearing mostly negative feedback are typically amazed at the amount of positive reactions they receive. These sessions give end-users a chance to verbalize their needs and hear what other end-user customers need. Fears that hearing other end users' needs would escalate all end users' expectations are typically unrealized. Instead, the sessions show users the true scope of demands the IS support department is juggling and attempting to meet. More realistic expectations are likely to follow.

Step 2: Analyzing the Data

Whether these feedback sessions or some other method is used to help support groups understand current and near-term customer expectations, analyzing and acting on the data is crucial. End users assume and expect changes to follow such inquiries about their expectations. If the IS department does not intend to explore new strategies for delivering service and support, it should not perform any kind of inquiry. Surveying needs and expectations with no visible attempts at change will simply solidify end users' views of IS as a nonresponsive bureaucracy. It may also reduce the customer response rate on future inquiries and surveys.

As the support group analyzes the data collected, it should consider the following points:

- There are many contributing factors to each response.
- Cause-and-effect deductions cannot be made from response data alone.
- Low-frequency responses are not automatically unimportant. They may be critical to the business of the organization.

- The responses should be scrutinized for misdefinitions and the differences between needs and solutions.
- The customer trends that indicate high dissatisfaction and high satisfaction should be carefully charted. Emotional components to these responses provide opportunities for early change and marketing of strengths.
- The organizational factors that contributed to these points of high dissatisfaction and high satisfaction should be listed. A short targeted meeting to create this list produces the best results. After the list has been created, it should be put aside for two to three days and then revisited in the first of IS's changing strategy meetings (which are discussed in the following section).

Step 3: Thinking Creatively in Client Support Strategy Sessions

Many IS professionals argue that if they could change the way they are providing services, they already would have. It is difficult to transform the way people think about technology service and support; however, it is not impossible. Changes in attitudes and thinking almost always occur when something or someone helps people see the particular situation from a different perspective.

Feedback sessions are one mechanism for reaching this new insight. Customers' discussion, examples, and frustrations may help the support group envision that different way of providing service. Assigning IS staff members to rotating stints in end-user customer departments frequently helps as well. Yet, a more concentrated effort may be necessary after the feedback sessions are over. Within six months of the feedback sessions, participants will want to see some change—however small.

Creative thinking and problem-solving techniques in a series of strategy meetings can bring IS staff to the new insight that is required. Many exercises have been designed to help support personnel break through mental blocks and status quo thinking. The IS manager may find that an expert facilitator can help create momentum and initiate creative thought in the first few meetings. Expert facilitators can be found in an organization's human resources department or outside the organization. Facilitators need to be impartial and unaffected by the decisions that are made in the meeting. End-user customers and IS support staff members are often too close to the issues to be objective facilitators.

The following practices are useful in running a strategy session:

- Questioning what has always been assumed to be fact.
- If IS support staff total six or more, breaking into pairs or trios for five-minute creative bursts and then sharing the results as a total group.
- As a whole group, expanding on the ideas from the creative bursts.
- Noting any comments on roadblocks to each idea.
- Having pairs argue in favor of ideas they believe will not work. This forces people to see the ideas from a different angle.
- Structuring each strategy session to allow time for introduction, creative bursts, discussion, and closure on at least two ideas. Each session should be a step closer to building the new customer-focused strategy.
- Resisting the tendency to analyze and discuss without coming to closure. IS

divisions often make this mistake. It may be the analytical personalities, the belief that a perfect solution exists, or a basic resistance to change that produces this detrimental behavior. In any case, the objective facilitator can help IS move past endless discussions and toward action.

- Visibly posting the reasons for changing or transforming the IS support group during every strategy session along with the question: What about the customer? Support staff members can look to these visual cues to avoid slipping into status quo thinking.

Communicating the New Strategy

At the end of the strategy sessions, IS will have a new mission statement that reflects its primary purpose for existence and its customer service philosophy. From that statement should flow new or revised processes, procedures, and service-level agreements. Once these changes have been drafted, a pilot to test the new strategy should be undertaken to determine how well it works.

If the new mission statement accurately reflects the overall business technology needs of the end-user departments, a trial implementation of the new service strategy is all that is needed to determine necessary modifications. Endless analysis, discussion, and planning do not test the efficacy of new procedures and processes.

For a pilot program to be effective, the support department must make sure end users are aware that the new strategy is in a pilot phase. This does not mean, however, that the program should be implemented in a lackluster manner. IS must be confident about its new strategy and simultaneously open to end-user feedback on the new strategy. In fact, the IS manager must solicit feedback at regular intervals to determine needed changes along the way.

The timing of a pilot is also important. Many departments want to stress test their new service strategy during peak periods of customer use. Although stress testing is an excellent idea, it should not be the first thing IS does in a pilot. End users need time to adjust to changes, and IS support needs an initial test of its understanding of business technology needs before it conducts a stress test.

An initial test requires introducing a new service strategy six weeks before an expected peak period. This provides time to modify processes and an adequate window to motivate end users to work with the support group in the short term to minimize the potential for crises during the peak period. If new technology platforms or systems for customer use are part of the new strategy, the timing of the initial test must be adjusted according to technical demands.

Communicating the changes to end users is critical to a new strategy's success. IS managers must be creative to catch the attention of jaded end users and to signal that changes really are in the works. The manager should improve the standard communication mechanism in place in the organization.

An option is to conduct kickoff sessions that end users attend during lunch or before work. Attending this event enables customers to meet the IS support staff, see the new technology they have been requesting, or attend a software package clinic. During the kickoff, the support staff can distribute information highlighting the new service strategy and processes. These highlights can be outlined in repeated 10- to 15-minute briefings. This event can also be customized for each end-user department and presented in each unit's area. Above all, the support group must reach out and market changes in the best possible light by showing confidence and enthusiasm.

Step 5: Phasing in the Final Plan

The pilot is a short, concentrated period to test the new strategy and changes in processes and procedures. During the pilot, the support group should collect end-user feedback, monitor its own assessments, and work to remain open to potential changes to the initial plan. IS support staff members may be tempted to rationalize the design of the new strategy and resist modifications because they experience creative ownership. The consultative approach, however, requires that support personnel create a strategy in partnership with end-user customer knowledge and input. The pilot phase is a partnership opportunity.

After revising the service strategy and processes as needed, the IS manager must finalize the plan and phase it in throughout the organization. Often a pilot period tests a plan with key end-user representatives. The final plan is phased in to eventually service all end users with the new processes and procedures. If IS does not phase in the services, end-user customers will expect 100 percent availability of all promised services the first time they make a request.

SKILLS FOR THE CONSULTATIVE APPROACH

The consultative approach to client support service, based on the productive customer philosophy, involves much more than technical acumen. The IS department's specialized technical analysts may not have the consulting skills needed for such an approach. The IS manager must therefore assess staff skills and provide appropriate training where necessary. The IS manager may also need to implement training to help support staff members shift from a focus on solving technical problems to a focus on addressing business technology challenges.

In assessing staff skills, the IS manager should look for:

- *Telephone skills.* These are required for gathering customer feedback and diagnosing and solving problems, especially at remote sites. This is not purely the domain of a front-line help desk.
- *Consultative communication skills.* Techniques include asking open-ended questions, assessing customer priorities, and opening exploratory discussions.
- *Interpersonal skills.* The key interpersonal skills are assessing personal space requirements, reading body language, estimating personality types and social styles, and adjusting behavior as needed.
- *Time management and organizational skills.* IS staff must juggle many priorities, keep communication flowing on status, market as they go, and of course, solve technical problems. This presents quite a challenge to IS management and staff, especially to IS members who were previously assigned only to long-term projects.

- *Negotiation skills.* Win-win negotiation skills do not come naturally to everyone. Yet all IS staff members can and should learn this valuable skill set. The productive customer philosophy requires IS staff to negotiate with end users whenever various options to solve service problems and meet service needs are explored.
- *Listening skills.* Listening is the most important skill for consultative service. Success in this endeavor is not possible without hearing end users' viewpoints.

This list is meant to guide an overall staff development effort. The organization's human resources department may be able to help assess these skills and then search for specific training and mechanisms to teach support personnel in unskilled areas. Customized courses are the most valuable because staff can spend the training time applying skills to the IS department's environment. Generalized customer service training courses provide overall principles and leave IS to translate them to their environment after the course.

IS managers need the same skills as the support staff. Moreover, managers must exemplify to the staff the attitudes and philosophy they want the staff to exhibit to end-user customers. For example an IS manager who wants the support staff to listen to end users can teach by example by listening carefully to staff members. The manager must outline the vision and strategy and then exemplify it to staff.

If IS managers want to encourage teamwork and participation with end users—both key aspects of a consultative service environment—they must develop the support group into its own team. A group rarely begins as an empowered team that is able to make strategic decisions without guidance.

CONCLUSION

The consultative approach to customer service is the basis for IS department service excellence. In everyday terms, it means anticipating and understanding the end-users' immediate needs and expectations, exploring options to meet their broader strategic needs, following through on details, communicating throughout the process, and delivering what is promised.

When dining out at a restaurant, for example, patrons evaluate the service according to these same criteria. Excellent service includes all of these elements. People are drawn to go back to similar experiences because they meet their needs and expectations without hassle. Even when mixups in service occur, the diner trusts that the service provider will aptly handle the mixup.

IS department customers respond in the same way if the support group has built that base of trust. Small steps that show the group is changing for the better help gain that trust. Thinking and planning alone do not.

III-2

User Involvement in Project Success

Stanley H. Stahl

A BASIC PRINCIPLE for implementing a sustainable software productivity improvement program is to make everyone a winner. A systems project that comes in on budget and schedule and meets user requirements makes winners out of users, senior management, and the IS department. Making winners of people helps get their commitment and involvement as well as helps them overcome their natural resistance to change. It is a critical component of quality improvement in pioneer W. Edwards Deming's precept of putting everyone to work to accomplish quality improvement.

Theory W is a way to make everyone a winner. This theory was developed by Barry Boehm in the late 1980s. At the time, Boehm was chief scientist in TRW's defense systems group and a professor of computer science at the University of California, Los Angeles. In their paper, "Theory-W Software Project Management: Principles and Examples," Boehm and Rony Ross presented a unifying theory of software project management that is simultaneously simple, general, and specific. In the introduction to this paper, Boehm and Ross wrote:

"The software project manager's primary problem is that a software project needs to simultaneously satisfy a variety of constituencies: the users, the customers, the development team, and management. . . . Each of these constituencies has its own desires with respect to the software project. . . . These desires create fundamental conflicts when taken together. . . . These conflicts are at the root of most software project management difficulties—both at the strategic level (e.g., setting goals, establishing major milestones, and responsibilities) and at the tactical level (e.g., resolving day-to-day conflicts, prioritizing assignments, and adapting to changes)."

Theory W is a way to help project managers cope with the difficulty of simultaneously satisfying different constituencies. Theory W has one simple but very far-reaching principle: make everyone a winner by setting up win-win conditions for everyone.

THEORY W: BACKGROUND AND BASICS

Theory W contrasts with such theories on management as Theory X, Theory Y, and Theory Z. The Theory-X approach to management originated in the work of Frederick Taylor, who was active at the beginning of this century. Taylor contended that the most efficient way to accomplish work was to organize jobs into a well-orchestrated sequence of efficient and predictable tasks. Management's responsibility was to keep the system running smoothly; this task was often accomplished by coercing and intimidating workers.

For obvious reasons, Taylor's Theory X is inappropriate for managing software projects. Theories Y and Z, dating from approximately 1960 and 1980, respectively, were intended as alternatives to Theory X. Theory Y's perspective is that management must stimulate creativity and initiative, which are both important qualities for a quality software project. The difficulty with Theory Y, however, is that it provides inadequate mechanisms for identifying and resolving conflicts.

Theory Z seeks to improve on Theory Y by emphasizing the development of shared values and building consensus. The problem with Theory Z is that consensus may not always be possible or desirable; this can be the case with different constituencies that have their own unique set of individual constraints and requirements.

If the Theory-X manager is an autocrat, the Theory-Y manager a coach, and the Theory-Z manager a facilitator, then the Theory-W manager is a negotiator. The manager in the Theory-W model must proactively seek out win-lose and lose-lose conflicts and negotiate them into win-win situations. Delivering software systems while making winners of all stakeholders seems, at first glance, to be hopelessly naive.

Users want systems delivered immediately and they want them with all the bells and whistles imaginable. Management not only wants systems delivered on schedule and within budget, they also want a short schedule and a low budget. Developers want technical challenges and opportunities for professional growth, and they often do not want to document their work. Maintainers want well-documented systems with few bugs and the opportunity for a promotion out of maintenance. How can a project manager expect to successfully negotiate the conflicting needs of all constituents?

Importance of Negotiating

Although it may seem like a naive theory, there is an accumulation of evidence that Theory W works. In fact, Theory W is coming to be seen as fundamental to project success. The reason lies in the character of a win-win negotiation. The objective in win-win negotiating is for all parties to recognize each other's specific needs and to craft a resolution that allows all participants to share in getting their needs met. This is very different from traditional styles of negotiation, which are too often win-lose.

In the absence of an explicit commitment to foster win-win relationships, software projects have the capability of becoming win-lose. For example, building a quick but bug-laden product may represent a low-cost win for an overpressured development organization but it is a loss for the users. Alternatively, when management and users force developers to add extra features without giving the development organization the time and resources needed to develop the extra features, the result may be a win for users and a loss for developers. Software maintenance personnel often lose as management, developers, and users fail to ensure that software is well-documented and easily maintainable.

At their worst, software projects can become lose-lose situations where no one wins. It is common for management to set unreasonable schedule expectations, and as a result, the development department tries to catch up by adding more and more people to the project. The result is, all too often, a poor product that comes in over cost and over schedule. In this case, everyone loses.

THE COSTS OF NOT NEGOTIATING

The following example illustrates how ignoring Theory W affects a project. Although this example is fictional, it is based on actual experience.

A Lose-Lose Project

A growing specialty retailer had just hired a new chief information officer. The new CIO was given the charter to modernize the company's antiquated information systems but had been explicitly told by the CEO that budgets were extremely limited and that the new systems would have to be implemented as the size of the IS staff was decreased.

The first task was to conduct a user-needs survey, which indicated that, except for the payroll systems, all of the company's existing systems were inadequate. The inventory control system was barely usable, there was no integration between different systems, and each system served, at best, only the limited needs of the department for which it had been designed. The survey also indicated that most users were unaware of the potential productivity boost that up-to-date information systems could give to the company's business.

After the survey had been analyzed, the following four recommendations were made:

- All existing systems should be replaced by a client/server system capable of supplying timely and accurate information to both operational personnel and senior management.
- The changeover should be implemented in stages. The first system should be a relatively simple, low-risk, standalone application.
- The system should be procured from an outside contractor, preferably a software house that has a package that could be used with minimal modifications.
- Training should be provided to middle managers to enable them to better guide the IS department in implementing the new systems.

Basics Were Ignored. These recommendations were enthusiastically approved. A request for proposal (RFP) for a new inventory distribution management control system, everyone's favorite candidate to be implemented first, was requested. However, nothing was said abut budgets, schedules, or personnel needs, and in their enthusiasm, everyone seemed to forget about training.

Lack of User Input. The RFP was developed with little input from distribution personnel, so it was rather open-ended and not very explicit. The result was that the IS group received from outside contractors eight responses ranging in price from $70,000 to $625,000. After lengthy negotiations, a contract was awarded to a single company that would provide both hardware and software for the new inventory control system.

Unclear RFP. The contractor was a leader in inventory management systems, though its largest account was only half the size of the retail company's. To land the account, the contractor promised to make any necessary modifications to the system free-of-charge. The contractor's reading of the RFP led its developers to believe that there was little technical risk in this promise.

The contractor's interpretation of the RFP was wrong. Although the contract called for the system to be up and running in six months at a cost of $240,000, a year later the contractor was still working on changing the system to meet the client's needs.

Neither was the retailer's IS department experiencing a good year. It was continually at odds with both distribution personnel and the contractor over the capabilities of the new inventory system. The users kept claiming that the system was not powerful enough to meet their needs, while the contractor argued that the system was in use by more than 200 satisfied companies.

Costly Failure. At the end of an acrimonious year, the contractor and retailer agreed to cancel the project. In the course of the year, the contractor was paid more than $150,000, and the contractor estimated that its programming staff had spent more than 10 worker-months modifying the system to meet the client's needs. The retailer estimated that it had invested the time of one senior analyst as well as several hundreds of hours of distribution personnel.

HOW THEORY W WOULD HAVE HELPED

Losers and the Consequences

The most apparent source of difficulty on the project was the explicit win-lose contract established between the retailer and the contractor. By requiring the contractor to cover any expenses incurred in modifying the system, the retailer set up a situation in which the contractor would only make changes reluctantly. This reduced the likelihood that distributors would get the modifications they needed and increased the likelihood that changes would be made in a slap-dash way, with too little attention paid to quality.

The IS department's relationship with senior management was also win-lose. There was little likelihood that the CIO could emerge victorious. The system had to be brought in on time and within budget, though the user community was inadequately trained to help properly identify its needs and requirements. The result was that neither the retailer nor the contractor had an adequate handle on the inventory system's requirements and were consequently unable to adequately budget or schedule the system's implementation. The IS department's situation was made worse because senior management wanted to decrease the size of the IS staff.

The users lost the most. Not only did they not receive the system they needed and had been promised, but they wasted time and money in diverting attention from their primary jobs to help develop the new system. Both the retailer's and the contractor's developers lost the time they invested in a failed project, the ability to grow professionally, and the opportunity to work on a successful project.

From a Process Perspective

Fault lies both in the contracting process and in the systems requirements management process by which the retailer and the contractor defined and managed systems requirements. These front-end processes are often the source of project management difficulties, but problems were aggravated in this case by the IS department's inability to identify the real needs of stakeholders and to negotiate an appropriate win-win package. Although the IS group was neglectful, it is not to blame—the problem lies with the process.

Steps to Improve the Process

To improve these processes, Theory-W principles of software management can be used. The following three steps, which are adapted from "Theory-W Software Project Management," can be used to implement Theory-W software management:

1. Establishing a set of win-win preconditions by performing the following:
   — Understanding what it is that people want to win.
   — Establishing an explicit set of win-win objectives based on reasonable expectations that match participants' objectives to their win conditions.
   — Providing an environment that supports win-win negotiations.
2. Structuring a win-win development process by accomplishing the following:
   — Establishing a realistic plan that highlights potential win-lose and lose-lose risk items.
   — Involving all affected parties.
   — Resolving win-lose and lose-lose situations.
3. Structuring a win-win software product that matches the following:
   — The users' and maintainers' win conditions.
   — Management's and supplier's financial and scheduling win conditions.

Application of Theory W

There are several actions that the retailer's IS department could have taken to increase the project's probability of success. It could have trained distribution personnel on the key role they have in properly identifying and articulating their needs. Following this training, IS staff could have worked with these users to draft a more thorough RFP. After receiving RFP responses, the IS department could have involved senior management in identifying limits on resources and schedules. It could have foreseen the difficulties the contractor would have if significant program modifications were needed.

By identifying constituent win-conditions, the IS department would then have been in a position to negotiate a fair contract that would have explicitly taken into account all win-conditions. Having done these critical up-front tasks, the IS department would then have been in a position to structure both a win-win development process and software product. Unfortunately, the IS department never set win-win preconditions.

In the absence of an explicit philosophy to make everyone a winner and an explicit process for accomplishing this, the IS department lacked the necessary support to identify stakeholders' needs and negotiate a reasonable set of win-win objectives. Thus, it was only a matter of time until incompatible and unobtainable win-conditions destroyed the project.

CONCLUSION

Boehm's work on Theory-W software project management continues. Currently, a professor of computer science at the University of Southern California and chairperson of its center for software engineering, he has a research program to develop a tool for computer-aided process engineering (CAPE) that has Theory W built in. As part of this research, he is prototyping an interactive system in which constituents can enter their win-conditions and all stakeholders can then simultaneously analyze and negotiate a combined set of win-conditions.

Theory W has been shown to be successful—both in terms of the paradigm it offers and in terms of its ability to help managers explicate and simultaneously manage the win-conditions of all constituents and stakeholders. Theory W is even more important for organizations embarking on a systematic program to improve productivity. Productivity improvement programs, and such similar programs as total quality management (TQM) or process reengineering, require the full and complete support of all stakeholders. Theory W offers both a theory and a process for getting and keeping this needed support.

III-3

Selecting User Members of an IS Development Team

Naveed Saleem

RAMPANT SYSTEMS FAILURES in organizations have fostered considerable research effort to devise strategies to enhance the likelihood of systems success. Researchers and practitioners alike consistently stress user participation in systems development as the effective strategy to achieve this goal. Generally, this participation is implemented through user membership in the design team. This strategy, however, has not proved effective in alleviating system failures.

Various factors can thwart the effectiveness of user participation. However, the qualifications of participant users and their roles during systems development are prime suspects. For instance, systems development directors express frustrations that functional managers are unwilling to assign qualified users to project development teams. On the other hand, some practitioners and researchers maintain that systems fail because designers talk to the wrong users during systems development. The question that logically follows is who is the right, qualified user to consult or to serve on a design team? Existing practice provides little insight into this issue.

The user characteristics deemed crucial to successful system development include: personality traits; functional, technical, and communication skills; and computing background. Only a few studies, however, have empirically investigated the significance of these characteristics.

In one case study, the relationship between personality traits of participant users and systems success was explored. It was found that systems personnel prefer technically oriented users to participate in systems development. It was concluded, however, that involving technically oriented users may facilitate a smooth design process but is likely to result in a failed system.

In another study, IS personnel from 20 large-sized firms were surveyed to form a list of the most critical factors responsible for systems success. The top three skills perceived as crucial to systems success included technical expertise, communication skills, and analytical skills. Therefore, contrary to earlier findings, the results supported participation of users with technical orientation.

Still another study suggests that user participation enhances the likelihood of systems success, because users possess the necessary systems-related functional expertise and business perspective. Other studies, however, indicate that user participation does not guarantee system success.

Therefore, empirical research provides conflicting guidelines for selecting users to serve on design teams. An adequate two-part approach to resolve this issue is to infer the essential user characteristics from the theories underlying the user participation concept; then to subject these characteristics to empirical testing.

This chapter examines the theories underlying the user participation or design team approach, and infers the key criteria for selecting users to serve on a design team. Finally, it reports the results of a field survey conducted to empirically test the merits of the inferred criteria. Such efforts are warranted, because a wrong user participant decreases the chances of systems success.

USER PARTICIPATION THEORIES

Two organizational paradigms usually advanced in the IS literature, as the theoretical basis for user participation, include participative decision making and planned organizational change. These paradigms assert that an organizational decision is less likely to face resistance if the employees who are to execute the decisions or who are affected by the decision participate in the decision making process.

Typically, this assertion is based on the argument that employees are more familiar with the practical implications and applications of a decision under consideration. Consequently, their input in decision making improves the quality of the decision. In addition, integration of employee expertise imparts a sense of control, commitment, and decision ownership. In turn, these factors enhance the chances of decision acceptance. Importantly, functional knowledge appears to be the primary reason for employee participation in decision making.

The argument generally advanced in support of user participation suggests that development of an information system requires the blending of two types of expertise: users' systems-related functional expertise and designers' technical expertise. User participation is believed to result in systems success through intervening mechanisms (e.g., user understanding of the systems content and objectives, sense of control, feelings of system ownership, better evaluation of the system, and an improved fit between user information needs and systems capabilities).

The argument for user participation is further refined in terms of users' level of functional expertise and the appropriate degree or extent of their influence on systems development. Accordingly, a low degree of user influence is deemed adequate when designing standard application systems (e.g., a payroll system). And, a high degree of user influence is recommended when designers lack the functional expertise required to develop the system, and the users possess such expertise.

These assertions imply a congruence between the level of a user's systems-related expertise and the user's influence on system design—the greater the expertise, the higher the influence. In fact, empirical evidence suggests group members expect congruence between their expertise and influence on the decision.

The effect of incongruence between expertise and influence on system quality is self-evident: restricting the input of more knowledgeable users can only result in diminished systems quality. In addition, this incongruence can create frustration and tension in the users and induce distrust and hostility within the design team. These factors, in turn, can precipitate negative attitudes toward the system.

The conceptual paradigms, underlying the concept of user participation, suggest that eliciting and incorporating users' functional expertise is the primary motive behind user participation. In addition, the level of user expertise determines the appropriate extent of the user influence on system design. Consequently, user participation paradigms imply that user expertise must be employed as the primary criterion for selecting users to serve on a design team and for determining their role during systems design.

A FIELD SURVEY OF DESIGN TEAMS

A field survey was conducted to empirically assess significance of users' functional expertise as a criterion to select users and determine their role during systems design. To accomplish this, systems development activities in 64 organizations were surveyed. Initially, the IS managers in these organizations identified systems that were developed through user participation as members of a design team and implemented during the last one year. The recency of systems was expected to help users recall their perceptions and experiences during the systems development process. The identified systems represented a cross section of information systems applications.

IS managers also identified the participant users. These users were requested to express their perceptions and experiences during systems development and were assured of strict confidentiality of their responses. Although the organizations and users were select, the large numbers of organizations and users enhanced the ability to generalize the findings. User perceptions of degree of participation (i.e., user influence on system design) and expertise were measured using a questionnaire (see Exhibit III-3-1). Users were also interviewed in person to confirm their participation in systems development.

User responses were used to place them within one of the four influence-expertise combinations. These combinations were based on two influence levels and two expertise levels. The first item of the questionnaire determined the level of user influence (high or low) and the next three questions determined the perceived user expertise (high or low).

High influence meant that a user perceived to have exerted a significant influence on systems design, relative to other participants. Low influence indicated that a user perceived to have exerted insignificant influence, relative to other participants. Likewise, high expertise implied that a user perceived to possess greater systems-related functional expertise than other participants, and low expertise meant that a user perceived to possess less expertise than other participants.

Notedly, the users with average influence (question 1) were placed in the high influence category. This approach seemed a logical one because if users did not perceive their influence as small, their input was viewed as significant, although others had the same amount of influence. This option, however, was placed in the

1. Compared to other members of the group, how would you describe the extent of your influence on system development?
   1. I was more influential
   2. All of us had equal influence
   3. I had little influence

2. If you were more influential, how would you describe your system-related functional knowledge compared to other members of the design team?
   1. I was more knowledgeable
   2. All had equal influence
   3. I was less knowledgeable

3. If you were equally influential, how would you describe your system-related functional knowledge compared to other members of the design team?
   1. I was more knowledgeable
   2. All had equal influence
   3. I was less knowledgeable

4. If you had little influence, how would you describe your system-related functional knowledge compared to the members who had significant influence on its development?
   1. I was more knowledgeable
   2. All had equal influence
   3. I was less knowledgeable

Exhibit III-3-1. User Perceptions of Degree of Participation and Expertise

---

questionnaire to help the users respond precisely to this item. Likewise, equally expert users were placed in the high expertise category.

This classification scheme provided the following category sizes: high expertise, high influence equals 183; high expertise, low influence equals 132; low expertise, high influence equals 143; and low expertise, low influence equals 147. To convert these numbers into a balanced design, observations were randomly dropped to attain a balanced design with 132 observations in each category. The test results reported next are based on this set of observations. Statistical analysis with original, unequal category sizes provided similar results.

DATA COLLECTION AND ANALYSIS

The indicators of systems success typically employed in empirical studies include user satisfaction with the system, user attitudes toward the system, perceived systems quality, and systems use. With the exception of system use, these indicators gauge users' perceptions concerning different aspects of systems. Accordingly, this study also focused on perceived measures of system success. The questionnaire listed in Exhibit III-3-2 was used for this purpose.

The first six items of the questionnaire measured user satisfaction with the system. These items were based on Jenkins and Ricketts' instrument. In preference to creating another instrument to measure user satisfaction, it was decided

Directions: Please react to the following statements about the system you participated in designing. There are no right or wrong answers; this is not a test. We are interested in your opinions of how well this system supports your information needs.

1. How satisfied are you with the user interface of the system?
   (Circle one number.)
   Very dissatisfied 1 2 3 4 5 6 7 Very satisfied

2. How satisfied are you with the format of the system reports?
   (Circle one number.)
   Very dissatisfied 1 2 3 4 5 6 7 Very satisfied

3. How satisfied are you with the content of the system reports?
   (Circle one number.)
   Very dissatisfied 1 2 3 4 5 6 7 Very satisfied

4. How satisfied are you with the relevance of the system reports?
   (Circle one number.)
   Very dissatisfied 1 2 3 4 5 6 7 Very satisfied

5. How satisfied are you with the timeliness of the system reports?
   (Circle one number.)
   Very dissatisfied 1 2 3 4 5 6 7 Very satisfied

6. Do you think the system needs modifications and enhancements.
   (Circle one number.)
   Definitely yes 1 2 3 4 5 6 7 Definitely no

7. If you had a viable alternative, how would you describe your likelihood to continue using the system under consideration.
   (Circle one number.)
   Very unlikely 1 2 3 4 5 6 7 Very likely

8. Are you satisfied with your contribution to the system design.
   (Circle one number.)
   Very dissatisfied 1 2 3 4 5 6 7 Very satisfied

9. If you were to participate in design of another system, will you prefer to work with the same system designer(s)?
   (Circle one number.)
   Definitely no 1 2 3 4 5 6 7 Definitely yes

Exhibit III-3-2. User Satisfaction Questionnaire

---

to use an instrument already developed and tested. Item 7 measured users' commitment to use the system, if an alternative were available (called user commitment hereafter). These variables indicated systems success.

Item 8 measured users' satisfaction with their roles and contributions, during the systems development process (called role satisfaction hereafter). Finally, item 9 measured users' attitudes toward the systems designers, with whom they worked during the development process (called attitudes toward designers hereafter).

Group	User Satisfaction	User Commitment	Role Satisfaction	Attitudes Towards Designers
HE,HI	31.03	5.28	5.19	5.30
HE,LI	27.19	4.54	4.52	4.42
LE,HI	30.12	5.07	5.11	5.23
LE,LI	29.97	5.11	5.14	5.17

Notes:

E   Expertise

I   Influence

H   High

L   Low

Exhibit III-3-3. Means of Users' Perceptions of Systems Success, Role Satisfaction, and Attitudes Toward Systems Designers

The Chronbach alpha measure of reliability for this instrument is 0.93. The corrected item-total correlations measure of validity ranges from 0.72 to 0.80, and all are significant at 0.0001 level. Exhibit III-3-3 lists means of perceptions of systems success, role satisfaction, and attitudes toward designers, of the four influence-expertise user groups.

To analyze the data, first the two high influence groups were compared with the two low influence groups. This analysis showed that the high influence users were more satisfied ($F = 25.03$, $p < .0001$), more committed ($F = 16.54$, $p < .0001$), more satisfied with their roles ($F = 18.90$, $p < .0001$), and happier with the system designers ($F = 35.02$, $p < .0001$), than the low influence users. It suggested that influential user participation enhanced the chances of systems success and increased users' satisfaction with their contribution and their appreciation of systems personnel.

The data also showed the significant interaction effect of influence and expertise on systems success and user attitudes (user satisfaction: $F = 21.37$, $p < .0001$; user commitment: $F = 19.44$, $p < .0001$; role satisfaction: $F = 22.63$, $p < .0001$; and attitudes toward designers: $F = 25.59$, $p < .0001$). This effect suggested that the amount of user influence required to achieve systems success and induce positive attitudes depended on the level of a user's systems-related functional expertise. To clarify this interaction, a simple effects analysis was conducted. Specifically, the two high expertise and the two low expertise groups were separately compared to evaluate how the variation in influence affected systems success and user attitudes between the two groups at a given expertise level.

This analysis revealed that the two high expertise groups significantly differed in their perceptions (user satisfaction: $F = 5.98$, $p < .0001$; user commitment: $F = 5.27$, $p < .0001$; role satisfaction: $F = 5.52$, $p < .0001$; and attitudes toward designers: $F = 6.68$, $p < .0001$). On the contrary, the two low expertise groups showed like perceptions of systems success and attitudes (user satisfaction:

$F=0.32$, $p=0.75$; user commitment: $F=0.28$, $p=0.77$; role satisfaction: $F=0.36$, $p=0.72$; and attitudes toward designers: $F=0.75$, $p=0.45$).

Variation in influence, consequently, affects systems success and user attitudes differently, depending on the systems-related functional expertise of the user. The expert users will accept a system only if they exert significant influence on its design. Nonexpert users, however, will likely accept a system regardless of the extent of their influence. Consequently, in a design team situation, it is imperative to elicit and incorporate expert users' inputs into systems design to enhance the likelihood of systems success among the user community.

Thus, the data provides strong evidence of the contingent significance of users' functional expertise to select users and to determine their role during system design.

CONCLUSION

Assigning qualified users to systems design teams, or talking with qualified users during systems design, may determine the ultimate success or failure of the system. Unfortunately, the existing research is highly inconclusive in providing the criteria guidelines for selecting qualified users to participate in the systems development process.

This chapter analyzed the conceptual paradigms underlying the user participation concept to infer the selection criteria. This analysis suggested that users' functional expertise was the most significant factor in this respect. A field survey of design teams supported this significance. The evidence suggested that users' functional expertise should be used as the primary criterion for selecting users to serve as members of design teams. Other criteria (e.g., users' communication skills, computing backgrounds, and personality traits) should be given secondary considerations.

Given that time and budget constraints affect the extent of user participation and systems scope, the study points out the situation in which substantive user participation is critical for system. In addition, the study suggests relying on users' functional expertise in determining systems scope and in resolving conflicts related to systems design and scope.

The research findings also posit a potential strategy to introduce a system to the larger, or geographically dispersed, user community, after developing the system through participation by a few, representative users. Because nonparticipant users form their attitudes toward a system based on their perceptions of the competence and contribution of participant users, communicating the criteria used in selecting participants and their contribution to systems design will enhance the overall chances of systems success.

Despite the emphasis on quality user-designer interaction, empirical research provides little insight on what constitutes quality interaction. This research fills in some gaps in defining such interaction. The research data supports correspondence between user expertise and user influence on systems design. Consequently, this study provides an important benchmark to systems personnel to monitor and improve the quality of user-designer interaction. It suggests system designers must seek and incorporate users' systems-related functional expertise in systems design and ensure substantive contribution by expert users to enhance the likelihood of system success.

The results of this study are based on the perceptions of the users about systems they helped develop. To further evaluate and validate these results, future research can examine perceptions of nonparticipant users.

III-4

Implementing Corporate Data Access

Robert Marcus

MANY CORPORATE BUSINESS PROCESSES are hampered by manual and paper-based methods. This results in excessive resources being used and a general lack of quality. Even when individual departments have electronic data available, a lack of uniformity and integration in accessing data still exists. The problem is compounded when data must be shared between application areas. It is impossible to simplify, automate, and dramatically improve these processes until robust electronic access to all necessary data is in place.

From the end-user perspective, robust electronic access to data has three levels of capabilities that must be achieved. In increasing order of difficulty, these are:

- Data available electronically when required.
- Data accessible easily and quickly from user platform.
- Data part of a logically integrated management system.

BUSINESS ISSUES

The main business issue associated with electronic access to data within a functional area is the need to reengineer business processes to take advantage of the technology as it becomes available. Without process improvements, electronic access to logically integrated data can only provide limited benefits at a very large cost. A key global long-range problem must be addressed by senior management as the data access technology spreads through the company. Within individual functional areas, systems are constructed to meet local requirements, budgets, and deadlines, and there is no incentive to promote data sharing across functional areas.

This situation is especially serious with the rapid growth of storage systems for nontraditional data (e.g., images, text, graphics, objects, models, and multimedia). The failure to build a strategy for accessing, transmitting, and integrating this data across applications will be very costly.

TRANSITIONS REQUIRED TO SOLVE DATA ACCESS PROBLEMS

Many transitions are needed to achieve the end-user vision. This section provides a detailed discussion of the rationale for assigning benefits to each of these transitions.

Data Converted to Managed Electronic Files

Much of the information in large companies is still stored or communicated in the form of paper or hard copy drawings. The value of converting this data to electronic files is as an enabler for further automation. A complete data resource management system must provide some type of tracking for this data. Imaging systems are needed to transform text and drawings into files. In some areas, most notably the factory floor, previously unrecorded data must be collected to store it in file form. Network connectivity is also essential to permit transference of files between users. The choice of which data to convert into electronic files should be done carefully based on the value of accessing and managing the information involved. In general, this conversion will add only moderate value and can be very costly.

File Management Systems to Active Data Dictionaries, Data Directories, and Workflow Automation

The main value of this transition is in enabling large increases in people productivity. These benefits come from reengineering, integrating, and automating key processes. The active data dictionaries and directories locate distributed data and translate it into the correct format for the user. Sophisticated information retrieval packages can help users locate data. Workflow automation provides automatic notification, configuration control, and release procedures for data and documents. Major productivity gains can be expected in key business processes that currently are based on manual, paper-based, and nonautomated procedures.

Simpler Data Bases to More Sophisticated Data Bases

The main value of this transition is in application productivity. It is possible to build more sophisticated applications on top of the new data bases. The benefits are not as great as the conversion from paper to file management systems, however, because the data is already in a managed data base. Some possible transitions and potential benefits are listed in Exhibit III-4-1.

File Management Systems to More Complex Data Bases

The main value of this transition is also in enabling application productivity. It provides an increased capability for multiuser and multiapplication access in

Data Model Transitions	Example of Benefit
Hierarchical to Relational	Ad hoc queries
Relational to Object-Oriented	Richer semantics
Textual to Multimedia	Better interface
Multimedia to Hyperbase	Improved browsing
Object-Oriented to Rulebase	Deductive retrieval
Relational to Rulebase	Deductive retrieval

Exhibit III-4-1. Transitions and Potential Benefits of Sophisticated Data Bases

---

Files to Data Base Transitions	Example of Benefit
Files to Relational	Concurrent multiuser access
Files to Object-Oriented	Preserves application semantics

Exhibit III-4-2. Benefits Gained from Converting File Management Systems to Complex Data Bases

---

such areas as CAD, CASE, and factory-floor control. It can also reduce the amount of customization and maintenance necessary. Converting file management systems to more complex models is necessary to build more sophisticated applications. The two important transitions are listed in Exhibit III-4-2.

Isolated Data Bases to Multi-Data Base Three-Schema Architectures

The main value of this transition is that it enables enterprise integration within and across functional areas. It combines the functional ability of an active data dictionary or directory with a multilevel architecture. The multi-data base three-schema architecture consists of external application view schemas, enterprise conceptual schemas, and internal physical schemas. The enterprise conceptual schema provides a central model that separates application views and physical data models. This permits applications and data bases to be changed in a modular fashion but can require at least two schema translations for each distributed transaction.

Significant benefits can be obtained by building large-scale conceptual models and repository managers, but an enormous amount of work is required. Localized three-schema architectures can provide initial benefits but can also cause integration and scale-up problems in the long run.

TECHNOLOGY ISSUES

Some enabling technologies must be available to fulfill the end-user data access vision even though they are not data management problems, including the following:

- Imaging or recognition systems to convert paper documents to electronic form.
- Network connectivity for data transmission.
- Robust user interfaces for data location and presentation.
- System development environments for distributed systems.
- Process models for workflow automation.
- Security for networks.
- Data compression and decompression algorithms and standards to ease network traffic and storage requirements.
- Continuous operation and high availability (COHA) will be necessary for critical systems.

The two main shortfall areas directly related to data management are the integration of heterogeneous data bases and models and the development of next-generation data bases including objects, text, and hypermedia. These technologies are required enablers across a broad spectrum of corporate applications. Many new products and architectures are being developed to attack these problems. For a more detailed discussion of data warehouse implementation, see Section IV of this handbook.

Heterogeneous Data Bases

The products and architectures for heterogeneous integration of data models and application are focused on specific functional areas. Some of the areas where repositories are being considered include software life cycle, systems management, product data management, office automation, and computer integrated manufacturing.

In general, the technology for integration within smaller groups sharing a local area network is relatively robust and getting better. The global integration problem is much more difficult for technical, organizational, and procedural reasons. This is the level where senior management involvement is necessary to guarantee that different organizations coordinate data, processes, models, platforms, and networks.

Next-Generation Data Bases

Next-generation data bases must have the capacity for storing and efficiently retrieving objects including compound documents, multimedia, hypertext, and knowledgebases. These data bases can also serve as the foundation for semantic integration of heterogeneous data bases. Once again, the technology for local area networks is approaching production capability very rapidly. Sophisticated new applications are also being built on top of object-oriented data bases. No large-scale systems or standards have emerged yet in these areas. The most important consideration is to avoid being locked into incompatible islands of data management while gradually introducing these new technologies.

PHASED TECHNOLOGY DEPLOYMENT STRATEGY

Key steps in solving the problem of electronic access to corporate data include:

- Moving data to files that can be accessed electronically.
- Building or buying active data resource managers that can control and facilitate data access within and across functional areas.
- Converting from files to more structured data bases to increase functional ability of applications whenever performance, cost, and technology robustness permit.
- Converting simple data bases to more sophisticated data bases.
- Using an enterprisewide three-schema architecture to logically integrate distributed heterogeneous data bases within and across functional areas.

The first two steps together will provide significant benefits in improving many corporate processes by reducing flow times, costs, and errors. The technology to begin accomplishing these changes is available today. There should be a major initiative in this area to ensure the rapid deployment of the technology, the redesign of processes, and the interoperability across functional areas.

The technology required for the third step will almost certainly be supplied by vendors during the next few years. Some internal enhancement and customization will be required. Corporations should track the development of the technology and implement it in production as it becomes robust and cost-effective. Tools to aid in the transition from legacy systems will be very important in this area.

The fourth step involves the reengineering of data bases and applications as more sophisticated technology becomes available. This should not be attempted until the new technology is robust and can produce significant benefits. Small pilot projects should be used, however, to evaluate vendor products and capabilities.

The last step requires the successful completion of the first four steps and major internal efforts in modeling, networking, and integration. It will probably be necessary to go through a long period of prototyping and pilot projects before the last step is attempted in large-scale production. There will be a strong requirement for the three-schema architecture driven by the introduction and the integration of complex data bases. Premature attempts to implement this type of integrated system based on paper architectures and early versions of products, however, could be disastrous.

CONCLUSION

The ability to store and access data of standard and nonstandard types across local and globally distributed systems is growing very rapidly. It is crucial that senior management step up to the responsibility of carefully supervising and controlling this growth. No project should be allowed to proceed unless it has demonstrated three essentials:

- It has a site where the technology has been used successfully for a similar problem in a production application or preproduction pilot.
- It has the process reengineering and associated cost benefit that will be facilitated by the new data management and access system.
- It has the ability for other corporate organizations to easily access the data managed by the projects when necessary.

III-5

Using Lotus Notes in Client Support Systems

Barbara J. Haley and Hugh J. Watson

THE PRIMARY PURPOSE OF AN EIS is to provide executives with the internal and external information required to effectively perform their jobs. Executives have always had systems to supply needed information. Traditionally, executives have relied on printed reports, subordinates, meetings, networks of people inside and outside the organization, telephone calls, newspapers, and industry newsletters as information sources. Contemporary EISs use computer and communications technology to deliver much the same kind of information as before, but in a better, more timely, accurate, and relevant manner. EISs have unique characteristics. For example, they:

- Are custom tailored to individual executives.
- Extract, filter, compress, and track critical data.
- Provide status information, trend analysis, and exception reports.
- Access and integrate a broad range of internal and external data.
- Are user-friendly and require little or no training.
- Are used directly by executives without intermediaries.
- Present graphical, tabular, and textual information.
- Provide support for electronic communications.
- Provide data analysis capabilities.
- Provide organizing tools.

The first EISs were implemented in the late 1970s using custom-built software. Although there were a few notable successes, there were more failures. These specially tailored systems were often too difficult to build, maintain, and use. In the mid-1980s, Comshare and Pilot Software introduced their Commander EIS and Command Center products, respectively. These mainframe-based offerings provided a set of tools that greatly facilitated EIS development and use. The emergence of appropriate software, combined with executives' demand for information, fueled a rapid growth in the number of EISs throughout the decade. The EIS software market has changed seriously, however, as firms have been moving from mainframe to client/server-based applications. Consequently, EIS software vendors have moved away from their more expensive mainframe offerings to less expensive client/server products.

EIS products were evolving concurrently with general-purpose software. In many ways, general-purpose software began to be more like EIS software in terms of the capabilities provided. For example, most data base and spreadsheet software evolved to include a graphical user interface. Many companies began to question what they should pay for EIS software when they could get nearly the same capabilities in Microsoft Excel, Powersoft's PowerBuilder, or Visual Basic, and at a lower cost. Although these general-purpose alternatives still do not match the functionality provided by specialized EIS software, the gap is narrowing.

The nature of EISs has also changed. Originally developed for a handful of senior executives, they evolved to support the top management team and now in many organizations have spread to serve hundreds or even thousands of users. For this reason, EIS now informally stands for "everybody's information system."

LOTUS NOTES

A relatively new entrant on the EIS software scene is Lotus Development Corp.'s Notes product. In 1988, Notes first appeared in the marketplace targeting groupware and work flow applications. It has been widely recognized as the first popular commercial product to serve this market. Today, Notes is used in more than 2,000 companies and on the desks of more than one million employees.

Notes serves a variety of purposes ranging from basic E-mail to complex work flow applications that are closely interwoven with critical business processes. Many companies have capitalized on the product's excellent data storage and sharing mechanisms. Others have been overwhelmed with Notes' extremely diverse capabilities and lack direction or an overarching strategy in their internal Notes development projects. Companies that learn how to harness the power of Notes to create well-planned, business-driven applications are much more satisfied with the results. The benefits from Notes surface when all of Notes' capabilities are integrated to create robust solutions.

What Notes Can Do

E-mail. An effective communications product, Notes provides the foundation for electronic mail exchange. Users can send and receive messages using standard mail forms that can be adapted to corporate standards or individual needs. Messages can include simple text or data that is saved in a variety of formats such as a Microsoft Excel spreadsheet or Lotus Ami Pro word-processed report. E-mail allows a company to reach beyond organizational boundaries through communications with customers and vendors.

Standard Templates. Notes also provides an applications development environment. Users can create applications from scratch or through templates. Notes users can select from several boilerplate applications for sales tracking or internal discussions. Developers can enhance or change these template applications to meet specialized needs. The result is an attractive, personalized form in which users can input data and, with proper access rights, later change or view the information.

Replication. After entering information into a repository through forms, workers are able to share the information that is spread over a variety of departments or locations. Notes' unique replicating ability facilitates information sharing among the most distributed of corporate structures. In a Notes network structure, distributed data bases periodically synchronize their information to create mirror images of data located throughout the company. Users can then access information locally regardless of the location of the original data source. A Notes administrator determines how often data needs to be refreshed and how to best meet user needs.

Searching and Viewing. A powerful full-text index search engine allows executives to filter out pertinent information once it has been distributed to users. In addition, flexible views can be created and manipulated to display the information.

Notes Applications

Broadcast. These applications often resemble electronic bulletin boards that display timely information that managers can check regularly for updates and posted messages. They also are popular repositories for news. Packages such as Newsedge and Hoover compile the day's news from numerous sources and store it in Notes data bases. The news can be filtered with user-defined criteria, such as a client name or a particular industry. The information is delivered to executives as conveniently as the morning paper, only the Notes solution supplies articles from news sources all over the world.

Reference. These applications are similar to broadcast applications and serve as libraries for robust, mostly static data. Meeting minutes, management reports, and policy manuals can be stored and categorized for users to access later. This application usually saves companies the cost of duplication and dissemination of documents that are best stored and updated centrally and accessed on an as-needed basis.

Tracking. These applications contain information that is valuable to a number of employees. Users can record an event and its current status. This event is then monitored, passed along to another user for action, or stored for future access. This dynamic manipulation of documents provides great benefits for processes that need to be automated.

Discussion. These applications provide forums for users to pose questions and dialogue through hierarchical replies. These saved discussions serve as an important part of organizational memory because they illustrate the thread of a decision-making process that can later be accessed when similar problems or situations arise.

THE TEN-COMPANY STUDY

A study was conducted to learn about the potential role of Notes in EISs. The study was exploratory in nature because of the relatively limited experience firms have, to date, had with the product.

First, firms using Notes for EIS purposes were identified. This information was compiled from a list of companies in the University of Georgia's EIS data base and references from vendors of EIS software. Ten firms agreed to participate in telephone interviews. The industries represented include gas distribution, natural gas, banking, consumer products, insurance, pharmaceuticals, consulting, and manufacturing. The companies are located throughout the US and Canada.

In each company, the person most knowledgeable about the use of Notes for EISs was interviewed. The interviews were scheduled in advance and took between 20 and 30 minutes to complete. The focus was on current and planned uses of Notes in the organization, specifically in regard to EISs. The interviews also explored the strengths and weaknesses of the use of Notes for EIS.

Why Use Notes for EIS?

Interviewees were first asked how Notes was chosen for EIS use. Answers revealed that the origins were either opportunistic or strategic. In the majority of cases, Notes was brought into the company for non-EIS applications. Its EIS potential was recognized quickly, however, was developers saw the opportunity to enhance their systems by using Notes. A few firms made the strategic decision to acquire Notes specifically for use with the EIS.

Already having Notes in-house increases the likelihood that it will be used with an EIS, especially if the licensing agreement covers the EIS user base. If not, the incremental cost of obtaining Notes may be prohibitive.

How Notes Is Used

The interviews revealed three different ways that Notes is being used for EIS: as part of the EIS software; as a separate, complementary EIS; or as the primary EIS software.

Using Notes as Part of EIS Software. Notes is often used in combination with other EIS software because users appreciate its capabilities for entering, maintaining, updating, and retrieving textual information. One of the banks profiled in the ten-company study is considering using Notes this way. Its EIS was originally developed using Lightship and Lightship Server from Pilot Software.

This software provided an effective solution for handling numerical data but was inadequate for textual information.

Notes, however, provides a management topics application that allows users to initiate topics for discussion and to enter and review comments made by others. All the information is textual and is used as a kind of electronic bulletin board for sharing soft information. The bank's EIS is designed to allow data suppliers and users to add textual commentaries to screens. For example, a comment entered by a data supplier might explain why performance as measured by a key service indicator has dropped. A user might add, for example, that certain actions should be taken to improve performance.

Using Notes as a Separate EIS. Lotus can also serve as a standalone system used to complement another EIS. The Notes-based system handles the kinds of applications for which it is inherently well suited. For example, one manufacturing firm in the study operates an EIS based on Commander EIS but uses Notes for document management applications. The EIS manager would like to integrate the two systems but has encountered compatibility problems. Both systems operate separately to serve the firms' executives.

Notes as the Primary EIS Software. Notes can also be used as the primary EIS software. This is the case at one company where a Notes-based EIS has replaced a system using more conventional EIS software. Several factors drove the decision to rebuild using Notes. First, there were bugs in the commercial EIS software, and the system's response time was too slow. In addition, the company recently decided on Lotus SmartSuite as an organizationwide desktop strategy, and Notes was compatible with this strategy. Finally, the company's EIS focuses on the display of information rather than on data analysis; this need could be well served by Notes. The company's new EIS was developed in six weeks using Notes, and the reactions of users have been positive.

EIS CAPABILITIES PROVIDED BY NOTES

Notes provides many capabilities that are associated with EISs. Exhibit III-5-1 shows the number of companies from the study that use Notes for these capabilities.

Support for Soft Information

Successful EISs often include soft information such as predictions, opinions, news, ideas, and even rumors. Most senior managers recognize that hard data is not always sufficient for decision making.

In the document management system for a consumer-products manufacturer, executives are able to add comments to forms that track standard reports at a corporate consolidated level. These comments provide a valuable exchange of reactions, explanations, and issues among the many executives who regularly use the application. This function, in fact, has become so popular that the company

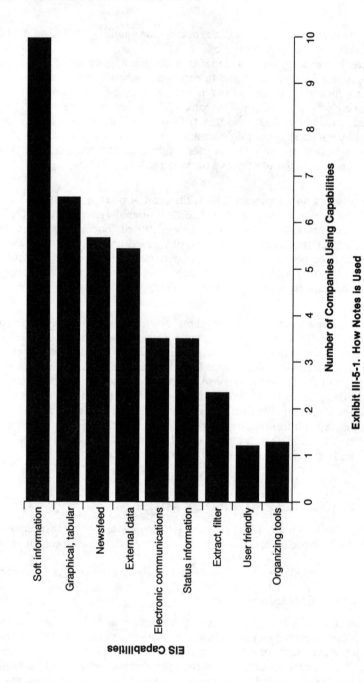

Exhibit III-5-1. How Notes Is Used

has added the ability for commentary as a standard for all of its internal Notes forms.

As shown in Exhibit III-5-1, every company in this study uses Notes to exchange soft information. In addition, each person interviewed noted the ease of incorporating soft information into Notes applications.

Presentation of Graphical, Tabular, and Textual Information

Executives often examine documents that contain graphics, tables, and formatted text. A rich presentation supports analysis and decision making. Notes manipulates robust documents much better than standard EIS packages. Graphics and tables created in Excel and PowerPoint can be embedded easily into Notes documents. Tools such as Lotus F/X can be used to link the graphics dynamically with their data sources, so that data changes are reflected in the graphical presentation.

For example, at BC Gas Utility Ltd., graphs and analyses are prepared by various functional area groups and deposited in Notes data bases. Executives can examine these graphs and tables instead of summary reports that are often more difficult to interpret. Furthermore, the company has used this process to implement management report standards. Users who once constructed numerous paper reports in various graphics packages now deposit reports into Notes documents that have a uniform look.

Support for Electronic Communications

Notes provides the primary E-mail system in some companies. Arthur Andersen & Co. first brought in Notes as a replacement for its Wang E-mail system. Notes E-mail unites its 35,000 consultants worldwide, offering companywide E-mail standards and customized forms. Other businesses integrate Notes E-mail capabilities with existing systems. For example, a consumer-products manufacturer uses Notes E-mail in parallel with MS-Mail, PROFS, and CompuServe's E-mail. Many companies, however, have invested in an E-mail infrastructure other than Notes and do not want to reinvest in an additional E-mail technology.

Presentation of Status and Trend Information

Many executives need to closely monitor events or processes to identify status, trends, or exceptions. Notes displays categorized documents so that users can easily identify the status of a process or event. At Toronto Dominion Bank, a Notes tracking system monitors and maintains relationships of customers for managers and executives. These relationships are vital to the bank's success, and their development is tracked carefully. A bank vice-president can access statistics on how many meetings have been conducted and by whom, presentations that have been given, and the number of prospects each person currently has.

Extracting, Filtering, Compressing, and Tracking Critical Data

Most EIS data resides on mainframe systems or in non-Notes applications, so companies need to download this data directly into EIS applications for their executives to access. Third-party products for Notes, such as InfoPump, offer developers the tools to set up links between various data stores so that data that was not created in Notes can still be used in Notes applications.

Arthur Andersen & Co., for example, is developing a system that can extract data about its consulting engagements from a mainframe using a medium dependent interface (MDI) gateway. The mainframe collects detailed information about client billing and employee time reporting. Periodically, this mainframe data will be summarized and exported into the Notes engagement information system where the data is categorized and reformatted. Executives can then view this information along with documents such as action items and status reports that are created within the Notes applications themselves.

COLLABORATIVE WORK SUPPORT AND OTHER BENEFITS

Notes provides a few capabilities not typically associated with EIS software. Especially noteworthy is support for work flow applications where the work task requires collaborative efforts.

For example, Toronto Dominion Bank plans to use Notes in its EIS for processing commercial loan applications. A loan officer performs the initial processing on a loan application and enters the information on a Notes form. This information is reviewed by higher-level officers, who add comments and conditions for the loan. The entire history of the loan application can thus be maintained in Notes.

In another example, an international bank has an EIS that provides considerable support for the personnel function. The bank plans to use Notes for processing employee requests for exceptions to personnel policies and procedures. A personnel manager can enter the request on a Notes form. Higher-level managers can review the request and enter comments as the request works its way through the approval chain. A powerful feature of the Notes-enhanced system is the ability to retrieve information about similar requests and the decisions that were made.

In both cases, multiple users are involved in the work and have the need to share information—an important benefit in a corporate environment.

Notes is a relatively inexpensive product to use with an EIS. If Notes has already been licensed for use within a firm, there may be no costs involved in integrating it with EIS software. Even if Notes requires additional expense, its per-user cost is typically less than that of traditional EIS software. Recently, Lotus released an inexpensive runtime version of Notes for use on computers that do not need to access development tools.

IS departments tend to choose generic rather than specialized software because of concerns about compatibility and technical support responsibilities. For this reason, Notes may be preferred over more specialized EIS software.

LIMITATIONS OF NOTES

Notes offers so many functions that it is difficult for some companies to find direction as to how to best leverage its capabilities. In addition, many of the Notes tools and third-party products are just now starting to mature. Although it is possible, it still is not simple to access mainframe-resident data or build applications that run on multiple platforms. The embedded data analysis and display capabilities are not as advanced as in traditional EIS software.

As for the user interface, users access documents through a nontraditional navigational system. They do not maneuver through a hierarchical menu structure but must learn how to manipulate views and forms to find the appropriate document or piece of information. All reporting must be created through views as well. In addition, building a graphical presentation of data is not inherent to Notes and must be created offline in other packages. The graphics are then pasted into Notes.

THE FUTURE OF NOTES FOR EIS

Future product upgrades and more enhanced toolsets are easing current limitations, and further improvements should make Notes more suitable for EISs. For example, a more robust user interface is expected in the new release of Notes. In the past, developers have been restricted to objects that follow the rules of Notes forms and views. Menus and complex macros required complicated workarounds. The increasing popularity of packages such as VIP and Power-Builder Library for Notes hint at the growth of more powerful user interface development resources. The high visibility of Notes resulting from IBM's takeover of the Lotus Development Corp. may motivate third-party vendors to create even more Notes-related products.

Integration between Notes and other data bases exists, but capabilities are expanding for companies that want to take advantage of data located in existing applications in a variety of formats. Toronto Dominion Bank is investigating how to integrate its credit processes in Notes with related mainframe information. Once the mainframe systems download customer information into Notes, and the credit is approved, the information will flow back into the financial systems. DataLens for Windows, for example, is a set of drivers that can connect Notes with leading relational data base management systems.

Overall, the consensus among the companies participating in this study is that there is an enormous amount of potential in using Notes with executive information systems in ways that reflect both traditional and nontraditional EIS characteristics. As more companies become familiar with Notes and realize its potential, its use for EISs should grow.

Section IV
Managing Information and Data

IN TODAY'S FAST-PACED technological environment, organizations are continually seeking ways to do business more effectively, efficiently and most of all, economically. The move to a client/server environment is one way to achieve those goals. To be successful in the move, however, IS managers need to take specific action to transform IS staff from one development methodology to another. Transforming a mainframe development and operations staff to a client/server environment involves four major tasks with 18 distinct steps. Chapter IV-1, "Moving to a Client/Server Environment," presents a detailed description of each of these steps. Managers who try to take shortcuts on the road to client/server run the risks of failing in the implementation of this new and promising technology.

Client/server technology is projected to be the de facto computing standard by the end of this decade. It is therefore imperative that companies planning to capitalize on the benefits of faster and greater access to corporate data understand the architectural and implementation issues they will encounter. Chapter IV-2 reviews the issues in "Client/Server Architecture and Implementation" and provides IS managers with the information they need to lead their companies' use of technology into the twenty-first century.

A complementary approach to capitalizing on new technology is object-oriented (OO) development. A company's decision to study and implement OO technology is just the beginning of a challenging and critical new role for software developers. Text-based, transaction processing-oriented programmers and designers can be retrained to take advantage of the benefits OO technologies offer. As Chapter IV-3's discussion of "Transition Strategies for OO Development" shows, these benefits include improved software quality, reusable objects, and the means to create truly distributed software across heterogeneous environments.

At the same time that organizations move toward newer technologies such as object orientation and client/server, supporting legacy systems remains a major chore for most IS managers. Even organizations committed to downsizing have business applications that need support and maintenance during the transition.

By ensuring that IS personnel keep a reasoned, objective perspective on legacy systems and their remaining business value, IS managers can help bolster the morale of their legacy maintenance staff. "Supporting Legacy Systems," Chapter IV-4, shows IS managers how to minimize apathy toward legacy systems maintenance.

To take full advantage of the data that has been accumulated in both newer and legacy systems, some companies are also moving toward the data warehouse concept. A dedicated plan and the activities of coordinated data management teams—the data team, the technical infrastructure team, and the direct-use tools team—are required to establish a data warehouse and directory. Chapter IV-5, "Building and Using a Data Warehouse," presents an approach to data access and availability that is both appropriate for most companies and vital for advancing a company's information architecture into the future.

The flexibility and ease of use of relational data base systems help to implement a data warehouse, but such systems create unique challenges to data and system security and control. New methods of making relational data bases more secure are being introduced, including enhancements to discretionary controls, as are more sophisticated multilevel secure data bases. Chapter IV-6, "Issues in Relational Data Base Control," explains how the IS management team can evaluate and use the new control technologies to guard against the weaknesses of relational data bases.

IV-1

Moving to a Client/Server Environment

Eileen Birge

Transforming current mainframe development and operations staff to a client/server environment is an intensive process with four major tasks. Foremost among them is establishing the environment necessary for success.

ESTABLISHING AN ENVIRONMENT FOR SUCCESS

Establishing the Technical Architecture and Operating Environment

Client/server technology offers a complex array of choices. A standard client/server architecture may involve more than 100 products from 30 or more vendors. Desktop hardware, server hardware, network operating systems, fourth-generation languages, virus detection, batch schedulers, remote connectivity, software distribution, relational data base management systems, object managers, methodologies, online transaction processors, and server operating systems represent just some of the areas where the organization will make product decisions. Adding to the problem is the pace of change; available choices change daily. Once an organization finds products that appear to meet its needs, it should test them together— this is the integration test of the technical architecture. The first test is usually a simple application, designed to ensure that all products are communicating. The second test should be a more complex application with higher volumes. (The tests are not real applications but tests of all the systems technology.)

The importance of this step should not be underestimated. During the first year of the move to client/server technology, the IS department makes critical decisions—decisions that will affect the systems development and operating environments for years to come. An organization can make decisions after deliberate reflection and testing or as the result of off-the-cuff thinking in its haste to implement its first application. Large mainframe shops probably have legacy systems written before the days of data dictionaries and naming, coding, and documentation standards. The results have been seen. Moving into a new environment provides the opportunity to put standards in place right from the beginning.

An experienced team can typically design a technical architecture within two to four months. Testing the technical architecture requires one month—more if the environment has very complex requirements.

Gaining Management Commitment

Companies have taken several approaches to gaining the commitment of management, including the following:

- Laying off existing resources and hiring personnel with the new skills.
- Using systems integrators to develop the initial applications and transferring knowledge to the current staff.
- Independently retraining the current staff and hiring (or contracting for) a minimum number of new skill resources.

Recruiting fees, reduced productivity while learning the organization's structure, culture and products, management time to recruit and interview, and high turnover from a work force with limited company loyalty are just a few of the costs associated with replacing current employees.

More than half of the companies moving to client/server have looked at the costs and the benefits of transforming their current staff and elected to retrain and retain. What are the benefits of retaining?

- *Employee loyalty.* Systems work often requires extra effort. Employees who recognize the investment the company has made in them will respond appropriately.
- *Retention of knowledge.* This includes retention of knowledge about the company and its values.
- *Knowledge of systems development process, audit trails, security, and controls.* Many of the skills associated with good development are not specifically technology related. It is usually less expensive to retain these skills and add the technology component than to buy pure technology knowledge and build development skills.

One research company has estimated the cost of retraining for a standard 200-person department at $5.5 million. Management must thoroughly understand that transformation is a process and that not all benefits of the new technology will be realized in the first few months. This whole project should be treated as a major capital expenditure with the same types of approvals and reviews that a company would give to a capital project of this magnitude.

Making the Partnering Decision

The next three years will be ones of major change. The IS department will face significant technical, personnel, and political challenges. Early in the process, the organization must determine the extent of involvement of outside resources. At one end of the spectrum is a partnership arrangement where the experienced outside resource has a long-term commitment throughout the process and provides or contracts for nearly all services. At the other extreme, an organization uses outside resources only in a limited manner, with an internal commitment to do it themselves, rather than use outsiders (i.e., make rather than buy) whenever possible. Regardless of the choice, the approach to a partnering decision should be articulated at the beginning. If the organization chooses significant partner involvement, time and effort should be spent in choosing the partner carefully. Key items to look for include the following:

- *Depth of commitment.* Does the prospect practice internally the methods, technologies, and organizational behavior of interest to the organization?
- *Corporate culture.* Is the prospect's culture one with which the organization feels comfortable?
- *Flexibility.* Will the prospect truly study the organization, or is the prospect wedded to one approach and ready to advocate that solution? For example, do they sell one particular vendor's products or only sell their own proprietary approach?
- *Track record.* How has the prospect performed in assisting other companies?
- *Risk acceptance.* Is the prospect willing to tie financial reward to successful outcomes?

Creating an Atmosphere of Change

There is an anecdote on change; the chair of a meeting says: "Change is good. Change is exciting. Let the change begin." Meanwhile all the meeting participants are thinking, Who's getting fired? If this ancedote represents thinking of the organization to be transformed, attitudes must be adjusted before proceeding.

The process of creating the right atmosphere for change is a major project in itself and beyond the scope of this chapter. Key points of creating this atmosphere, however, include the following:

- Allowing room for participation.
- Leaving choices.
- Providing a clear picture.
- Sharing information.
- Taking a small step first.
- Minimizing surprises.
- Allowing for digestion.
- Demonstrating IS management commitment repeatedly.
- Making standards and requirements clear.

- Offering positive reinforcement.
- Looking for and rewarding pioneers.
- Compensating extra time and energy.
- Avoiding creating obvious losers.
- Creating excitement about the future.

ESTABLISHING THE VISION OF THE IS GROUP OF THE FUTURE

The Vision Statement

What will be the role of IS in the future of the organization? How will success be measured? Is the mission and strategy of the IS department in concert with that of the organization as a whole? Regardless of how client/server technology is implemented, it will be a major financial commitment. Before that commitment is made, the role of IS should be reexamined and optimal use of financial resources ensured.

A Functional Organization Chart for the IS Department

The current organization probably reflects many assumptions from mainframe technology roots, with offshoots reflective of the growth of LAN technology. For the transition to client/server to be effective, an organization must do more than merely layer technology onto the existing organization. A sample new functional client/server-legacy organization chart is shown in Exhibit IV-1-1.

The sample organization emphasizes tools and methods. The client/server environment can be an intensively productive environment—some companies have reported throughput improvements of two to four times in the effort to design and implement systems, with similar increases in user satisfaction. Companies can only realize these gains when the developers have an understanding of the tools they are to use, the design guidelines to follow, data base standards, and version control procedures, among other issues. It is also important to note the position of Manager—IS Professional Development in the exhibit. Transitioning the staff, updating the plan, tracking progress, and managing a multimillion dollar budget requires full-time commitment.

Position Descriptions for the Future Department

IS managers should create a picture of what their staff will be doing in the not-so-distant future. To create the transformation plan, they must know where they are going. They should write descriptions that are as clear as possible, giving serious thought to how performance will be measured for each item on the position description (a sample is included in Exhibit IV-1-2). Managers should make a preliminary estimate of how many of each type of skill set they will need.

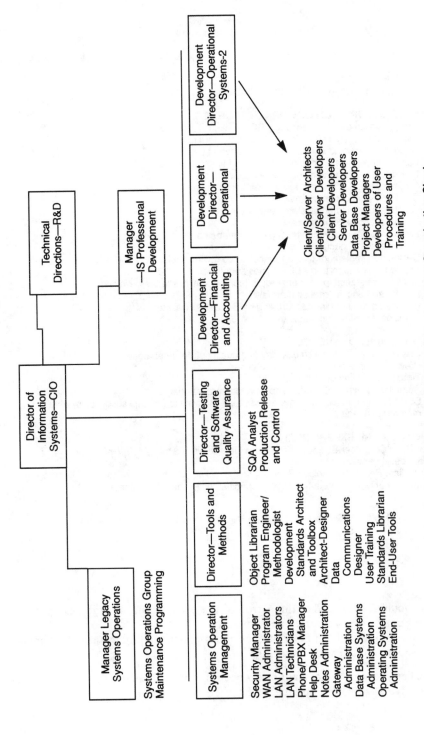

Exhibit IV-1-1. Sample Functional Client/Server Legacy Organization Chart

Company ABC
Position Description

Date: 8/1/96   Position Title: Client/Server Developer

PRIMARY FUNCTION
Develop and maintain ABC business applications.

GENERAL DESCRIPTION OF WORK PERFORMED:
1. Design logical data bases using ABC development platforms.
2. Work with data administration staff to implement and tune data bases.
3. Conduct and record facilitated joint application sessions.
4. Lead prototyping sessions and implement user requests.
5. Interview users and document user requirements.
6. Create detailed program specification packages and test plans.
7. Code and unit test programs.
8. Create and implement systems test plans.
9. Implement conversion plans.
10. Provide quality assurance testing of programs coded by others.
11. Create systems documentation.
12. Design and implement user interfaces in compliance with CUA and ABC standards.
13. Provide user support on ABC business applications.
14. Provide assistance to user procedure/training analysts in the development of user training and documentation manuals.
15. Interview and assist in the recruiting of IS professional staff.
16. Participate in staff and status meetings.

KEY MEASURES OF SUCCESS:
1. Customer satisfaction with usability and quality of delivered software.
2. Programming accuracy and completeness.
3. Timely completion of assigned tasks.
4. Compliance with ABC design and development standards.
5. Customer and project manager assessment of ability to function successfully as a member of a team.

EDUCATION AND EXPERIENCE:
BA or BS in Computer Science or Business Degree with IS minor
2 years development experience
ABC's Client/Server Technology Series
Organizational Development training (as specified by Human Resources)

Exhibit IV-1-2. Sample Position Description: Client/Server Developer

---

They should focus on what the person in the position will be doing as opposed to the place in the organizational hierarchy.

In developing position descriptions and estimated staffing quantities, IS managers should consider the following:

- Client/server development teams should be kept as small as possible. Teams of five to seven are optimal, eight to 10 are manageable.

- A development team requires a full-time manager, three to four developers, a part-time or full-time data base analyst, a part-time or full-time client/server architect, and (in the latter stages of the project) a full-time user procedure analyst/training specialist. (If the project affects a large number of users and has a significant training component, these metrics do not apply. The project to design and deliver the training material may dwarf the systems project.) One architect and one data base analyst can be assumed for eight developers.

- Client/server developers work with users to identify requirements, reengineer processes, design, code, and test. Development methodologies in this environment are most effective when they stress iterative prototyping and refinement. For optimal efficiency, the roles of analyst and programmer should not be separated.

- A client/server architect works with members of the tools and methods group to set up development environments and to identify components of production environments. If a production environment will involve use of previously untested products or new releases of products, the architect tests the technical architecture before significant development efforts are expended.

- The tools and methods group can be highly leveraged. One tool builder-designer should be assumed for each 50 developers-architects-analysts.

- If software is being developed for internal use only, one tester should be assumed for every two developers.

- One LAN administrator should be assumed for every 200 users and one groupware administrator for every 400 users. Growth in management tools should reduce staffing requirements over time.

This is an area where most organizations look to consultants for assistance—both for identifying the responsibilities and to work with human resources to determine the impact on pay scales and incentive plans.

Skills and Performance Needed

In the preceding step, responsibilities and work performed were defined by each position. In this step, they are translated into the types of skills and levels of proficiency required. For example, a client/server developer position description may include some of the following responsibilities:

- Interviewing users and documenting user requirements.
- Preparing logical data models.
- Preparing unit-test plans and executing plans.
- Managing own time against task deadlines.

Those responsibilities can then be translated into skills. Interviewing users requires the following:

- Interviewing techniques.

- Effective listening.
- Interview planning.

Documenting user requirements requires:

- Effective writing skills.
- Understanding of the selected methodology and associated documentation techniques.

It is tempting to declare that all staff be expert in all skills required for their positions, but that is both unrealistic and unaffordable. It is necessary to identify the minimal skill level needed to perform in the position in a satisfactory manner.

The translation of job responsibilities into skills requirements is difficult. Doing this job well, however, has a tremendous payoff. It affects the evaluation process and has a dramatic affect on explaining the role of training and staff development to senior management. It focuses the work force. Setting the expected skill levels assists staff in planning their own self-study activities.

Hiring and Arranging for Skills from the Outside

At this stage, IS managers should have an initial feel for the skills that are likely candidates for acquisition from new hires or consultants. They should start the process for acquiring these skills now so that the candidates will be on board when they are ready to start implementing the plan. The hiring and acquisition process will continue at the same time as the next seven steps.

CREATING THE PLAN

After establishing the environment needed for success and also establishing the vision of the IS group of the future, companies are ready to tackle the nuts and bolts of the transformation to a client/server environment.

Mapping Current Staff to Future Positions

For this task, managers must look at their current organization and personnel and attempt to fit the individuals and positions into their future roles. During the mapping operation, interests and individuals should be matched rather than it being assumed that programmers will become client/server developers. All staff members should have access to materials developed so far. The position descriptions help staff identify what roles they believe are most suited to their own abilities.

How do managers decide who is best suited to be a client/server developer? A client/server architect? No fixed rules exist, but there are some guidelines. The client/server architect will typically be more technical than his or her developer counterparts. The architect usually has less user involvement and interacts more with the development team. Managers should look for persons and development positions that focus on the technical versus the functional aspects of the work.

Aptitude should be considered. One report concluded that 26% of existing mainframe personnel could not be converted to client/server. In other experience, this figure has been closer to 35%. These persons are clearly the candidates to maintain legacy systems during a transition period.

Skills Analysis

The positions of the future and the skills they require have been identified. The probable candidates for each position have also been identified. In this step, managers identify what skills the candidates have already to avoid wasting training dollars.

A skills assessment document should be prepared. The document asks individuals to rate themselves as 0 (no knowledge), 1 (conceptual), and so forth. Guidelines are given so that the staff understands the indicators for these levels. Guidelines are not meant to be all inclusive (i.e., the guidelines should help individuals assess themselves, not delineate the total knowledge requirements for that level). Sample guidelines for a developer's knowledge of Microsoft Windows are:

- *Novice.* Can explain the purpose for Windows. Knows which version of Windows is running. Can reset, minimize, and open windows. Can explain the concept of the active Window.
- *Needs supervision.* Can explain the functions of the three main Windows programs, can differentiate the various kinds of memory, can explain and use the terms DDE and OLE appropriately. Can list and define the various components of a window. Has developed at least one application program in the Windows environment using a standard 4GL tool (i.e., PowerBuilder or Visual Basic). Can explain the function of the WIN.INI.
- *Works independently.* Can explain the purpose of the Windows API. Has written at least three production programs in the Windows environment. Has written at least one application involving the use of OLE or DDE.
- *Expert.* Has written three or more native Windows programs.

First, each staff member should self-assess without knowledge of the suggested skill levels for the proposed positions. Next, an independent party should assess each individual. Managers should meet with the staff member to discuss any significant variations between the self assessment and the independent assessment. The final, agreed-upon skill level should be documented.

The manager responsible for implementing the transition plan now has a picture of each individual: current skills, current skill levels, and the target skills and levels needed to perform in the future. Managers must analyze and summarize to develop the profile of the typical staff person slotted for any position for which six or more staff will be assigned. These positions may include: project managers, client/server developers, data base administrators, client/server architects, LAN administrators, and software quality assurance testers. For such positions as WAN administrator or object librarian, plans can be tailored to individual needs. Little benefit will be gained from summarization because there will be only a few candidates for each position.

The Training or Job Assignment Plan

Armed with the profile of typical current skill levels and the target skill levels, a training assignment plan designed to raise skills levels to the targets can be created. The following rules apply:

- Training alone cannot create level 3 (works independently) or level 4 (expert) personnel. Although training often only creates a level 1 (conceptual understanding) rating, effective training can create a level 2 (works under supervision) rating. Training also helps level 3 and 4 performers maintain currency in their skills. For example, training should help a level 4 Oracle V 6.0 data base administrator move to Oracle V 7.0.
- Within two months after training and using a major new tool on a daily basis, productivity should be at 50% of target. By six months, productivity should be at 100% (and skill level should be at 3).
- Training not followed quickly by job-reinforcing experience is wasted.

Given these rules, it is helpful to look at a sample training or assignment plan for an organization's first group of client/server developers.

1. *Form a team of 6–8 people.* Provide a high-level description of the system to be implemented (people learn best when they can relate the knowledge to what they need to know—so as they take classes, they can relate the concepts taught to the system they will work on). Plan on training the team together.
2. *Provide initial technology awareness training and needed soft skills training in the following areas:*
   - Client/server and LAN basics (e.g., terminology and theory).
   - Client and server operating systems.
   - Office suite productivity training (e.g., for word processors, spreadsheets, and graphics tools—tailored to the documentation and probable uses).
   - Data analysis and documentation tool (relational or object oriented).
   - Effective listening and writing.
   - Methodology orientation.
   - Facilitation (developers only).
   - LAN administration (LAN administrators only).
3. *Assign the first job.* The first job assignment within the department should not be a mission-critical system nor have a deadline that is critical to success. One company elected to make its first client/server implementation a companywide budgeting system, to be delivered in September to coincide with the beginning of the annual budget cycle. Not surprisingly, the system failed to make the deadline: everyone in the company knew and IS's judgment was seriously questioned. Preferably, the project should have some

kind of high impact when delivered so that the first client/server application helps fuel the excitement about the change to this architecture. The assignment should be sufficiently complex to test most aspects of the technical architecture and reinforce the needed technical skills.

Plan to have this team conduct initial user-requirements definition—using the data design tool, methodology, and writing techniques. The LAN administrators should set up the development environment and productivity tools.

4. *Provide second-level training after the requirements.* Typically, the developers and architects will need training in user-interface design, the specific development tool, and prototyping. The architect may require additional training on the components of the technical architecture assumed for use in this application. Other members of the team may require training in data base administration and performance tuning.

5. *Build prototypes and the technical architecture.* Plan to have the team return to the project and conduct prototyping sessions with the user. Critical functional ability and performance features should be developed to the point where the technical architecture can be tested and modified, if necessary.

6. *Complete the system.* Integrate the completion with methodology training appropriate for the project phase.

An Infrastructure to Manage the Plan

With a 200+ person department, a three-year plan, dozens of vendors, more than 2,500 person-skill combinations, as much as $2 million in hard costs to budget, classrooms to equip and schedule, and as many as 300 official and unofficial training courses to track, management is a challenge. For the typical Fortune 1,000 company, executing this plan requires a full-time commitment and appropriate systems support.

TESTING AND EXECUTING THE PLAN

Testing and Refining the Plan

A plan has already been developed for the first team. Now, the plan must be executed. The manager responsible for all professional development should participate in as much of the training as possible to observe the participants and the material. Participants should be debriefed after each training session to determine strengths and weaknesses. Participants should also be interviewed at intervals after the training to find out what worked and what did not. The project managers can help determine how job-ready the participants were after returning from training. The suggestions from the first project team should be incorporated into the training plan.

1. Establishing the environment needed for success, including:
   - Making the partnering decision.
   - Establishing the technical architecture and operating environment.
   - Gaining management commitment to the staff transformation approach.
   - Creating an atmosphere of change.
2. Establishing the vision of the IS group of the future, including:
   - Creating a vision statement for IS.
   - Creating an organization chart for the EUC department in the future.
   - Creating position descriptions for the future department.
   - Identifying the skills and performance levels that will be needed.
3. Creating the plan, including:
   - Making a preliminary cap of current personnel to future positions.
   - Performing a skills analysis
   - Determining which skills must be acquired versus built.
   - Creating a training and job assignment plan.
   - Creating an infrastructure to help manage the plan.
   - Initiating hiring or arranging for skills from the outside.
4. Testing and executing the plan, including:
   - Testing the plan.
   - Executing the plan with the remaining staff.
   - Evaluating and refining the training plan.
   - Incorporating continuing change and development into the culture.

Exhibit IV-1-3. Major Tasks in Moving to a Client/Server Environment

---

Executing the Plan with the Remaining Staff

The remaining staff should be scheduled into the refined training plan. Again, the mode of training development teams together should be followed once a project has been identified. It should be assumed that a new group can be started through the process every four to eight weeks. The schedule should be modified to reflect current assignments.

Refining the Training Plan

Feedback should be collected from system users regarding satisfaction levels. Additional feedback can be obtained from staff going through the plan and incorporated into the plan on a continuing basis. Staff who went through the training earlier may need refresher or catch-up topics to reflect new thinking or new technology. The plan should be verified at least quarterly with the group responsible for technology to update tools and architecture information.

Incorporating Continuing Change and Development Into the Culture

The environment will continue to change. Business and strategies will change faster. It is important for the IS staff to realize that the transformation process will never end. At least semi-annually, each staff member should reassess current

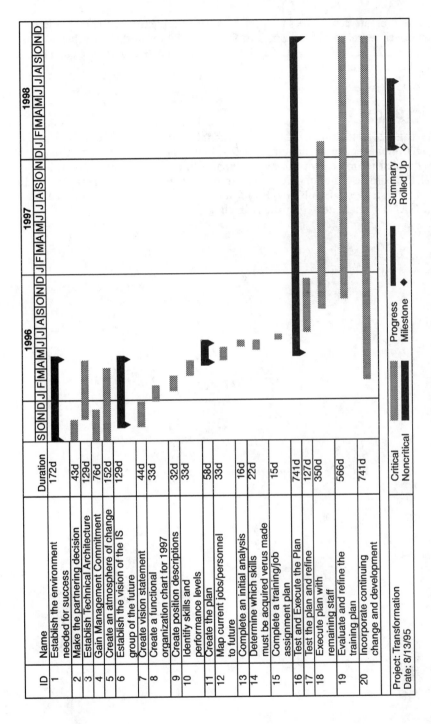

Exhibit IV-1-4. GANTT Chart for Transformation Process

skill levels, create new targets for performance, and identify the combinations of job experience, self-development, and formal training needed to achieve those skills. Preferably, achievement of skill development goals should be a component of the bonus or raise process.

CONCLUSION

As can be seen, moving a staff to client/server is just like most systems projects: managers must determine what they want, refine the requirements, create a plan to implement the requirements, and then test and refine the plan. What seems to be a monumental task can be broken down into manageable and measurable steps; see Exhibit IV-1-3 for a review of the steps and Exhibit IV-1-4 for a GANTT chart depicting their timeline.

IV-2

Client/Server Architecture and Implementation

Nathan J. Muller

CLIENT/SERVER COMPUTING gives users faster and greater access to corporate data at a lower cost than that of conventional terminal-to-host systems. According to Forrester Research (Cambridge MA), the cost per user is approximately $9,000 for client/server computing versus $13,000 to $15,000 for mainframes and $25,000 for high-performance UNIX systems. This helps explain the appeal of client/server computing.

In the client/server model shown in Exhibit IV-2-1, an application program is broken out into two parts on the network. The client portion of the program, or front end, is run by individual users at their desktops and performs such tasks as querying a data base, producing a printed report, or entering a new record. These functions are carried out through structured query language (SQL), which operates in conjunction with existing applications. The front-end part of the program executes on the user's workstation.

The server portion of the program, or back end, resides on a computer configured to support multiple clients, offering them shared access to a variety of application programs as well as to printers, file storage, data base management, communications, and other resources. The server must not only handle simultaneous requests from multiple clients but perform such administrative tasks as transaction management, security, logging, data base creation and updating, concurrency management, and maintaining the data dictionary. The data dictionary standardizes terminology so data base records can be maintained across a broad base of users.

THE CLIENT/SERVER NETWORK

The migration from central to distributed computing has produced two types of networks involving servers: the traditional hierarchical architecture employed by mainframe vendors and the distributed architecture employed by LANs. The hierarchical approach uses layers of servers that are subordinate to a central server. In this case, PCs and workstations are connected to servers that are connected to a remote server or servers. This server contains extensive files of addresses of individuals, data bases and programs, as well as a corporate SQL

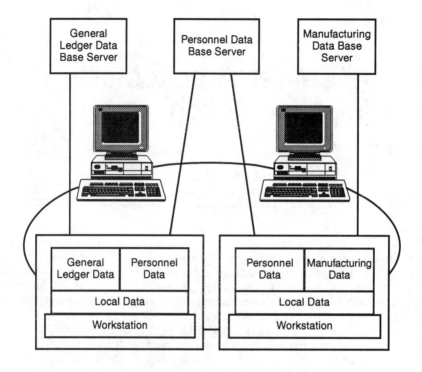

Exhibit IV-2-1. The Client/Server Model

data base or a file of common read-only information (e.g., a data dictionary). A terminal on a LAN making a request for data not on the LAN has its request routed to the central server. The server adds any pertinent information from its own data base and sends the combined message to the end user as a unit. To the end user it appears to be a single, integrated request. Also, the local LAN server passes data base updates to the central server, where the most recent files reside.

This type of server network maintains the hierarchical relationship of mainframe communications architectures (e.g., IBM Corp.'s SNA), thereby simplifying software development. An added benefit is that more programming expertise is available here than in the distributed environment. The disadvantage is in the vulnerability of the hierarchical network to congestion or failure of the central server, unless standby links and redundant server subsystems are employed at considerable expense.

In contrast, the distributed server architecture maintains the peer-to-peer relationship employed in LANs. Each microcomputer on the LAN can connect to multiple specialized servers as needed, regardless of where the servers are located. Local servers enable such services as data bases, user authentication, facsimile, and electronic mail, among others. There are also servers responsible for managing connections to servers outside the LAN. The microcomputer merges data from the server with its own local data and presents the data as a composite whole to the user (see Exhibit IV-2-2).

Distributed client/server architectures can be difficult to apply because the software to manage them still needs considerable development. After all, microcomputers must know where to find each necessary service, know the access codes, and have the software to access each service. Such software has been developed for traditional mainframe-based architectures. But centralized architectures are beginning to run out of steam and distributed server networks, when combined with LAN internetworking devices like routers and bridges, are coming into the mainstream of LAN internets. Keeping the network and computing process transparent to the end user is rapidly becoming a requirement for future networks.

The network also consists of the transmission medium and communications protocol used between clients and servers. The transmission medium used is no different from that found in any other computing environment. Among the commonly used media for LANs is coaxial cable (thick and thin), twisted-pair wiring (shielded and unshielded), and optical fiber (single- and multimode). Emerging media include infrared and radio signals for wireless transmission.

A medium-access protocol is used to convey information over the transmission facility. Ethernet and token ring are the two most popular medium-access protocols used over LANs. When linking client/server computing environments over long distances, other communications protocols used over private facilities (e.g., point-to-point T1 links) come into play, which provide a transmission rate of as much as 1.544M bps. Frame relay and other fast-packet technologies are rapidly emerging communications protocols for carrying LAN traffic over the wide area network (WAN), while the Internet protocol (IP) remains the most common transport protocol used over the WAN. Each of these must be evaluated for their price-performance and reliability factors.

OBSTACLES TO IMPLEMENTATION

Although many organizations have embraced the concepts behind client/server, many are still wary about entrusting their mission-critical applications to the new architecture. Despite all the vendor hoopla, today's client/server environment is still burdened by the lack of diagnostic and applications development tools, which are readily available for the mainframe environment. In particular, such troubleshooting tools as debuggers and other diagnostic programs, although more powerful than they were just two years ago, are still less robust than those found in the mainframe world.

Another important concern is the inability to centrally control client/server networks linked to one another and to larger host machines. For the most part, the tools used locally on LANs to diagnose, correct, and troubleshoot problems cannot be used remotely or across different platforms. The lack of such tools as autobackup and autorecovery in current client/server configurations is a big concern for many organizations, as is the lack of integrated data dictionaries and development tools.

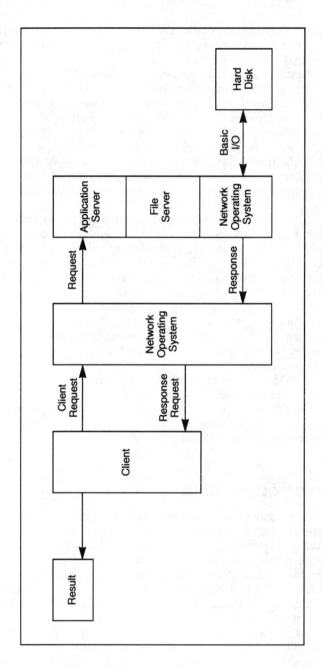

Exhibit IV-2-2. How Data Is Retrieved in a Matrix Server Environment

Because PC-based networks can be unstable, the hardware platform should be thoroughly tested before it is entrusted with mission-critical applications. Isolating a problem on the LAN can be a very time-consuming task because of the difficulty in tracking it down, whereas on a mainframe, the cause of a problem is often immediately apparent.

Although management tools are emerging for the client/server environment, they are still few and far between. Therefore, it is important to have knowledgeable staff who understand the nuts-and-bolts of the operating system, the interrelationships of the applications, and the networking environment. The reason for this is disaster recovery. Many companies do not fully appreciate or understand how they are going to manage distributed data on multiple servers that may be scattered all over the country. When disaster strikes, it is important to have a recovery plan already in place so that vital data does not get lost. An effective disaster recovery plan will not only be thoroughly scripted to correspond with various disaster scenarios, but be tested periodically, and refined if necessary.

INTEGRATION ISSUES

Even where development and diagnostic tools do exist, users often find they must wrestle with complex integration issues, as well as learn a whole new language. Until there is more collaboration among mainframe and microcomputer vendors to make integration easier, users may want to consider a systems integrator to facilitate the transition to client/server and use them for knowledge transfer.

Integrators can play a key role in managing the complex relationships and problems—both technical and administrative—that arise in a multivendor environment. They not only help integrate products from many different vendors, but smooth out incompatibilities between communications protocols. Integrators also lend valuable assistance in negotiating service and support contracts.

When choosing a systems integrator, it is important that it share the organization's vision. One area in which shared vision is particularly important is that of technological innovation. If the organization wants to implement leading-edge solutions, the integrator must be willing and capable to support that vision with investments in emerging technologies and cutting-edge concepts.

Most integrators are concerned with the problem at hand so they can get on with solving the next problem. They generally do not help clients articulate a vision that will provide essential guideposts into the future. An integrator that can provide business process reengineering services for select applications, for example, is a better choice than a vendor that provides basic service only.

Until corporate management sees the client/server platform providing equivalent stability, performance, consistency, and reliability to the mainframe, they will not be comfortable moving mission-critical applications. Pilot programs can help organizations evaluate the client/server platform in terms of performance, reliability, and disaster recovery. The time to initiate a pilot program and try new techniques is when new programs must be developed. Small, manageable applications allow time for staff to get through the learning curve, which can greatly facilitate the transition to client/server.

NETWORK SUPPORT

Those who have taken the plunge into client/server applications have noted that their organizations are becoming increasingly dependent on enterprise networks. Managers must now invest more heavily in internal and external network support.

Behind the growth in expenditures for network support is the confusing array of communications challenges that are confronting managers, from evaluating new internetworking technologies needed to create enterprise networks to maintaining, managing, and leveraging far-flung corporate data bases. The hope of saving money by using client/server applications may be dashed once managers realize that the cost required to make each program work remains the same. Although it does make end users more productive, by itself, the client/server approach does not really save money. For faster applications development and cost savings, the client/server approach may have to be coupled with computer assisted software engineering (CASE) or object-oriented programming (OOP).

THE CASE FOR OBJECTS

The basic premise of OOP is that business functions and applications can be broken up into classes of objects that can be reused. This greatly reduces applications development time, simplifies maintenance, and increases reliability.

Objects provide functional ability by tightly coupling the traditionally separate domains of programming code and data. As separate domains, it is difficult to maintain systems over time. Eventually the point is reached when the entire system must be scrapped and a new one put into place at great expense and disruption to business processes. In the object-oriented approach, data structures are more closely coupled with the code, which is allowed to modify that structure. This permits more frequent enhancements of applications, while resulting in less disruption to end users' work habits. With each object viewed as a separate functional entity, reliability is improved because there is less chance that a change will produce new bugs in previously stable sections of code.

The object-oriented approach also improves the productivity of programmers in that the various objects are reusable. Each instance of an object draws on the same piece of error-free code, resulting in less applications development time. Once the object method of programming is learned, developers can bring applications and enhancements to users more quickly, thereby realizing the full potential of client/server networks. This approach also makes it easier to maintain program integrity with changes in personnel.

CASE tools, fourth-generation languages (4GLs) and various code generators have been used over the years to help improve applications development, but they have yet to offer the breakthrough improvements demanded by an increasingly competitive business environment. In fact, although these tools have been around for years, the applications development backlog has not diminished appreciably.

This is because many CASE tools are too confining, forcing programmers to build applications in one structured way. This can result in redesign efforts often falling behind schedule and over budget. In addition, CASE tools are not typically compatible with each other. This would require a CASE framework with widely disclosed integration interfaces. Complicating matters is the growing number of government and industry standards organizations that are offering proposals that supersede and overlap one another.

Object-oriented technologies, however, are starting to deliver on the breakthrough promise. In some instances, OOP technology has brought an order of magnitude improvement in productivity and systems development time over that of CASE tools—it is not unheard of for some IS staffs to compress five or six months of applications development time to only five or six weeks. Few technologies available to the applications development community hold as much promise as object orientation.

Transitioning to Objects

Several concrete steps can be taken to ensure the successful transition to object technology in the applications development environment. The success of any large-scale project hinges on the support and financial commitment of senior management, who must be made aware of the benefits as well as the return on investment. Fortunately, this not hard to do with object-oriented technology.

To demonstrate the potential advantages of object-oriented technology, IS managers should seize the opportunity to apply it to a new project. Projects that lend themselves to object-oriented technology include any applications that are being downsized from the mainframe to the client/server environment, because the applications will have to be rewritten anyway.

It is a wise idea to prepare for object-oriented technology now by determining the availability of training and consulting services and reference materials. If senior management wants to know about object-oriented technology and its potential advantages, IS managers will elicit more trust and confidence by demonstrating immediate knowledge and understanding of the topic, rather than begging off until they can become more informed.

Like the move from mainframes to client/server, the skills mix necessary in object-oriented technology differs from that in conventional methods of applications development, if only because the shift in activities is toward the front-end of the applications development cycle. This means there is more emphasis on such things as needs assessment and understanding the workflow processes in various workgroups and departments. This affects the design of the applications in terms of the modularity and reusability of various objects.

New incentives may be needed to encourage systems analysts and programmers to learn and adhere to object-oriented analysis and design methods, and to reward those who create and implement reusable code. The object-oriented paradigm signals a fundamental shift in the way networks, applications, data bases, and operating systems are put together as well as how they are used, upgraded, and managed. The ability to create new objects from existing objects, change them to suit specific needs, and otherwise reuse them across different applications promises compelling new efficiencies and economies, especially in the client/server environment.

STAFFING

A potential obstacle that may hinder the smooth migration to client/server is the apparent lack of skills among programmers outside of the traditional mainframe or standalone personal computer environments. Those with PC experience typically have never worked in an IS shop and are not familiar with the control procedures and testing rigor that a formal shop expects in mission-critical applications development. Alternatively, moving from the mainframe to client/server environment requires knowledge of multiple platforms, rapid applications development tools, relational data base design, and, ultimately, the principles of object-oriented programming.

One difference for many mainframe operators switching to client/server environments is the heavier involvement with users. This often means reconciling system wants and needs among end users. Also, IS managers usually have more contact with senior management, who want to know how the new technology can benefit the company and what to anticipate in terms of return on investment. For more on object-oriented technology, see Chapter IV-3.

TRAINING

The shortage of skilled object-oriented programmers is perhaps the biggest obstacle to speedy implementation. Object-oriented methods require that programmers think about things differently, and thinking in terms of objects as opposed to lines of code is certainly different. Even with the three to four months needed to train staff members in the object-oriented approach, once programming staff are up to speed they can develop applications faster and more efficiently.

The client/server environment tends to require more staff experts, because no one person typically understands all of the pieces. As if to underscore this point, there seems to be more trial and error in developing applications for client/server than on older, well-understood legacy mainframe systems.

One of the trends driving training for the rest of this decade is that the whole information technology arena is undergoing a paradigm shift—from mainframe to client/server systems. This means a major retooling of organizations around the country, requiring substantial increases in training dollars.

Only two possibilities exist for obtaining the necessary skill base required for moving from a mainframe orientation to a client/server orientation. One is to fire everyone and start over, which is not viewed by very many companies as even remotely feasible. The other is to work with existing professionals to upgrade their skill base with training. Within the context of most companies, training is the best solution because the people already have the underlying knowledge base. The object of training is to apply an existing knowledge base in a new direction.

Managers should endeavor to become as well versed in client/server issues as they are about mainframe issues. Such people will be a greater asset to companies making the transition to smaller, diverse platforms. The person most valuable is somebody who has the desire to learn the client/server environment and has the flexibility to go back and do work on the mainframe when it is appropriate.

Outside consultants can be brought in to provide the necessary training, but programmers and systems analysts must learn more than just the details of how products and software work. Working closely with senior management doing strategic planning and getting hands-on experience with how applications are being used can be equally important.

CONCLUSION

The path to client/server nirvana is long and winding, with many technical and organizational issues to be hashed out along the way. The trouble is that many companies are more focused on the technical issues and ill-prepared to deal with equally important management issues. Failure to consider such management issues as support requirements, the skills mix of staff, and training needs can sidetrack the best-laid technical plans for making the transition to the client/server environment. Even on the technical side, attention must be paid to the availability of diagnostic and applications development tools, as well as the opportunities presented by such complementary technologies as object-oriented programming, so that the full potential of client/server networks is realized.

IV-3

Transition Strategies for OO Development

Steven Rabin

THE BENEFITS OF OO DEVELOPMENT include greatly improved software quality, reusable objects, and a means of creating truly distributed software across heterogeneous environments. The most sophisticated development organizations and their tools are, however, no substitute for enlightened developers, organizationwide, as object-oriented techniques change the way systems development is done.

The use of OO concepts and techniques must be carefully planned and introduced into the development environment. All too often, top management has unreasonable expectations while developers are unsure how to design, much less develop, in this new environment. Rather than improving software quality, this situation has the opposite effect of producing inferior code and problem-plagued objects. Integrating objects into the development mix must be done transitionally. It is an evolutionary rather than revolutionary process.

This chapter explores the three fundamental aspects of a successful OO implementation. These are:

- Preparing people for a new way of developing systems.
- Integrating new tools into the organization's development hierarchy.
- Revising the organization's methodology to ensure that the highest-quality reusable objects are created.

Development methods must be reviewed so that changes can be accomplished with as little negative impact on current productivity as is reasonable. It is therefore important to approach the transition of development methods in such a way as to effectively get people involved and motivated.

READINESS TO MOVE TO OO

Businesses are actively pursuing ways to move applications that have traditionally run in a closed mainframe environmental to distributed environments.

At the same time, analysts are examining and reengineering the business processes that have been encapsulated in these existing applications. Concurrently, many IS organizations are using this time to consider the advantages of object orientation.

Object orientation may be the wave of the future, but COBOL has been the language of choice for more than 30 years. Business logic is encapsulated in the millions of lines of COBOL code that exist today. If a company is looking for an opportunity to reengineer business processes, and associated code, it should also be examining the use of object orientation as a possible vehicle for all or some of this reengineering.

OO transition issues affect programmers, applications designers, quality assurance personnel, and development management. Developers face an uncertain future as they move away from the professional skills they have acquired over their careers. The skills required to design and develop a 3270-based, action-oriented host system using proprietary architectures and host system services (e.g., VTAM, SNA, CICS) do not easily transfer into this new environment. A variety of questions need to be answered to determine what is required and the best way to proceed. IS management should ask:

- Is a replacement strategy realistic?
- What are the ways to conserve (or optimize) the current investment in resources (both code and skill sets)?
- How can object systems be integrated into existing systems?
- What are the tools and skill sets required to move to this new environment?

The remainder of this chapter addresses these questions from both the management and developer's perspectives.

A DISTRIBUTED SYSTEMS STRATEGY

A good way to begin is to consider the future of object technologies and development tools. There is no shortage of bold claims about object-oriented tools (all of which potentially lead to unrealistic expectations); nonetheless, many IS shops are already in the process of (or will soon be) adopting this technology for the development of their next-generation applications (see Exhibit IV-3-1). By 1998, robust distributed, client/server object-oriented tools and system services will be available. By the year 2000, more than 80% of development organizations are expected to be using object technologies as the basis for their distributed development strategies.

Design Considerations

Cross-platform OO tools are one of the key ingredients required for the success and implementation of this technology. They must be able to handle mission-critical applications and provide the key system services required for enterprise

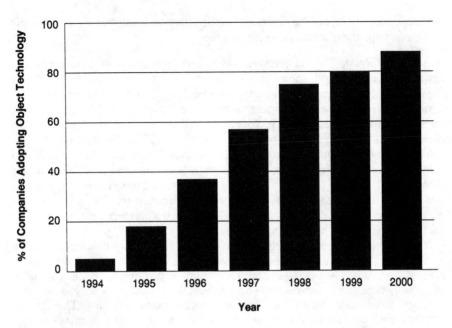

Source: IDC Enterprise Technology Study

Exhibit IV-3-1. Future of Object Technology

applications, including data management, transaction management, and messaging in a high-volume application processing environment.

Object projects differ from traditional development projects for several reasons. Analysis and design procedures are different; so are the methodologies and tools used. The code structure/syntax is new also. There is C++ instead of C, and OO COBOL instead of COBOL, for example. Development and runtime facilities also must change to exploit the use of objects across the enterprise. The composition and role of the development team changes as well. Finally, new means of testing and maintaining object-based systems need to be implemented.

Development Cycle Changes. The conventional development cycle incorporates rigid development phases. These phases usually have specific start and stop points that are difficult to alter. Systems design is performed in one of the initial phases, so any subsequent changes to the design cause confusion, delays, and misplaced logic. This is certainly true when no design/development tool is being used and in many cases is true even when an integrated CASE (ICASE) tool is used. This approach to development is best characterized as a big bang approach.

After months or years of development, the application is implemented in one big push; out with the old and in with the new.

Rapid Prototyping. Object-oriented development is much more of an evolutionary process. Rapid application prototyping is one method often used. This allows for a series of ever-improving prototypes to be developed until the application is ready for delivery. The initial prototype has basic functionality. This prototype is improved and enhanced until it is close to the deliverable. Finally, the application is delivered even though it continues to evolve through maintenance.

The reason this approach works well is because the prototype is developed using component objects. These objects define basic business functions and are incorporated into the prototype as required. Individual objects are easily modified and enhanced as the application is readied for delivery. Even after implementation, system modification is best characterized as further refinement of the prototype (excluding programming bugs).

Rapid application prototyping offers a variety of benefits to developers as they make the transition to OO. Simple objects that are easy to understand can be created first, then used as a learning tool in initial prototypes. Even if some of these early objects need to be thrown away and re-created, they serve a valuable purpose, from both the training and application points of view. The idea of working with simple objects (maybe as part of the desktop presentation) is a reasonable way to introduce people to the technology and ease developers' worries.

Incorporating New Methods and CASE. Current design practices incorporate a variety of methodologies and procedures, including some relatively old practices such as structured analysis, design, and programming. They also include newer facilities like ICASE and entity-relationship modeling. The further advanced an organization is with regard to applications design methods, the easier will be its transition to object-based design.

Several techniques are used in conjunction with object-oriented applications development. The point of this chapter is not to review or compare each of them but to emphasize that one of them must be selected and incorporated into the environment. It is difficult if not impossible to move people to OO without the use of a design facility specifically geared to OO development. One technique is not necessarily better suited to the task than any of the others. Selection must be based solely on its applicability to the organization and its current methodology. A sampling of the methods to study includes:

- Object-oriented recursive design.
- Object modeling technique.
- Object-oriented software construction.
- Object-oriented software engineering.

Much has been written about the use of CASE tools, both good and bad. In the mid-1980s there was as much hype about the benefits of CASE as there is today about object orientation. Although all of the promises did not meet user expectations, CASE still offers value to the art of software development and design.

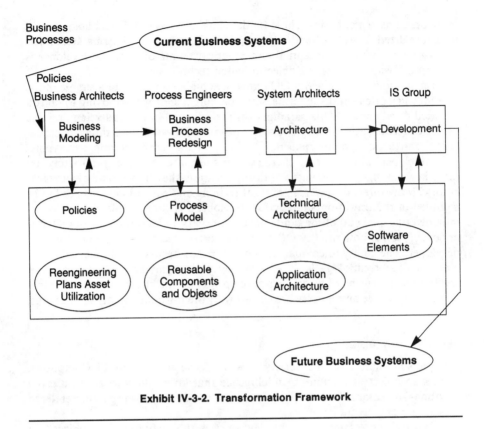

Exhibit IV-3-2. Transformation Framework

The same is true of object-oriented development. Exhibit IV-3-2 offers a framework that can serve as the basis of transforming applications development.

So many organizations use some form of CASE tool that it is important to consider the tools in the light of this discussion. Host developers accustomed to using CASE facilities face several significant differences when reviewing OO-CASE tools for object-oriented analysis and design. First and most important is that OO tools incorporate real-world modeling as the basis of the method. Once defined, these models are converted into objects. The better these objects simulate the business environment, the easier it is to create specific instances through the use of an objects method. These objects are finally encapsulated with their data and thus have the potential of being logically distributed across the enterprise.

OO CONCEPTS FOR THE HOST DEVELOPER

For the people who actually create, enhance, and maintain code, one of the major challenges is understanding how object technology translates to the developer's specific environment (i.e., language, tools, and services). Developers must first master the basics. These fundamental aspects of OO technology must be internalized, activated, and then applied. Once basic OO terms are understood—from both the conceptual and practical points of view—a developer is well on the way to mastering object-oriented technology.

Keep in mind that the use of OO terms in actual practice is not a simple thing. The industry often speaks in terms of the paradigm shift when moving to object-oriented development. This paradigm shift is reflected in the understanding and use of concepts such as objects, classes, instances, messages, methods, encapsulation, abstraction, polymorphism, inheritance, persistence, binding, and typing.

If developers already grasp these concepts and are able to appropriately use them in the design/development of the application, they understand object technology. More often, however, significant training and education plans need to be included in the transition strategy for developers. Although this chapter is not intended to explain all of the fundamental concepts and terminology of OO, it is important to see how the key OO terms can be related to the world of the host developer. The ability to compare and describe new technology in light of older, more familiar technology is an excellent way to begin the transition process. Devising some means of bridging a developer's current knowledge to new technology can reduce any anxiety associated with the introduction of OO methods.

Familiar Concepts

Objects are described in a variety of ways. Steve Jobs, of NeXT Computers, defines an object as a chunk of intelligence that knows how to act in a given situation—a reasonable definition but not one that helps a programmer learn how to use and create an object.

Somewhat more familiar to the developer is this definition: An object is a "program" made up of methods (or subroutines) that simulate the activities of the object. Objects always capture or simulate the activities of real-world events; each method represents one specific state of the object.

Messages. Objects communicate via messages. There is little physical difference between messages sent between objects and calls between programs. The difference lies in the fact that calls between programs are static, based on the linkage between subprograms. Accessing another object's methods is dynamic because the called object is able to inherit the characteristics (and data) of the calling object.

Instances and Persistence. The idea of object instances and persistence are also concepts that can be related to things the host developer is familiar with. Instances are nothing more than the specific occurrence of an object, similar to a row of data in a relational table or the execution of a specific program. Persistence refers to the storing of objects in a data base or file. One of the foundations of business data processing is that information can subsequently be retrieved in the same way (or state) in which it was stored.

New Concepts

Terms such as messages, instances, and persistence are simply new names for relatively old concepts. Object technology is obviously a lot more than these few simple terms, however. In fact, the following two concepts are much more difficult for the host developer to grasp because there are no corresponding notions in legacy systems.

Encapsulation. The concept of encapsulation is a basic underlying principle of object orientation. It states the requirement that an object's data and processes are bound and distributed together. This directly contradicts the idea of data independence, which is one of the principles of traditional computing.

One of the goals of mainframe development has always been to get as many programs as possible to share as many subroutines as possible. A corresponding goal is getting as many programs/subroutines as possible to share the same data. Encapsulation represents a direct departure from this philosophy. Object development attempts to ensure that every object is shielded and protected from all of the other objects it comes in contact with. Each object owns its own data, methods, and protocols. Any other object requiring access to those items must "ask" the owning object to pass them over. Objects inherit data/methods from objects (especially related objects of the same class, as in object class libraries) they come in contact with.

Polymorphism. The concept of polymorphism is the process of making the same name do different things depending on the object that inherits it. In traditional development environments, variable names are, for the most part meaningless. Although they may have meaning to the developer, they have little if any meaning to the operating environment. A field named NET-AMOUNT-DUE would provide the same results as one entitled SDFDSF-ZFSZFD-ND as long as they were defined similarly (i.e., numeric versus alphanumeric).

Under polymorphism, not only do the names of things have meaning, but the same names can exhibit or trigger different behaviors based on the object receiving it. A simple example is the idea of a currency conversion object. This object behaves differently when confronted with frames as compared to dollars.

One problem often encountered by developers new to OO is the creation of "dead objects." These objects look exactly like other objects but when faced with changing circumstances cannot adapt. These objects are not able to exhibit different behavior. They consume resources in the system but never provide adequate results.

Although encapsulation and polymorphism may be difficult for the host developer to grasp, they are the key reasons object orientation offers such promise for the development of distributed applications. Encapsulation and polymorphism can be incredibly helpful and efficient in those situations where the developer of an object does not wish to be concerned about the details of how or where things get done.

LANGUAGE ISSUES

Sometimes knowing one thing makes learning new things easier. In this case the transfer of learning is positive. In the programming arena, however, it is often the case that being experienced in one paradigm gets in the way of learning a new one, resulting in a negative transfer of learning. This should not come as a surprise to many readers. Conventional programming has been mainly focused on functional decomposition and structured programming. These are disciplines that work in a variety of development environments but are quite different from the OO way of approaching problems.

Unlearning a paradigm (especially one that works) is usually difficult. This problem is compounded when a new programming language must be learned as well. Take the case of COBOL programmers wanting to migrate to the emerging world of objects. If a new language must be learned in addition to the new way of approaching a problem, it can be overwhelming. It is hard enough developing an application in a new environment let alone in a new environment with radically different rules and a new language.

For the developer to be able to work in an object-oriented environment, languages and tools need be considered. The use of C++ is one choice but not necessarily the best one for host developers who usually have a wealth of experience using COBOL. In addition, there is nothing intrinsically better about using C++ as compared to any other language, COBOL included. Excellent OO programs can be written in C++ or OOCOBOL just as easily as terrible programs can be developed in these languages.

Flavors of Languages

Object-oriented languages are available in three flavors:

- Enhanced languages.
- Native languages.
- Visual languages.

Enhanced languages are third-generation languages that have been modified to include the constructs necessary to develop OO programs. C++, OOCOBOL, and Visual Basic fall into this category.

Native languages are languages specifically designed to develop OO programs. These languages are often scripted and tied to specific tools. Eiffel, Actor, and Smalltalk fall into this category.

Visual languages are high-level languages that are tied to specific development environments. PARTS and Visual Age are members of this group.

Regardless of the language and tools selected, it is important to consider the entire gamut of OO development and where each piece fits (see Exhibit IV-3-3).

Smalltalk is becoming popular in the business community because it is a high-level language that enforces, as a pure object-oriented language, rules of encapsulation. Smalltalk is considered by many to be especially applicable for business applications because of its ease of learning, its mature class library, and its enforcement of OO discipline. In addition, Smalltalk has a fairly rich infra-

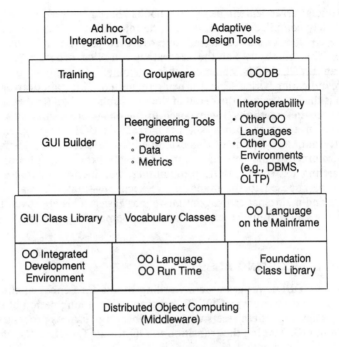

Exhibit IV-3-3. The Big Picture of OO

structure in terms of its development tools and interfaces to other subsystems, such as OO data bases and other languages and system services (i.e., CICS).

Although there are advantages and disadvantages to each OO language, some are better adapted to helping developers move to this new environment. COBOL is already familiar to developers and allows organizations to use their existing assets. These assets are both the developers' expertise and knowledge and the millions of lines of existing business application code. Although much of this code requires reengineering, it contains the operational logic and business rules of the organization.

OOCOBOL is an extension of the existing COBOL standard and so is familiar to most developers. Although the issues of development environments and object libraries still hold, the experience in using OOCOBOL for people with a COBOL background (which includes most host developers) often produces much less of an obstacle in making the transition to problem solving using the OO approach.

For example, one way to engage COBOL programmers is to ask them to think of ways in which they can extend the range of data types found in standard ANSI 85 COBOL. COBOL has a built-in set of classes (e.g., COMPUTATIONAL, PACKED DECIMAL). They have polymorphic methods called ADD and SUBTRACT. In fact, these data types can be extended. The result is usually a rather artificial arrangement using copybooks shared between client programs and separately compiled that implement the interface to the data type.

Because copybooks can be nested, one can even contrive a semblance of inheritance. The "methods" in the separately compiled programs are reached through an EVALUATE statement that examines a parameter of the called procedure indicating which service is being requested. The main drawback of this approach is that so much of the detail of the encapsulated data (and even the code used to select the "methods") is exposed to the client programs.

It is a bit of a stretch to describe the current COBOL language in terms of object orientation. The value of this example is to describe scenarios familiar to host programmers. This approach not only teaches the principles of OO in a familiar setting for the COBOL programmer, but it also convinces the programmer—as opposed to the manager or executive—that OO makes the programmer's and maintenance programmer's jobs easier. This approach is the key to promoting OO within the applications development department.

LEVERAGING EXISTING ASSETS

The many COBOL programmers working today have encoded the business processes of the companies in COBOL programs over a long period of time. It is important to leverage these assets when reengineering business processes into the new world of OO. Making the transition to OO from COBOL is therefore a key issue for IS management.

The idea of migrating applications developers and code to leverage existing assets to the maximum extent is a sensible, practical, and cost-efficient approach. It involves a concentrated code analysis process to understand the current state of the code and how it can best be used. Once the analysis phase is complete the serious work of redevelopment engineering can proceed.

Transformation Methodology

The heart of the redevelopment process is the transformation methodology that combines the business and technology visions into a coherent whole. This is actually the coalescence of top-down (business vision) and bottom-up (technical vision) approaches. The result is the overall organization's transformation policy: a strategic statement or contract defining what the system will be and what it will take to get there.

Once the plan is formalized and in place, the business of redeveloping the system can begin in earnest. The analysis of the existing system now helps identify overlapping functions—that is, the functions the target system and current system have in common. A variety of projects have shown that as much as 60% of an existing system's code can be reused in the new system.

Because these functions may be used repeatedly during the development process, reusable code in the form of objects is suggested. In addition to determining functional code that already exists, all other functions should be identified and catalogued. These catalogued functions are natural candidates for objects and an excellent way to get developers to understand how to identify and create objects.

Functions, processes, and the application code comprise only half of the equation. Data relationships and requirements must also be examined. Overlapping data—common data between the current and target system—needs to be analyzed and catalogued. A data repository can track the data requirements of the system and ensure that data is not duplicated. The idea of encapsulation must be used to help define how the data is used, how it is modified, who uses it, and in what instances. In this way, the developer learns about the data requirements of the application at the detailed function or object level.

These techniques do not by themselves create an OO application. COBOL expertise does not equal OOCOBOL expertise. It does, however, suggest an approach to get host developers to start thinking in the right direction. Once the application is defined at the object and nonobject levels, the user interface may be considered.

STARTING OO DEVELOPMENT

GUI Builders. There are a variety of tools and facilities available for creating sophisticated OO GUI interfaces. These interfaces need to be highly intuitive and often contain common components across screen sets. Common components or screen objects are relatively easy to build and have value because they can be easily reused.

Starting OO development at the user interface portion of applications not only makes sense, it is something that can be accomplished through the use of a variety of OO GUI tools. Implementations of Smalltalk all exploit the window-icon-mouse-pointer approach and, more important, take advantage of the transfer of learning that comes about through the use of protocols such as IBM's Common User Access specification. Another example is the Dialog presentation development system from MicroFocus that directly interfaces to COBOL programs. That the user interface can be created at the same time the fundamental principles of OO are being learned is a double advantage.

Business Processes. It must be pointed out that the common belief that sexy user interfaces are what OO is all about is misleading. Business processes are equally amenable to OO.

Many of the problems of creating, extending, and maintaining business applications stem from the amount of translation that occurs between the problem being addressed and its computational solution. A simple request from the shop floor to the warehouse becomes a transaction involving terminals, files, and synchronization points in the non-OO world. Using object technology this is simply a message that is sent from the shop floor object to the warehouse object. The complexities involving this activity are hidden within the implementation of each object.

Done properly, the objects in the original problem specification and the objects in the computational solution are directly related, making for easier understanding and hence maintenance. In other words, the business definition of the problem is also the computational solution to the problem. This is, however, different from the way most organizations and certainly host developers design and develop applications.

Team Development. OO development uses teams to create different aspects of the application. A framework team develops the reusable objects while an application team develops or assembles the application. This means that the application team owns the application but the framework team owns the components of that application. This is different from traditional code ownership and requires flexibility and communication among the different teams.

Data Acquisition. The next issue of concern is the aspect of data acquisition and persistence. How does the application store the data and what is the bridge between the non-OO aspects of the code possibly using a relational data base management system and the OO aspects of the code that possibly use an object-oriented data base? This dual data base strategy must tie relational legacy data with objects—that is, data residing on the host using DB2, for example, must interface with objects residing on distributed servers using Object Store. The migration process thus involves not only developers but technologies that must be carefully considered.

The least confrontational solution is to use SQL as a common access mechanism. Not only do host developers know SQL, but it is able (or almost able) to bridge the gap between these environments. SQL2 is the current ANSI standard that most developers are familiar with. It is being successfully used with the current implementation of relational data bases on a variety of platforms. Of particular importance is its support of referential integrity and stored procedures.

The definition work on SQL3 is currently in progress. It will replace the current ANSI standard SQL and provide support for objects, including object identification, classes, methods, and inheritance. Once completed, SQL (or what some are now calling OQL) will be able to provide distributed access to objects similar to its ability to provide distributed access to data.

Eventually all aspects of object management will be handled via standard SQL calls. As the SQL language adds capabilities and new syntax, it will be able to accommodate new object environments, including OMG's CORBA, IBM's SOM, and Microsoft's OLE, thus allowing for the transition of SQL to incorporate objects along with a long-term blueprint for full object-oriented systems. Developers can adapt the data acquisition portion of application code by taking advantage of new features as required. This represents an evolutionary, not revolutionary, path to object technologies.

OO CLIENT/SERVER INTEGRATION

The integration of OO technology with the demands of distributed client/ server applications is another significant issue. OO must be able to integrate with existing technology, both legacy and distributed models.

OO's Role in Current and Future Generations of Systems

First-generation client/server systems now under development are rather modest in their design owing to the absence of sophisticated tools (both development and system services) and the lack of expertise in this relatively new technology. The next generation of client/server applications will be more robust, providing transparency of data, transparency of process location, and the ability to access local, relational, and nonrelational data. The third generation of client/server solutions will incorporate most of the features organizations have been looking for in distributed solutions. In this case, systems include distributed client platforms, reliance on middleware, heterogeneous data sources, mixed access technologies, high transaction volumes, and mission-critical integrity.

Object-oriented features will be incorporated throughout each generation of client/server systems. As distributed technologies and associated tools mature, so will the use of OO, though its use will vary depending on the expertise of the organization. First-generation applications are allowing developers to experiment with OO but, for the most part, not export them to the production solution. The time is nonetheless well spent by developers, who are learning the basic concepts of OO while attempting to develop component pieces for use in actual applications. Second- and third-generations of client/server applications will use OO in ever-increasing amounts. By necessity, the third-generation of these systems will require OO to efficiently provide the required solution.

The use of Smalltalk, OOCOBOL, and other tools offers developers a means to satisfy the requirements of each generation of client/server applications. For example, Smalltalk may be initially used to develop the desktop-presentation portions of the application. As the requirements of the application increase in complexity, reusable Smalltalk application objects can be developed for distribution across the enterprise (Smalltalk can be integrated with standard language calls)—for example, a COBOL program calling a Smalltalk object or a Smalltalk object calling a COBOL (or OOCOBOL) routine.

The functional requirements of the third generation of client/server applications require object-oriented data bases, object request brokers, and object request servers. The object request broker acts as sophisticated middleware transparently transporting objects across the enterprise. A combination of Smalltalk and language objects will all be serviced in this scenario. From the developer's point of view, the use of Smalltalk and OOCOBOL objects means that the work done early in the transitional phase can be used in later stages to a large extent.

Anticipating the Costs of the Transition

In the early stages of transition to OO techniques, it is reasonable to expect an average of three redesigns before a set of objects are suitable for use in production. The organization must be willing to invest in these "lost objects" and consider it a part of the expense of training. One study found that more than 13 reuses are required to cover the cost of developing a reusable component. This situation is in part due to the current state of the technology, especially tools, but a portion of the problem must also be attributed to the design methodologies currently being practiced (thus the criticality of moving to one of the OO design methods). As development organizations gain experience and their inventory of available objects increases, this number will go down.

Key decisions must also be made about the applications operating environment before any code is developed. Are the facilities of a relational data base management system to be used, an online transaction processing system, or a combination of the two? Is the data base relational or OO? If an OLTP is required, how can that be effectively interfaced to the OO portions of the system? Because both technologies may be required, how are they to be integrated and what communication methods handle the distributed object management? The realities of the current state of OO middleware are important to understand if the application is to be architected.

LANs, multiuser environments, GUI interfaces, and distributed processing facilities must also be modeled to determine where each piece fits and the tools available to integrate the application into a seamless unit. For example, PM, Windows, and Motif each specify a different GUI interface. Each GUI has specific requirements (to go along with individual APIs) and requires careful consideration (regardless of the tool being used to create the interface). The next generation of operating systems and interfaces should also be looked at.

Building reusable components and then distributing those components is critical to the success of the distributed client/server application—that is, different objects executing on the platform best suited to provide the solution. A common example is a system that has been distributed with front-end processing occurring on distributed clients with data acquisition elements residing on a host or hosts (including distributed servers). Managing these diverse resources in an effective and optimal manner is key to the success of any mission-critical application.

CONCLUSION

Migrating a development organization to object-oriented methods is a long-term investment decision involving all aspects of the development environment and affecting the way the organization will conduct business. The transition process is not limited to but certainly includes the actual developers who may have little understanding of OO concepts. System architects, designers, analysts, and programmers must all understand the basic paradigm shift that moving to an OO environment entails.

While object-oriented technology brings certain benefits to the table, it also raises many concerns. How much training is required and what is the expense? What will it take to actually move current application methods to OO and what is the cost of this conversion? Other concerns include the maturity of the technology and related tools, lack of standards, and execution speed.

Integrating OO technology into the current production mix will require tools that are open and do not include proprietary technology. Finally, the enterprise model for the organization's next-generation applications must be supported. This requirement includes robust performance, data integrity, and the services provided by a transaction processing monitor.

Although these concerns are real and need careful consideration, OO technology offers the only realistic solution to the promise of truly distributed client/server applications. Faster development, higher-quality code, reduced costs, and easier maintenance have been promised by each new development technology. In each case, improvements have been made, but none compare to the results experienced by early OO adopters. Increased scalability through the use of objects as building blocks allows heterogeneous environments to be transparently supported.

As development organizations move to OO environments, they are facing and resolving problems related to interfacing objects to current technology, training and design methodology issues, and the basic conflict developers face when moving away from data independence principles to encapsulation.

The biggest investment the organization will be required to make is in training. The second biggest investment is ignoring the cost of training. Many organizations that make the mistake of selecting tools (both development and system services) before or in conjunction with formalized training find themselves lost in the technology and select tools that do not match the way the organization will ultimately develop objects and applications. The richness and stability of the selected environment is critical along with its potential for growth and its ability to interact with both object and nonobject environments.

Regardless of the development methodology, language, and tools eventually selected, it is important to spend as much time as required to consider this move and how to effectively transition the organization and its developers to this new world.

IV-4

Supporting Legacy Systems

Nancy Blumenstalk Mingus

LEGACY SYSTEMS continue to be used because they continue to add some value to the business and because they are so expensive to replace. Yet staff members responsible for supporting and maintaining 10- to 20-year-old mission-critical systems may feel they are being denied a chance to acquire new skills. IS managers can protect staff morale in their departments by conveying the business reasons for using legacy systems to the staff assigned the job of maintaining and supporting them. This chapter outlines various ways to minimize apathy among support staff, with tips for helping maintenance employees keep the job fresh.

RECOGNIZING LEGACY SYSTEMS

Any of the following conditions may be true of a legacy system:

- It was programmed by someone who left the company 10 years ago.
- It uses data base technology or a programming language rooted in the 1970s.
- It was translated from one language or operating system to another by an automated translating utility.
- It has been modified so many times, the code looks like spaghetti; there are pages of variable names that are never referenced and whole sections never executed.
- It is so old, the source code is missing.

Although physical age and old technology are hallmarks of a legacy system, another equally important identifier is that a company still uses the system in production. If the system is a purchasing, order entry, inventory, human resources, or even an executive information system, odds are the company still trains or supports the users and maintains or enhances these systems even though they are past their prime.

Many companies call their older systems legacy systems. Legacy is a nicer name than dinosaur, though the idea is basically the same. More specifically, however, legacy systems are usually financial or human resources systems left over from the 1970s. Legacy systems are mainframe-based. Whereas most dinosaur systems are mainframe-based, they need not be. A 10-year-old dBase II or

Lotus 1-2-3 application can also be a dinosaur, especially if the corporate standards for PC software packages have changed.

WHY LEGACY SYSTEMS LINGER ON

These systems got to be legacy systems in a variety of ways. Here are just a few:

- They were state-of-the-art when implemented. Many of the systems still running today were ahead of their time when they were written. They used the latest technology, and in ways the product developers never intended.
- The systems were passed from person to person, until finally ending up with the one or two employees who know them now. Unfortunately, the documentation never made it past the third or fourth handoff.
- The systems continued to be patched instead of redesigned as corporate conditions changed.

Many systems that became legacy for these reasons continue to be used for similar reasons. The most common rationale is: If it's not broken, why fix it?

Business and Financial Reasons

Even though code is patched, often several layers thick, the system continues to serve its function. A company may be leery about investing time in a redesign of something that still works. What companies often fail to realize, however, is that in many cases, when these systems do break, they might not be fixable. This is especially true of those systems with hard-code date routines that will not be able to handle the year 2000.

Another reason why these systems linger on is that they meet a need no preprogrammed package can meet, even today. Legacy systems are almost universally in-house written and fit the organization so well that no one wants to change procedures so they can upgrade the system.

In addition, other higher-priority jobs continue to push legacy system rewrites to the back burner. This reasoning ties in with the first one: As long as these systems continue to perform their function, a company may determine that it is better to invest in systems that can save money or make money.

Converting legacy systems to new technology is costly in terms of redesigning and recoding the software, as well as purchasing new hardware. Furthermore, current staff may not have the required skill sets for recoding the systems, so new staff, consultants, or extensive training become necessary. Also, the terminals, controllers, and mainframes generally used with existing systems are paid for. Networks and PCs require additional capital.

The company's legacy systems were often the first automated systems, so they usually contain sensitive corporate financial, personnel, and product data. Some companies maintain that rewriting the systems could jeopardize data confidentiality and potentially affect data integrity and for this reason opt to keep their legacy systems.

OBJECTIVELY EVALUATING LEGACY SYSTEMS

Drawbacks of Legacy Maintenance

The drawbacks to maintaining existing systems are fairly obvious. IS professionals confront them daily. Some of the major drawbacks are that:

- *Only a few people know the system, so they end up doing all the training, support, and maintenance.* This deprives the staff of time to learn new systems, which virtually every employee would rather be doing.
- *These systems were installed before data entry validity checks were popular, so bad data is often entered.* It takes extra support time to fix errors, extra maintenance time to fix the system, and extra training time to tell people how to enter data correctly. Furthermore, these systems are often used in departments with high turnover, which adds to the problem of training and support.
- *Training generally must be designed and delivered in-house.* Because the systems are not standard packages, there are no canned or vendor-delivered courses available. Even if they were originally written in a standard, supported product, the product may be so old that it is difficult to find anyone who teaches courses on it anymore.
- *Every time operating systems, file structures, or other support programs change, the existing systems might not work.* This often requires significant support time to get them running again, if they will run at all.

Benefits of Legacy Maintenance

There are some benefits to providing quality training, support, and maintenance on existing systems. Among them:

- *Maintenance can add another five or more years to their life span.* Although this strategy often makes the technology of the legacy system even further removed from state-of-the-art, it also buys time for the company as it makes plans to migrate to newer strategic systems and downsized platforms.
- *Proper maintenance minimizes system errors.* Because legacy systems are often complicated to use, it is easy to create errors and difficult to correct them. Proper training and support minimize the chance of operator error.
- *Unlike off-the-shelf PC or mainframe packages, legacy systems do not change significantly.* The benefit in this case is that there is no need to update the training materials or support procedures every time the vendor introduces a change.

MINIMIZING APATHY TOWARD LEGACY SYSTEMS

Burnout is probably the number-one problem where maintenance staff is concerned. IS managers attentive to the morale of their departments can encourage IS maintenance personnel to regain interest in their work in several ways.

Maintenance staff should be encouraged to dig through the fossil record. For example, one method is to allow the people responsible for legacy systems to investigate the history of the systems, to find out who wrote them and what particular design or programming problems they overcame. This information can give the staff new respect for the systems. By compiling a list of the ages of the various production systems, the people charged with these systems may also be surprised to find that these systems are not as old as some others.

It helps to explain to staff members doing legacy maintenance assignments why the systems are still being used. There is a strong inclination to want to scrap systems simply because they are old. This thinking obscures the real reasons that management and users may be reluctant to bury their existing information systems. It also erodes the sense of purpose maintenance staff members need to remain motivated.

IS managers can take several measures to keep legacy systems and their remaining business value in perspective. At the same time, these practices will help to minimize low morale among employees responsible for legacy systems maintenance.

Do Not Give Responsibility for Legacy Systems as a Punishment. If IS employees have had problems adjusting to new systems, the manager's first urge might be to pull them off that assignment and relegate them to the job of providing maintenance or support for existing systems. This action will always be seen as punishment. In many companies, junior-level people with limited experience or senior-level people nearing retirement are also saddled with older systems. Whether this decision is intentional, this action is generally viewed as a punishment, too. IS managers may be inviting trouble if they give legacy maintenance assignments as a punishment.

Consider Adding a GUI Front-End. Adding a graphical user interface (GUI) to an existing system is a common first step in migrating to new platforms. Customers (i.e., users) reap the benefits of a consistent look and feel; at the same time, the GUI front-end gives maintenance staff a taste of new technology, trainers new screens to work with, and support people fewer data entry errors to contend with.

Suggest That Trainers Change the Exercises in the Training Course. This simple suggestion takes less time to implement than developing a completely new course, yet it will make the course feel new and give trainers a chance to propose new ideas.

Allow Staff to Find an Undocumented Feature of the System and Publicize It. This is like uncovering a new type of dinosaur bone. It can stimulate more interest in the whole system and give the department some additional visibility.

Encourage People to Train Others as Backup. For maintenance staff, backup usually comes from a colleague, but for trainers and support staff, backup might come from an end user who favors the system, a colleague, or even a consultant.

Regardless of the source, having a backup gives the regular maintenance, training, and support staff room to breathe.

Perform a Full Systems Analysis on Existing Systems. The purpose is to find out why the system is still in use. A full systems analysis usually reveals that the documentation for the company's legacy systems is missing, dated, or incomplete. That is why only one or two people know the system. A full systems analysis will provide documentation or bring it up to date.

A full systems analysis that includes a cost/benefit section for replacing the existing system can be used to explain to the staff why management has decided to keep and maintain the existing system. Conversely, a cost/benefit analysis may convince management that the benefits of keeping the system are overstated and that it is time to retire the system, thus paving the way for redeploying current training, support, and maintenance personnel to learn new systems.

Allow Training, Support, and Maintenance Staff to Learn New Technology.
The entire staff should be granted time to keep up with new systems. Consider having each person on the maintenance staff pick a technology area they would like to learn about and present the latest developments at weekly staff meetings.

Encourage More Business Knowledge. If IS personnel are working on accounting systems, for example, suggest that they take an accounting course so they can better understand how their system fits in the overall business scheme.

Outsource the Training, Support, and Maintenance of Existing Systems. Although in-house people might view legacy assignments as punishment or a dead-end job, consultants tend to view them simply as work. Outsiders taking over existing maintenance are also likely to lend a fresh perspective to uncovering opportunities to improve efficiency.

CONCLUSION

Even companies committed to downsizing need people to provide training, support, and maintenance for their existing systems that keep the business functioning. But that does not have to mean a step backward for the IS staff involved. By viewing legacy systems objectively, and helping employees do what they can to keep their job fresh, IS managers can help their employees avoid becoming dinosaurs themselves.

IV-5

Building and Using a Data Warehouse

Robert E. Typanski

INTERVIEWS WITH BUSINESS PERSONNEL, which are used to determine their major concerns about the effectiveness of an existing information environment, yield surprisingly consistent results. Management, business professionals, and administrative personnel express dissatisfaction with data availability and development of computer systems to support fundamental company operations, such as manufacturing, order entry, inventory control, and payroll. Their primary needs are:

- Total solutions that met their needs, with a lower price tag.
- Flexible access to company data for decision support purposes.
- Greater accuracy in the applications systems they use to run their daily operations.
- Easier identification of data contained within the company.
- Friendly, easy-to-use software tools, along with responsive training and support.
- Delivery of the applications system within the time constraints of the business need.

To address these needs, information systems organizations must change the way they do things. The entire process of identifying requirements, developing and maintaining applications systems, and making data available to company employees requires a major overhaul.

WHAT NEEDS TO BE DONE

First, a strategic planning process involving all of IS management and many company management and professional personnel must be established. This effort is needed to determine overall goals and objectives and to obtain buy-in. Only then can specific strategies be developed to address the applications systems and data availability concerns.

Key strategies relating to the major needs are:

- Eliminate bottlenecks that make applications systems development and support unresponsive.
- Maximize applications systems development, productivity, and accuracy by using high-level tools that emphasize design-level development.
- Involve company personnel who will need to work in conjunction with the new environment.
- Provide company personnel with a unified view of the company's data, regardless of its physical location.
- Create a data directory for easy access to company data definitions and descriptions.
- Provide easy access to data through supported, direct-use software tools.

These strategies are the guiding principles. Once they are firmly established it is time to put a structure to these goals.

THE STRUCTURE TO SUPPORT THE STRATEGIES

To implement these strategies, an architecture must be built to provide overall guidance for the next stages—that of changing the IS development and support functions. This architecture is illustrated in Exhibit IV-5-1.

The key characteristics of this architecture is the creation of two distinctive information systems types: information retrieval/decision support systems and applications systems.

Information Retrieval/Decision Support. IR/DS systems are the basis for the informational processing activities of the company. They perform business analysis and reporting functions using data extracted from the applications systems data bases and other sources. This data is then placed in a new data base focused and oriented to the specific needs of the users. This data base is called a data warehouse.

Applications Systems. These types of information systems are the basis for supporting the operational activities of the company. They support fundamental company operations, such as manufacturing, order entry, inventory control, and payroll. These systems enter data into the applications systems data bases, usually through the use of a highly optimized transaction- and batch-processing environment.

THE COOKBOOK: HOW TO DO IT

The processes of the new environment—planning, development, execution, data management, and data enhancement—are created to complement the overall architecture. These processes are the recipes that allow IS to produce the products, programs, and data that are required by a company to support its business goals.

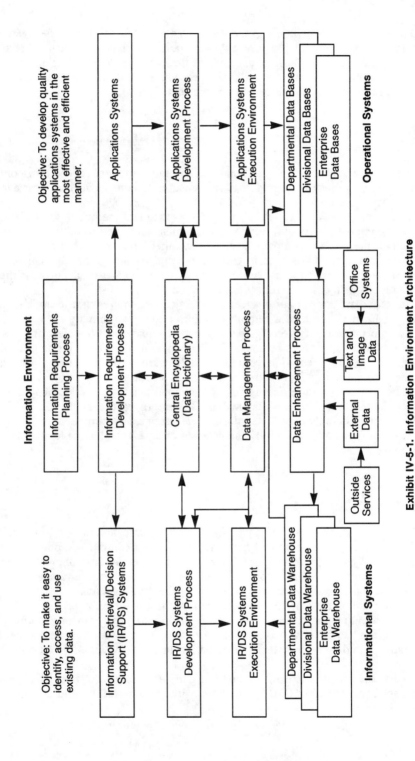

Exhibit IV-5-1. Information Environment Architecture

Documentation of these processes in a printed or online form must be created as part of the overall effort, to ensure that the information environment achieves its objectives in a way that is structured yet flexible. The documentation of the processes contains the process activities, procedures, and standards as well as guidelines that maximize the benefits of the environment.

DOING IT THE RIGHT WAY

To eliminate the bottlenecks that make IS development and support unresponsive, it is best to select a methodology that ensures responsive development and support activities.

The first criterion used to select a systems development methodology is that it not only complement the information environment architecture but that it also address the needs of the company business personnel. To address the needs of the company, the methodology has to emphasize requirements gathering. This criterion is consistent with the emphasis on quality by companies today, because the definition of quality is "meeting the requirements."

The second criterion used to select a methodology requires that it emphasize data, the major resource of a company's information environment.

The Information Engineering methodology combined with object-oriented (OO) techniques appears to be a good fit as the base methodology for an overall information environment that contains a data warehouse. It places a strong emphasis on gathering data requirements before a solution is attempted.

Inherent to Information Engineering is its emphasis on the development of an information system from a data model. This improves the ability of the IS organization to quickly modify its information systems, adapting them to changing business needs and facilitating the creation of data base designs for the data warehouse.

THE KEY TO SUCCESS

Throughout the process of changing the entire information environment, non-IS business personnel must be involved in steering committees, one-on-one meetings, and group presentations to make sure that the new environment meets their expectations. Feedback from this involvement is used to fine-tune the new environment and verify assumptions regarding the requirements.

A major component of this involvement is the use of pilot projects. Pilot projects determine and ensure the feasibility of the new environment. Company personnel need to be interviewed by IS personnel to apprise them of the new environment and to request their participation in pilot projects used as a final verification.

Finally, success also depends on providing the data administration (DA) and data base administration (DBA) functions with proper staffing and organizational placement.

Organizing and Staffing Data Management Functions

DBA is responsible for the physical placement of data in the data warehouse. It is primarily a technical infrastructure consideration and can be placed in the more technically oriented groups within IS. In some companies the DBA function is outsourced to contract personnel because knowledge of the company business environment is not crucial to its effectiveness.

Data administration is the logical structuring of the data is concert with the business needs of the company and is critical to the usability of the data warehouse by company business personnel. Because of the emphasis on data in a new information environment, this function is created to safeguard that data—the fundamental asset of the information environment—is consistently defined and modeled within the context of company business activities. Just as the financial controllers of the company provide assurance regarding the consistent handling of cash assets, so it is that data administration provides assurance regarding the handling of the data assets.

Although data is usually maintained through the collective actions of many seemingly isolated applications systems efforts, it is the responsibility of the data administration function to define data and model it in a manner that makes it useful to all interested parties.

The data administration function can be optionally placed in several organizations. The most common is to combine DA with DBA in a data management organization within IS. This type of organization helps ensure that the data designs created by the DA function are implemented by DBA if at all possible.

In a company with a strong commitment to data integration and close matching of the data structure to the business needs of the company, both functions need to be staffed with an equal number of employees—this staffing level for data administration is greater than what is usually found in a company, however. It is necessary, though, because of the emphasis on data modeling activities that uncover the business rules and relationships that properly match the data structure to the business. In addition, the data directory usually becomes the responsibility of data administrators, who must establish extensive interactions with company business personnel to accurately define the business definitions for maximum ease of data identification for use by company business analysts.

Other organizational placements for data administrators are in the applications systems development function and, more idealistically, in the company business areas outside of IS. If this last approach is taken, then the DA function truly becomes a company function responsible for the optimal use of the data assets analogous to the financial controller function's responsibility for the optimal use of the cash assets of the company.

In any case, a data administrator must be identified for each company business area. Each of these individuals works with the other data administrators to ensure that all information systems are synchronized to minimize data redundancy. A primary result of the data administrator's activities is the birth of the data warehouse.

THE DATA WAREHOUSE

The data warehouse environment is the final step in the development of a new information environment. It serves as the foundation for strategic and tactical decision making of the company.

A data warehouse is usually defined as a selection of historical data, extracted from the operational data bases, that is organized to facilitate analysis for strategic and tactical decision-making activities. It is time-stamped and contains both detailed and summarized views of the data.

Past efforts to create this environment at most companies have resulted in a fragmentation and duplication of the data. Key components such as data administration and a user-friendly data directory are usually missing. Company personnel cannot readily find the data, and costly coming. Company personnel can not readily find the data, and costly computer resources are needed to store the duplicated data.

To facilitate use of the data warehouse, the IS organization also creates a data directory, which provides definitions and descriptions of all company data and offers an overview of all data available. This directory is a key factor in making the data warehouse a success.

ROLES AND RESPONSIBILITIES OF COORDINATED TEAMS

Because of the complexity of developing a complete data warehouse environment and the usual preoccupation with technologies and tools rather than data, a separation of the responsibility for selecting components of a data warehouse is sometimes required. Three coordinated teams, each with a special focus, can be created to address the requirements:

- A data team.
- A technical infrastructure team.
- A direct-use tools team.

The teams should comprise both IS and business professionals. The team approach helps to emphasize the focus of attention. A coordinator or steering committee to consolidate the recommendations is also a valuable component. Final recommendations should be tested in a laboratory-style environment (to verify the right technologies were selected) and a pilot data warehouse system developed (to demonstrate the overall capabilities to all company business areas).

The Data Team

This team is the most important of the three teams because it is responsible for ensuring that the data is structured in close coordination with the business needs of the company. Without the proper emphasis on this facet of the data warehouse environment, the contents of the data warehouse would not meet the requirements of the business users. Key objectives of this team are the overall business-oriented data structure, the data enhancement process, and the data warehouse directory.

Data Structure. Business-oriented, logical data structures establish a unified view of company data to users of the data warehouse. Data structure deals with issues of:

- Enterprise versus departmental scope.
- Levels of detail and summarization.
- An overall approach to data modeling.

Pragmatism and Data Integration. The standard approach to data warehouse logical data structures is an enterprisewide, subject-oriented view that helps integrate the functionally oriented, fragmented application data structures. This ideal approach is practical in companies with a strong central IS direction coming from a common company authority body, such as the chief executive or an executive committee that has control over divisional and staff department initiatives.

In today's environment, however, this is seldom the case. Divisions and staff departments are given much more autonomy and are held responsible for their bottom line rather than having to adhere to an overall company policy. Consequently, a more pragmatic approach to data integration is needed.

Generally, although business functions within a company are realizing that they want easier access to their data for information retrieval/decision support purposes, they are not interested in delaying it for the sake of developing an enterprisewide data model that they would then fit into. They want their data to be made available quickly and are not necessarily concerned with standardizing and integrating with other company organizations that have similar needs.

It is the responsibility of the data administration function, therefore, to achieve an enterprisewide view of the data in the data warehouse. This is achieved through close coordination among the various data administrators in standardizing on naming conventions and on business definitions, and in identifying the common sources of data that are requested. The use of a sophisticated data modeling tool that facilitates the sharing of data models and extending them when necessary is also crucial to this approach.

This approach places a large burden or responsibility on the DA function, but the results are a highly integrated view of company data with minimal redundancy. This integration is then accomplished as a by-product of the creation of data warehouses rather than as a preliminary prerequisite activity that delays the warehouse's creation. To achieve data integration in this way requires a DA staff that is:

- Technically proficient in data modeling.
- Skilled in interpersonal and facilitation skills.
- Knowledgeable in the various facets of the company business environment.

These personal attributes, combined with the use of sophisticated data modeling tools, lead to the creation of an integrated data warehouse logical business structure almost in spite of the individual business area demands.

Data Enhancement Process—Gateway to the Data Warehouse. As depicted in the information environment architecture in Exhibit IV-5-1, the data enhancement process is the gateway to the data warehouse. All data must go through this process to ensure that the data warehouse is not only integrated from a logical business perspective but is also operationally maintainable.

The data enhancement process is designed to be used by data warehouse programmers to create the programs that extract data from the operational data bases, outside sources, and office systems. All of these sources must be accessed and data extracted and mapped to the logical business designs of the data warehouse. Programs are created to access the operational data and created time-stamps, perform edits, calculate common derived values, and eliminate operationally oriented indicators and flags.

The development of these programs can be accomplished by several methods. Programs can be hand-coded in a procedural language or generated from a computer-aided software engineering (CASE) tool. The most common method used today is to purchase a specially designed data extract tool for creation of a data warehouse. These tools also help to develop the data directory of technical and business information that is used to maintain and access the data warehouse environment.

These programs are then placed in a production environment for scheduling in combination with the business needs that are addressed. Usually these programs are run during the night-time processing schedule.

The Data Warehouse Directory. More than anything else, the success of a data warehouse depends on the content and ease of use of the data warehouse directory. Its purpose is to provide easy identification of the data in the data warehouse to the company's business analysts and managers.

Although the directory contains technical information regarding data lengths, characteristics, and access names, the most important information about data is the business-oriented information that facilitates the identification of data items as the correct ones for the business problem at hand. Key information about this facet of the data warehouse data are:

- Company functional and business area names responsible for the data.
- Subject area names and description.
- Relational data base management systems (RDBMS) table names.
- Data owner name with access authority.
- Access security requirements.
- Frequency of update cycle.
- Update method (e.g., append/replace).
- Physical data base vendor.

Ideally, the directory should provide this information in a manner that is usable by direct-use tools. Recent data warehouse directory products are moving in this direction by including query tools as an integral part of the directory system.

Technical Infrastructure Team

This team is responsible for a more dynamic facet of the information environment—the technical environment that will support the physical data warehouse. The primary requirement placed on this team is that a single image of the data must be provided to users of the data warehouse regardless of its physical distribution. Major components that must be addressed are: physical data base system, hardware/software platform, and middleware.

Physical Data Base System—A Distributed Approach. The prerequisite decision that must be made before a data base management system is selected is whether the data warehouse environment is to be in one physical location or distributed across many hardware environments.

Although one large data warehouse has several advantages, the trend is to the client/server model that allows the implementation of small portions of the data warehouse as business areas of the company develop their requirements and funding approvals. The client/server approach to data warehousing, therefore, dictates a distributed physical data base architecture.

To minimize the complexity of providing a single image of data to users in a distributed architecture, a single data base management system should be used on all distributed hardware platforms. A few such data base management systems are available today that support different hardware vendors and operating systems.

Hardware Platforms. A common operating system should be used, maximizing the flexibility of selecting a hardware vendor to take advantage of periodic vendor price-performance advantages. UNIX is now fulfilling this role; even though all UNIX versions are not identical, they are closer to one another in functionality than proprietary operating systems and require minimal work to migrate from one flavor to another. The actual hardware vendors under consideration should therefore be studied to determine if they provide a UNIX operating system and support the selected data base management system.

Middleware. In today's distributed, client/server environment, middleware has become a major decision. Middleware in the context of this discussion is all the hardware, software, and communications facilities that make it possible to access data across multiple server hardware platforms from multiple client workstations.

Although a myriad of routers, network operating systems, and bridges must be used, two key components need to be selected that have a long-lasting implication in the area of personnel required to develop expertise in their use.

The Communications Protocol—TCP/IP. A single communications protocol is highly desirable to simplify the conductivity issues. Because UNIX is probably the operating system, Transmission Control Protocol/Internet Protocol (TCP/IP) is practically a default choice. TCP/IP's past security deficiencies are being corrected and it is becoming widely available and universally accepted for at least the type of processing incurred in a data warehouse environment.

Data Base-Oriented Middleware. The data base integration middleware decision is very complex. The decision here is influenced by the type of client/server computing used.

In a data warehouse environment, the remote data access type is most common. In this type of client/server computing, the program logic and presentation facets are resident on a client workstation and only data base calls are sent to the server. This type of processing is handled very well by the data base management vendors if their products are used on all hardware platforms.

Middleware supplied by the data base vendors is called data base-oriented middleware. It is usually the responsibility of the data base administration function to maintain the tables within this middleware that are required to provide a single image of the data to users of the data warehouse environment.

Direct-Use Tools Team

Many new tools are available that can access a data warehouse through standard structured query language (SQL) calls. However, because of the very dynamic nature of this facet of the data warehouse environment, it is the most difficult to standardize. In addition, once a particular tool is evaluated and recommended, it usually does not meet the personal preferences of the company's business analysts.

Direct-use tools usually fall into three categories: query and reporting, decision support, and executive information system (EIS). The trend is for tools to combine features of two of the three types. It is now common to have tools classified as either:

- Query and reporting/decision support.
- Decision support/EIS.

In addition, commonly used office software such as spreadsheets are now including query and reporting SQL capabilities, and object-oriented 4GL (fourth-generation language) tools are being used for development of EIS.

IS departments should be careful not to spend too much effort in this area. It is of limited long-term value and the business areas of the company usually want to pick their own favorites.

MARKETING AND DEPLOYMENT OF THE DATA WAREHOUSE

In market-driven environments, new products and services must be packaged and marketed to the customers. So it is with a new product such as the data warehouse. Marketing is a new world for IS organizations, and it is usually not one of its strengths.

Although the data warehouse benefits the company as a whole, the IS department cannot assume that all company personnel readily appreciate it. The re-

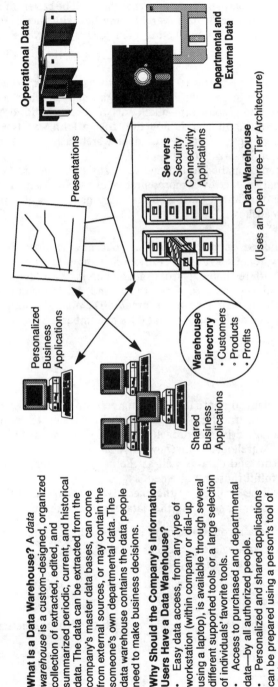

Operational Data

Departmental and External Data

Presentations

Servers
Security
Connectivity
Applications

Personalized Business Applications

Warehouse Directory
· Customers
· Products
· Profits

Shared Business Applications

Data Warehouse
(Uses an Open Three-Tier Architecture)

What Is a Data Warehouse? A *data warehouse* is a custom-designed, organized collection of extracted, edited, and summarized periodic, current, and historical data. The data can be extracted from the company's master data bases, can come from external sources, or may contain the someone's own departmental data. The data warehouse contains the data people need to make business decisions.

Why Should the Company's Information Users Have a Data Warehouse?
• Easy data access, from any type of workstation (within company or dial-up using a laptop), is available through several different supported tools or a large selection of individuals' favorite tools.
• Access to purchased and departmental data—by all authorized people.
• Personalized and shared applications can be prepared using a person's tool of choice.
• Presentation of results is customized using the person's tool of choice.
• Periodic data is available, so people do not have to wade through several months of reports to find all the data they need.
• Organized directory means no one has to scroll through irrelevant data.

• Summarized data is available, so users do not have to look at all the details to find exactly the data they need for decision making.
• Customized data means that the data in the warehouse is defined by the users themselves.
• Extracted data is available, so the data a user needs is already there and available.

◦ The data is current, updated regularly, according to a user's business needs. No one has to wait for the end of the week, month, or quarter.
◦ New data requests can be addressed by managers or their staffs by using the data warehouse directory.

Exhibit IV-5-2. Sample Marketing Sheet from a Data Warehouse Brochure for Users

sponsibility for convincing the company personnel that they will be better off and more effective in their jobs because of data warehousing lies with the IS staff. Toward this end, IS must develop a marketing plan for its data warehouse product.

The Marketing Brochure. The first step to take is to develop a marketing brochure that provides a more interesting depiction of the data warehouse environment. The use of color and graphic arts–quality artwork, along with down-to-earth wording that whets the audience's appetite, goes a long way toward generating interest. A sample page from a real data warehousing marketing brochure is shown in Exhibit IV-5-2.

This kind of brochure can be mailed to internal company personnel and then followed up with a personal contact by a representative of the IS organization. The brochure can also be distributed during special demonstrations of a pilot data warehouse called a roadshow.

Taking the Data Warehouse on the Road. This roadshow is more than a demonstration of a data warehouse. It is carefully orchestrated to provide potential internal customers with testimonials from satisfied users, introductions to key support personnel who are there to serve them, and an opportunity to test-drive a data warehouse in their own environment. Technology should be discussed only if it is requested and at a level that does not embarrass any of the participants.

CONCLUSION

By taking a structured, planned approach involving personnel from all facets of the business, companies can transform the business of providing IS services from a fragmented, technology-driven approach to a unified, data-driven environment including a data warehouse. This new environment emphasizes the identification of requirements and data as well as the use of appropriate technologies and processes to fulfill those requirements.

Even greater benefits will be realized by the executives, managers, business analysts, and administrative personnel using the data warehouse through:

- Easy identification of data through use of the data warehouse directory.
- Unified data to support strategic and tactical decision making.
- Flexibility in hardware vendor selection.
- Comprehensive training on direct-use software tools.
- Effective management of the data assets of the company.

The data warehouse environment is here. The more it is used, the better it becomes.

IV-6

Issues in Relational Data Base Control

Sean D. Doyle

===

THE EARLY DEVELOPMENT of relational data base management systems (RDBMSs) focused primarily on basic system functions and performance. As organizations began to use relational technologies to build mission-critical applications, they became increasingly concerned about the potential legal and financial consequences of poorly managed systems. As a result, the market demanded that software developers provide effective protection mechanisms. As the relational data base industry matured, it became better positioned to provide the needed solutions.

This chapter describes contemporary challenges in managing data and describes how new relational data base technologies help meet those challenges. Discretionary access controls and related security and audit capabilities of new relational data base products are discussed. The chapter also addresses such emerging technologies as multilevel secure (MLS) data base systems. Practical tips on how to evaluate these technologies are provided. Although the issues discussed are applicable to most relational data base products, specific security capabilities are illustrated using the Oracle RDBMS, Version 7.0, and the MLS Oracle RDBMS, Version 1.0.

CHALLENGES IN RELATIONAL DATA BASE MANAGEMENT

Relational systems have been designed to provide increased ease of use and availability of data. These characteristics can create unique challenges to system control. Relational systems allow end users to manipulate and share data in ways that were not possible with more traditional hierarchical, network, and flat file data base applications. For example, the capabilities of Structured Query Language (SQL) allow users to enter real-time, ad hoc queries to access and modify data; such power and flexibility create risks that may not be anticipated by IS managers who are unfamiliar with relational systems.

The inherent flexibility of relational systems must be balanced by control policies that limit users' access to only the data they need to perform their jobs.

A policy of least privilege can be implemented, requiring that each user be granted the most restrictive set of privileges needed to perform a set of authorized tasks. The use of such a policy helps limit the damage that can result from accident and error as well as from unauthorized use.

Highly granular access controls can also be used to enforce separation of functions. Separation of functions involves dividing sensitive tasks into smaller subtasks and then assigning these subtasks to different individuals. This practice prevents one person from performing, and perhaps compromising, the entire function.

Unfortunately, most systems do not support a sufficiently granular assignment of privileges to enforce an effective level of separation of functions; for example, under most systems, the data base administrator is assigned all privileges. This is problematic because it is particularly important to enforce such controls on data base administrators and security personnel. It should also be noted that managing privileges on large, multiuser systems running complex data bases can be tedious and can consume significant resources.

The control of relational systems is further complicated by the increased use of distributed processing. With distributed systems, several issues arise:

- Should the data base be administered globally or by each site?
- How should users of networked data base resources be identified and authenticated to the system?
- Can such distributed system use be audited centrally?

To be accepted, controls must not introduce undue complication or inconvenience to users and data base administrators; end users should be insulated as much as possible from the security mechanisms of the underlying operating systems, networks, and data base management systems. Controls should not inhibit the use of such sophisticated front ends to data base applications as graphical user interfaces and fourth-generation languages. Security mechanisms must also support the full range of data base functions and interfaces (in fact, to gain user acceptance, these controls should be seen to simplify data base use).

With these objectives in mind, the IS management team must evaluate the ability of data base products to meet security requirements. Fortunately, data base security standards and product evaluation criteria have been developed to help in the process.

DATA BASE SYSTEM CONTROL STANDARDS

Standards provide a good starting point for gaining a relatively broad perspective on the control issues related to relational technologies. Relevant standards include the US Department of Defense's Trusted Computer System Evaluation Criteria (TCSEC, also referred to as the Orange Book) and the corresponding Trusted Database Interpretation (TDI) of the TCSEC, which interprets the TCSEC guidelines and applies them to data base management systems. A similar effort in Europe has produced the Information Technology Security Evaluation Criteria (ITSEC), which is gaining in popularity among security professionals.

Class	Description
A1	Verified Design
B3	Security Domains
B2	Structured Protection
B1	Labeled Security Protection
C2	Controlled Access Protection
C1	Discretionary Security Protection
D	Minimal Protection

Exhibit IV-6-1. TCSEC Security Levels

Control standards are also being developed by other countries, and several professional organizations are working to define the requirements of the commercial sector.

Government-Sponsored Standards

As shown in Exhibit IV-6-1, the TCSEC identifies seven classes of trusted products, ranging from the highest level of security (class A1) to the lowest level (class D). Each rating class specifies the required functional abilities of such features as user identification and authentication, auditing, and data labeling; it also defines the level of assurance required to ensure that the product's control mechanisms are properly implemented and cannot be circumvented. The criteria for each class of controls are cumulative; for example, whereas class C products incorporate discretionary security controls, class B products include mandatory controls and other requirements in addition to discretionary controls.

Many users have accepted the C2 rating as the minimum level of security for data base and other systems processing sensitive business data. At a C2 level, users are individually accountable for their actions through the use of log-on procedures, audit trails, and resource isolation.

The B1 rating is considered appropriate for systems that process classified and other more highly sensitive information. The B1 level enforces the use of data labeling and mandatory access control over specified subjects and objects.

Many currently available relational data base products provide a subset of class C2 features; some vendors are developing products to meet the complete range of C2 requirements. Multilevel secure data base products that satisfy B1 and higher criteria are also now entering the market.

In the US, a new initiative is under way at the National Institute of Standards and Technology and the National Computer Security Center to develop a more comprehensive set of criteria that reflect international standards, advances in computer and security technologies, and the requirements of the commercial sector.

The Europeans have taken an approach to control that differs from that of the Orange Book in several respects. Unlike the Orange Book, the European ITSEC addresses assurance-related criteria separately from the criteria for evaluating system functional abilities. Whereas the Orange Book focuses on protecting the confidentiality of information, the European criteria also address the integrity and availability of information.

Professional Standards Organizations

New standards are also being developed by various professional organizations that, though not focused primarily on security issues, may affect the integrity of data bases and other systems. For example, the American National Standards Institute has developed data integrity specifications for SQL. Relational data base product standards can also be expected from such sources as the International Standards Organization, the Institute of Electrical and Electronics Engineers, Portable Operating System Interface for Computer Environments, Federal Information Processing Standards, Open Systems Interconnection, and SQL Access. These standards should be referred to during the evaluation of trusted data base products to ensure that they meet the full set of operational standards appropriate for their processing environments.

DISCRETIONARY ACCESS AND CONTROLS

Discretionary access control is the most general form of access control in relational data base products today. Discretionary access control mediates access to information through the assignment of privileges—the subject, which can refer to either the user or the processes run by the user, must have the appropriate privilege to access an object (e.g., a data table or view). This type of access control is referred to as discretionary because appropriately authorized users can grant other users access privileges at their discretion. For example, the owner of a data base table may grant another user permission to select data from that table.

In most relational data base systems, discretionary controls are implemented by means of SQL, which is the standard query language for relational systems. Under SQL, users can be granted various privileges to access tables and other objects. The implementation of discretionary controls varies according to the vendor-specific extensions of SQL and the degree of granularity enforced.

In a relational data base, views can support the enforcement of discretionary controls. Views are virtual tables consisting of a subset, union, or join of the columns of one or more tables. Data managers can provide users with access to relevant subsets of data, in the form of views, while restricting them from direct access to complete data base tables. Data access privileges can also be stored in data dictionary views, providing an effective method of managing these privileges.

Although discretionary controls are sufficient for many applications, they do not always provide necessary security. For example, the management of privileges may be difficult, as illustrated by the following scenario. User A grants user B access to a table, with the intention that no other users be granted such access; however, user B may promulgate access privileges to user C, thereby defeating user A's intention to limit access to the table. With discretionary controls, this problem can be avoided only through painstaking management of privileges.

Newer relational data base products that implement mandatory access controls can virtually eliminate the problem.

All relational data base systems offer some audit capabilities, but the audit capabilities of most products are marginal and the tools for analyzing audit data are insufficient. In addition, audit facilities are often unused because of concerns that these facilities may degrade overall system performance. As discussed in the next section, new data base products are being developed that provide more comprehensive and efficient review features.

To be effective, both discretionary access and audit controls require that a system properly identify users. Typically, users identify themselves to a data base system by entering a user ID, and they authenticate themselves by entering a password. The management system typically stores the password in encrypted format in the data base. Although these measures can provide an effective level of security, their use is burdensome for users, who must remember passwords for at least one operating system and data base system. This problem may be compounded in distributed environments.

In summary, although the control capabilities of relational data base systems have improved in recent years, many areas still require improvement. The next section describes features of newly emerging data base products that are designed to provide more effective controls that are also more easily managed.

ADVANCES IN DATA BASE CONTROL

New methods of securing data bases are being introduced that should simplify administrative tasks, facilitate implementation of least privilege and separation of functions, and offer improved overall data base capabilities. These features shift more of the burden of enforcing controls from the application to the data base, thereby providing greater consistency of control across multiple applications that use the same data.

Privilege Management

The proper enforcement of system and object privileges is of primary importance in data base management. An object privilege refers to the right to perform a particular action on a specified table, view, or other named data base object (e.g., to update the DEPARTMENT table). A system privilege refers to the right to execute a particular system command or to globally perform a particular action on a class of objects (e.g., to select from any table).

A new trend is to provide a finer granularity of data base privileges, in particular, system privileges. It is possible to more narrowly define roles among administrative staff by unbundling system privileges from a fixed set of three or four present definitions. For example, rather than the data base administrator having all system privileges, appropriate privileges can be granted for such specific functions as system backup, user account management, security, auditing, and application administration. This capability makes it easier to enforce controls on the basis of the principle of least privilege.

For example, Oracle Corp.'s relational data base product, ORACLE RDBMS, Version 7.0, allows data base privileges to be grouped into entities called roles. The data base administrator can create a role named CLERK and then grant to that role the data base privileges needed for clerks to perform their duties. This role can be granted to all clerks in the organization, making it unnecessary to grant individual privileges to each clerk. The Clerk role can also be granted to the CLERK/MANAGER role, conveniently giving the manager all staff privileges. The use of roles greatly simplifies the assignment and maintenance of privileges in a relational data base.

Cooperative System Controls

Various system controls are becoming available that enhance data base security. Data base systems are being designed to interface with operating system mechanisms for user identification and authentication so that users need only identify themselves once to the operating system, rather than to both the operating system and the data base system. Users must remember only one password; passwords are stored only once, and audit trail records reflect a one-to-one mapping between operating system users and data base users.

Vendors are also beginning to provide data base audit capabilities that meet TCSEC class C2 criteria. Several products now offer auditing of statement executions or failures, auditing of objects, auditing of individual users or groups of users, and auditing of audit trail management. This ability to specify areas to be audited should result in more concise audit reporting and reduce the need for additional tools for audit trail analysis. However, extensive use of these more comprehensive audit capabilities may degrade system performance and increase the time required for audit trail review; consequently, audit options should be carefully selected and used. Audit features should permit the auditor to examine only those actions necessary to ensure system security.

The ability to enforce limits on the use of data base system resources can also enhance security. For example, the data base administrator can set limits on the number of concurrent sessions allowed per use of the data base, idle time per session, CPU use, and logical block reads. In some systems, this can be done by specifying a resource limit profile for either individual users or roles. The use of such profiles can help protect against denial of service and ensure the availability of system resources. For example, limits can be imposed to control the use of long-running, resource-intensive queries during peak hours.

Data Base Integrity Controls

Four principal types of data integrity controls—referential integrity, transaction integrity, entity integrity, and value constraints—are supported in varying degrees by relational data base products. Because product capabilities vary widely in this area, it is important to review these controls carefully in evaluating data base products. It should be noted that data base integrity is of particular importance in multilevel environments, as is discussed later in this chapter.

Referential integrity controls involve the comparison of a foreign key value to a primary key value. In the case of relational data bases, for example, a rule may

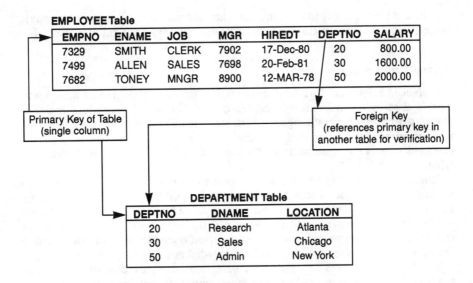

EMPLOYEE Table

EMPNO	ENAME	JOB	MGR	HIREDT	DEPTNO	SALARY
7329	SMITH	CLERK	7902	17-Dec-80	20	800.00
7499	ALLEN	SALES	7698	20-Feb-81	30	1600.00
7682	TONEY	MNGR	8900	12-MAR-78	50	2000.00

Primary Key of Table
(single column)

Foreign Key
(references primary key in
another table for verification)

DEPARTMENT Table

DEPTNO	DNAME	LOCATION
20	Research	Atlanta
30	Sales	Chicago
50	Admin	New York

Exhibit IV-6-2. Sample Referential Integrity Controls

be defined for a column of a table to permit modification of a row only if the foreign key value associated with the column matches the primary key value associated with a column of a related table. In Exhibit IV-6-2, for example, to ensure that all department numbers assigned to employees are valid, the foreign key value DEPTNO from the column in the EMPLOYEE table containing the department identification number of each employee is compared with the primary key value DEPTNO in the column of the DEPARTMENT table containing all valid department numbers. Some relational data base products allow users to code their own integrity constraints into data base applications. With other products, SQL is used to declare integrity constraints to the data base; the data base stores these constraints in the data dictionary and automatically enforces them.

Transaction integrity controls are designed to ensure that a transaction can be rolled back if it is not executed successfully in its entirety. For example, if a financial posting involving a debit and credit transaction is not completely executed and stored, it must be rolled back to the stage before execution. To ensure transaction integrity, relational data base products provide such features as on-line redo log files, rollback segments, and distributed data base recovery functions.

Entity integrity controls identify each record in the data base to ensure that the record is unique. For example, an automated sequence generator can be used to ensure unique primary key values in a relational data base.

Value constraints can be used to check a data value to ensure that it falls within the limit of a predefined constraint; for example, salaries in the EMPLOYEE data base table are checked to verify that they are within an appropriate numeric range. Value constraints can be defined using SQL when the table is created.

Stored Procedures

Enhanced relational data base systems use stored procedures to access and modify data in a consistent and secure manner. A stored procedure logically groups a set of procedural language SQL statements that perform a specific task when the procedure is executed. A trigger is a type of procedure that is implicitly executed when such statements as INSERT or DELETE are entered against a table.

Stored procedures can be used to restrict the way in which data is accessed and updated. For example, a user may be allowed to update a specified table only executing a stored procedure; the use of this procedure ensures that all updates are performed consistently. In this example, the user is authorized only to execute the procedure; because the procedure itself owns the privilege of updating the table, the user does not have to be granted that privilege explicitly.

Triggers can be used to implement unique or complex business rules. For example, a trigger can be used to enforce referential integrity in a distributed data base in which parent and child records reside on different network nodes and in which referential integrity between the parent and child records cannot be enforced using declarative SQL statements. If a change is made to the child's record in a table, a trigger associated with that table can execute a query against the remote table in which the parental record resides to perform the required integrity check. Triggers can also be used to enforce complex security rules, such as restrictions on data access and modification based on time of day.

Triggers can also support auditing activities. For example, a trigger can be written to record table values before and after an update to provide a detailed audit trail of change transactions.

MULTILEVEL DATA BASES

A new generation of multilevel relational data bases has been developed to provide a high degree of protection for proprietary and other sensitive data. Multilevel secure systems allow the simultaneous processing of data of various sensitivities by multiple users with various clearances. Most organizations have been hesitant to mix proprietary data with public data on the same system, preferring instead to segregate such data on separate computer systems. This approach is both costly and inefficient. Under multilevel secure systems, data residing on the same system is explicitly labeled or classified according to its degree of sensitivity to compromise; such classification schemes permit data isolation while simplifying management and reducing costs.

Multilevel secure data base systems enforce mandatory access controls in addition to the discretionary controls commonly found in most current products. Mandatory controls restrict access to objects using two types of information: the security classification of the object, as represented by its sensitivity label; and the authority of the user to access and use the object. In a relational data base,

High	Hierarchical Levels	Nonhierarchical Categories Within Each Level		
	Proprietary	Finance	Research	Marketing
	Confidential	Accounting	Development	Marketing
Low	Public	No Separate Categories		

(left axis label: Sensitivity — arrow pointing from Low to High)

Exhibit IV-6-3. Sample Labels

control is typically enforced on each row of a data base table. If a user has not been authorized to the classification level associated with that row of data, access to the data will be denied regardless of any discretionary access rules that might otherwise permit access.

For example, a company might classify its data as being either proprietary, company confidential, or public. Each of these hierarchical classifications constitutes a security level within the data base. Within each level, however, data can be further divided into descriptive, nonhierarchical categories. One category might identify proprietary data that belongs to a certain special project; another category might identify the department that controls the proprietary information. It is the combination of security level and category that forms the sensitivity label associated with the data object. Therefore, as shown in Exhibit IV-6-3, access to a relational data base row labeled PROPRIETARY:FINANCE would be restricted to those users with sufficient clearance to access proprietary information belonging to the finance department.

Under a multilevel secure system, sensitivity labels are stored with the data object and can be changed only by users who have certain powerful mandatory access control privileges. Similarly, only users with such privileges are permitted to transfer access authority from one user to another; end users cannot transfer access privileges at their discretion. Mandatory access control privileges must be carefully administered and monitored to protect against their misuse.

Control Conflicts in Multilevel Data Base Applications

The use of multilevel data systems can create conflicts between data confidentiality and integrity. The enforcement of integrity rules can create covert channels for discovering confidential information and, in general, lead to conflicts between other business rules and security policies.

For example, enforcement of entity integrity requires that each data base row be identified by its primary key, which cannot be a null value. A conflict between data confidentiality and integrity can arise if a user with a low-level access classification (e.g., unclassified) attempts to add a primary key that, in fact, already exists at a higher classification level (e.g., confidential). (A primary key at this high security level is not visible to an unclassified user.) If the data base system permits the addition of this duplicate key, entity integrity is compromised; if the addition is denied, the secrecy of the existing key value for the confidential information is compromised. This problem can be avoided by using the security label as part of the primary key or by using an automated sequence generator to assign primary keys within a specified value range for each security level.

It may also be possible to infer information about a data base entity if referential integrity is enforced across multiple access classes. For example, if a user with a low-level access classification attempts to delete data at a higher classification level, a violation of referential integrity may occur. The user may be able to infer information about the targeted data item if the system returns an error on the basis of the access classification of the data item.

Transaction integrity conflicts can also arise in a multilevel data base system. To maintain transaction integrity, all steps in a given transaction must be processed as an entire unit. Any expected transactions that pass across different security levels should be carefully reviewed to identify potential conflicts. These problems should be eliminated either by modification of the data base design or through decomposition of multilevel transactions.

Weighing the Pros and Cons of Multilevel Security

Although multilevel secure data base systems provide an enhanced level of control not previously available, this advantage must be weighed against the costs required to implement this technology and the requirements of the organization. For some organizations, enhanced discretionary controls provide a more cost-effective alternative.

For organizations that process highly sensitive information, the implementation of a multilevel system is readily justified. Through the use of mandatory access controls, data access rules can be more explicitly defined and enforced, and controls can be more easily established around each category of system user. For organizations that rely solely on procedural or physical control measures, multilevel systems can provide an additional layer of controls. Reliance on redundant hardware and software systems and redundant data can be greatly reduced or eliminated, providing significant savings in system maintenance costs. For example, hardware systems that were formerly dedicated to processing confidential data can now be used for multiple applications that access data of differing sensitivities.

These advantages, however, must be weighed against the additional complexity of multilevel applications design and implementation. The data base design must be analyzed to identify and eliminate conflicts in enforcing data integrity controls. The data must be thoroughly classified, and users must be assigned specific authorizations. Multilevel applications must also be run on secure operating systems because mandatory controls cannot be reliably enforced by the relational data base on nonsecure systems.

Some organizations may consider implementing multilevel data bases only for selected applications that process proprietary information, while continuing to run other applications at a single security level on existing systems. If this configuration is selected, it should be verified that the multilevel product can support the interoperability of multilevel and single-level applications.

There are now several multilevel relational data base products from which to choose. These products can be run either on standard multilevel operating systems or compartmented mode workstations, which are multilevel secure workstations, that offer window capabilities.

IDENTIFYING SECURITY REQUIREMENTS

In reviewing the appropriateness of a data base system, the IS management team should not simply evaluate just the security features of the data base product itself. It is also important to identify the security requirements of the overall system, of which the data base is only one component. What is the minimum level of control required by the organization as a whole? Are there any specific applications that require enhanced data protection? Answers to such questions help determine whether discretionary or mandatory access controls are required.

The architecture of the relational data base should also be evaluated to determine whether it provides a portable, transparent, and secure foundation for applications processing. A data base management architecture that is independent of the operating system platform provides improved system portability as well as greater ease in evaluating and implementing system controls.

The prospective data base system should be designed also to interface smoothly with other components of the overall system, including the operating system, network, user authentication devices, and other applications that affect security. Such a transparent user interface offers users a more seamless view of controls by providing the appropriate protection at each level of the system (e.g., log-on security at the system access level, file security at the operating system level, and data base security at the object level).

IMPLEMENTING DATA BASE CONTROLS

There are two basic approaches to implementing improved data base controls. As is done in most environments, existing data base applications can be migrated to a more secure data base management system; or, where possible, completely new applications can be built. In the case of migration, assuming that there are no major compatibility problems, implementation efforts focus on the transfer of data using export-import (i.e., migration) utilities and on the implementation of any new system control features.

In general, new data base applications should be designed to make effective use of the data base system's security features. The design should be carefully planned and executed. Each data base component should be reviewed to ensure that the appropriate controls have been incorporated in the design for that component.

The following sections briefly describe the process of designing and building new data base applications. It should be emphasized that the first step involves development of a sound policy that defines how the organization manages, distributes, and protects sensitive information. A comprehensive policy provides useful guidelines for designing the data base and related controls and results in a cleaner, more simplified set of controls.

CASE Tools

Computer-aided software engineering (CASE) tools can be used to design and build data base applications. These tools can be used to model data flows and entity relationships and to build a unified repository of system data. Some CASE tools generate data base application code from the repository data. CASE tools can also be useful in analyzing the design to ensure that the data base conforms with the organization's policy objectives.

The Data Dictionary

A data dictionary can be used to store such information as the user names of data base users, user privileges, the names of data base objects, integrity constraints, and audit-related data. The data dictionary can serve as a reference guide during data base development. It is also a useful tool for auditing data base operations after implementation.

Because of the importance of the information stored in the data dictionary, access to it should be carefully controlled. In general, end users should be granted read-only privileges; write privileges should be restricted to data base administrators.

APPLICATIONS DEVELOPMENT

The standard approach in building Oracle RDBMS applications, for example, requires that the data be normalized, as needed, and tables created according to design specifications. Referential integrity and value constraints should be included in table definitions. Upon loading tables, the Oracle data base system automatically checks that the data conforms to the rules. Triggers can be written after the tables have been developed or at a later date.

Views should be created to provide controlled access to portions of multiple tables rather than to the tables themselves. Views can be used to grant users access only to that subset of data they require to perform their jobs. For example, a view of the EMPLOYEE table could be created and granted to managers so that only the records of employees in the manager's department can be accessed.

In the planning and design stages, the privileges to manipulate objects should be defined for all users. To facilitate this process, common data base privileges can be grouped into roles, usually on the basis of shared job functions. Using roles eliminates the need to create and maintain individual privileges for each user. In building applications, therefore, systems developers should create previously identified roles, grant privileges to these roles, and assign the roles to users who share related job duties.

As a final step, audit controls should be put into place. It is important to audit only those areas essential for ensuring system security. Audit options should be carefully selected to avoid performing superfluous audits that might degrade system performance and to ensure that audit reports are as concise as possible.

CONCLUSION

Data base control should be well supported by a relational data base product. The mechanisms used to manage users and data base privileges and the availability of roles and of other enhanced features should provide sufficient flexibility to implement the organization's control and protection policies.

Because today's computing environment changes rapidly, it is also important for a product to be able to evolve to take advantage of emerging technologies. The challenges posed by recent developments in client/server computing and distributed data bases only dramatize the need for data base systems that can adapt to the computing environment of the future.

Section V
Delivering Products and Services

A MAJOR SHIFT is occurring in the mechanisms used by the IS organization to deliver information. IS professionals are moving away from the job of operating machines, mostly large mainframes and mass storage devices, and toward the operation of networks; they now deliver information that users can manipulate rather than preprogrammed reports. The large central processing unit—that is, those that continue to exist as a part of the delivery structure—is becoming a node on the network.

This shift means that IS management requires better and more in-depth planning to stay on top of rapidly changing technology. Better metrics are needed to indicate when IS is doing a good job and when it is not. Thinking has to be refocused from machine uptime to customer satisfaction, and goals have to be broadened. Answering 75% to 85% of calls to the help desk correctly on the first call is not good enough—to be competitive, IS has to resolve first calls 93% to 98% of the time. IS customers do not want machine or network availability as much as they want a problem solved or a business need satisfied. In today's competitive world, machine availability can be part of customer service, but 99.9% uptime will not always buy customer satisfaction.

IS customers also want help in using technology to meet their information needs. It is probably accurate to say that in most companies today, technology is misapplied as often as it is appropriately used. That means money is wasted, opportunity is lost, and competitive position is diminished. In addition, in many organizations, lines of responsibility between the data center and data administration/management functions have blurred, just as they have blurred between the systems development and data management groups. This situation does not always help IS customers access the data they need to make their business decisions and do their jobs. Users do not care who has the responsibility for data, they want access to it.

Satisfying the needs of IS customers is not easy. If it were, outsourcing would be less popular and IS customers would be less determined to set up their own personal computers and workstations. Better planning is needed to ensure that the resources are available and appropriate to users' needs; better and broadly accepted standards are needed, especially for data networks; and better procedures are needed for acquiring information processing resources. In addition, IS must explore alternative ways of delivering this data and information to users. The chapters in Section V address each of these needs.

Chapter V-1, "Points of Failure Planning in the Client/Server Environment," presents ideas on better resource planning. IS managers can more effectively control and manage the processing environment, especially client/server computing environments, by planning for a series of potential points of failure and laying the groundwork for mitigating service disruptions should they occur.

"Adding Multimedia to the Corporate Network" also affects the processing environment, and Chapter V-2 discusses the implications of the increasing use of digitized audio and video on LAN servers. The chapter outlines the transmission requirements IS managers need to know about to deliver multimedia applications without adversely affecting other network users; it also discusses methods of restructuring an existing network to cost-effectively accommodate transportation of multimedia.

Multiple protocols on LANs combined with legacy systems and newer applications, like multimedia applications, have led to chaotic situations in many organizations. IS professionals often lack the training and experience needed to manage complex networks, yet they often face the task of doing just that. Chapter V-3 addresses methods of connectivity, including multistacking and the use of software-based gateway technology, to help IS managers deal with "Multiple Protocols" in the LAN environment.

The more complex networking environment has broadened the IS manager's responsibility to include the acquisition of a vast array of information processing and network equipment. IS managers are also often involved in the decision regarding purchasing methodology. Whether to purchase or lease involves many considerations, some of which are technical. Chapter V-4, "Equipment Leasing," discusses types of leases and offers advice on issues that should be considered in the lease-versus-buy decision.

Improving standards should be an ongoing objective of the IS manager. Operating standards for LANs offer certain advantages for keeping expenses for procurement and maintenance under control. Chapter V-5, "Operating Standards for LANs," reviews the basics to include in a LAN standards document.

V-1

Points of Failure Planning in the Client/Server Environment

John P. Murray

THE MOVE TO CLIENT/SERVER processing brings new opportunities, challenges, and risks to the management of the data center. Although client/server hardware and operating software differs from that used in mainframes, many methods and procedures that applied in the mainframe environment still apply to distributed systems.

Some organizations have successfully mastered the transition to client/server computing and removed all their mainframe hardware. Most organizations, however, are only currently considering how to make the transition. In these cases, the function of the mainframe is shifting from the primary processing tool to that of a large file server. With this shift, the vulnerability of the organization's data center operation is going to grow. As reliance on the mainframe lessens, a series of new management concerns arises for IS managers.

OPERATING ISSUES IN CLIENT/SERVER ENVIRONMENTS

A primary concern is managing a processing environment that consists of many more components distributed over a much larger geographical area. In addition, the work being processed on those components covers a greater span of business functions than was the case in the past.

Data center personnel may be unaware of the specific work being done at the remote sites. The first time the data center staff hears about difficulty with a particular processing problem may be the first time it has heard of the application. This situation highlights the scope of the work done in the client/server environment and the fact that much of this work is carried out beyond the direct control of the IS staff.

Support Issues. While the scope of the activity in the client/server environment expands, the responsibility of the data center staff is not going to change.

Although client/server processing gives more autonomy to business users outside the IS department, IS personnel remain responsible for support functions, which may include:

- The availability of the processing environment.
- Response time across the network.
- Easy access to files and training.
- The protection of the data on the various networks.

Hardware/Software Reliability. Another issue is the reliability of the client/server hardware and software. Client/server hardware and software have become more reliable over the past few years, but they have not yet reached the levels found in mainframe processing. Whereas the data center staff has a great deal of experience handling the nuances of the mainframe processing environment —including being able to anticipate problems and solve them before they disrupt the environment—potential problems in client/server environments are less apparent. Not only are there more problems in the distributed environment, but they may take longer to resolve.

SERVICE ORIENTATION NEEDED

The client/server model presents new challenges and opportunities for data center operations. The challenges include managing a more diverse environment with greater levels of customer service and satisfaction. Delivering those services must be accomplished while moving from the traditional command-and-control environment to a service-oriented environment.

Because the effective use of increased IT processing power plays a key role in helping the enterprise grow and prosper, the development and management of a solid client/server infrastructure throughout the organization is a major concern. Data center personnel who cannot, for whatever reason, adjust to this environment face the prospect of outsourcing. Business users of information technology are increasingly sophisticated, with little tolerance for anything less than a high-quality data center service. Today, and increasingly in the future, IS customers are going to enjoy many processing options, and they will be able to do more for themselves—including choosing some source other than the in-house data processing function.

Management and Control Issues

Many business functions, especially those at higher levels in the organization, want shorter delivery time for information. Disruptions will assume greater levels of urgency than they did in the past. For example, given the work and travel patterns of executives, they expect the systems they want to use to be available, accurate, and fast, whenever and wherever they want to use them.

More organizations are moving to processing environments where the IT resources must be available 24-hours a day, 7 days a week for anyone who may want to use those resources. This is a customer service issue, because the ability of customers to contact an organization any time of the day or night is a competitive tool. Serious customer service and public relations issues must be overcome when the availability of these systems is impaired. Failure to provide the array of products and services expected by customers, because of technology-based constraints, opens opportunities for the organization's competitors.

RECOGNIZING THE POINTS OF FAILURE

A key issue for the IS manager is how to move to a position that can ensure the continued operation of the organization's critical applications at all times. The challenge is to get to 100% availability and remain at that level. Nothing less than total availability is going to be acceptable.

IS management and staff can address the control and management of the client/server processing environment by thinking about the issue as a series of potential points of failure. The idea is that any entity within the client/server processing environment that has the potential to disrupt that environment—a point of failure—must be identified and managed. Once the points of failure are identified, the next step is to develop a set of plans to help the organization anticipate the potential for damage from those point of failure entities. The final step in the process is to lay the groundwork to mitigate any point of failure damage should it occur.

Most data center personnel think first about the vulnerability of the IT hardware. Although the continued availability of the hardware is critical to the smooth functioning of the production processing environment, other items have to be included in any consideration of the client/server points of failure.

Recognition of all the items that carry the potential to disrupt the processing environment is not enough, however; the IS team has to be ready to move aggressively when any of the identified points of failure create difficulty. The potential damage, depending on the circumstances, may range from inconvenience to disaster.

The items that need to be considered as client/server processing points of failure are:

- *Hardware.* Hardware includes the mainframe and associated traditional data center components plus network hardware (e.g., servers, disk storage components, routers, and bridges). Communications components such as telephone switches and lines must also be considered as points of failure under the rubric of hardware.

- *Software.* Both operating and applications (either products developed in-house or purchased applications software).

- *Change control.* This area is easily overlooked when identifying client/server processing points of failure. However, the ineffective management of the introduction of change into the client/server processing environment can create great difficulty.

No one point of failure category should be seen as more important than the other two. Management and staff must position themselves to be able to manage any disruption that might arise in any of the three point of failure areas. That management must be based on an understanding of each of the point of failure areas and the development of appropriate controls for each area. In addition, the three categories cannot be thought of as separate. There are linkages between the three areas that must be taken into consideration.

For example, the introduction of a new piece of hardware on the network raises an obvious point of failure concern. The primary issue is that of the reliability of the particular hardware component. However, concern with reliability cannot be the only concern. There is also the issue of the ability to integrate this piece of hardware with the rest of the network components, including the operating software.

In addition, change control problems have to be acknowledged. The timing of the placement of the hardware should be planned to reduce the likelihood of difficulty. Bringing in the new hardware during a period of heavy business activity may not be a sound approach. Another change control task is to make certain that those who may be affected by the changes are informed of those changes well before they occur.

Containing Risk

In as far as it is practical, an important aspect of management and control of the points of failure is to limit the variety of the components, both hardware and software, installed throughout the organization. The idea here is simple. The potential risk can be reduced by reducing the overall variances within the processing environment.

Often a case will be made to move to some specialized piece of hardware or software to solve some limited problem. A careful analysis of the actual benefit of that component should be made against the risk associated with the increased processing complexity that may occur as a result of the installation. If the introduction of the piece of equipment or software increases the vulnerability of the processing environment to disruption, then the benefit associated with that installation must be sufficiently strong to help offset that risk.

IT installations have to come to grips with the result of the uncontrolled addition of different network components. That problem becomes apparent when network difficulties arise that require a considerable amount of time and effort to resolve. Usually the network environment has become encumbered with so many different types of hardware, software, and special tools that tracking the cause of problems is itself a problem.

MAPPING THE POINTS OF FAILURE

The place to begin the process of managing the hardware environment is with the development of a series of hardware maps. These maps should show, in some detail, all the IT hardware components within the organization. Hardware maps for one corporate data center are shown in Exhibits V-1-1 and V-1-2.

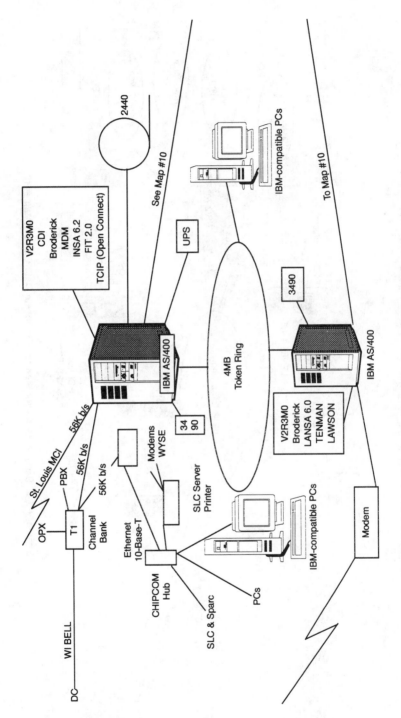

Exhibit V-1-1. Sample Hardware Map for Corporate Data Center (Map # 9)

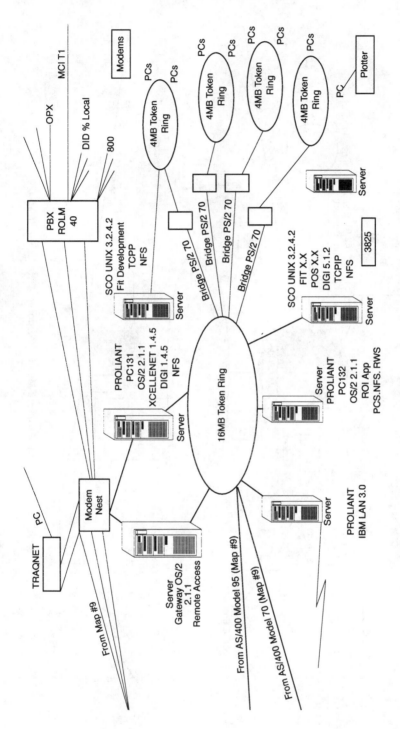

Exhibit V-1-2. Sample Hardware Map for Corporate Data Center (Map # 10)

Because this effort should be considered a mapping process in every sense, not only must the location of each entity be shown, but the relationships of those entities to each other need to be identified. Identifying those relationships is important because the effect of the failure of one component on other areas of the processing environment may not be readily apparent.

Besides the graphic representation of those components, additional detail should be provided about the size and age of each component. The vendor of each piece of hardware should be identified. Should a critical component (a point of failure) crash, bringing the function back online as soon as possible is going to be crucial. Having as much detailed information as possible helps make this happen.

Hardware maps can be constructed easily with the use of PC-based drawing tools that provide a series of stencils and templates for laying out the environment. Well-designed drawing tool packages provide a full array of stencils for laying out all types of IT processing environments; all that is required is selecting an item from the stencil and dragging and dropping it into the map. If a particular item is not available in the stencil, other drawing tools are usually available in the package that can be used to represent a particular entity. The use of the drawing tools is also invaluable for keeping the maps current. It is possible to make changes to the environment quickly, as needed, which is especially useful in large organizations where there may be many changes to the components in the various client/server installations.

Beyond mapping the hardware components, the maps should also contain information about other components of the processing environment that pertain to managing point of failure situations. Examples of those other components would include the operating system being used on a given network and the use of packaged applications products on the network and special hardware or software tools on the network.

To ensure that the mapping work is done correctly and that the maps are kept up-to-date, the responsibility for the process should be assigned to a data center employee. Without a specific assignment for that responsibility, the maps are not going to be kept current. Unless the maps are current and accurate, they are not going to be of much assistance in the event of a disruption of the processing environment. The initial effort to construct the maps may be time-consuming, but once the maps are in place, less work is needed to keep them current.

BUILDING THE CASE FOR HARDWARE BACKUP

The next step in the development of the processing environment maps is to devise an approach that ensures, in case of difficulty at a point of failure, that the problem is going to be rapidly corrected. There are several ways the issue of adequate backup for the hardware components can be managed. The approach selected must reflect the business requirements of the organization.

The hardware maps can be used to good advantage in developing the case for hardware backup. In many organizations, at best only a handful of people fully understand the magnitude of the client/server processing environment. Using the maps to show the scope and, as a result, the vulnerability of that environment is an effective way for data center management to acquire redundant processing capacity.

A point of failure contingency plan should be prepared by data center management for senior management review and approval. Several options with corresponding expense estimates should be presented. The key in corporate management's decision on which of the several proposals to approve will depend on how much they are willing to pay for a given level of reliability in a particular part of the processing environment. In as far as it is practical, IS should carefully outline the expense and risk associated with each option presented. A plan done well makes senior management's decision easier.

Emphasizing Business, Not Technology, Support

As an example, with respect to a particular hardware component, one option would be to use some level of hardware redundancy within the processing environment. One way to deal with redundancy would be to provide, in the case of file servers and disk storage on the network, mirror processors that would immediately take over if the primary component fails. Another hardware approach would be to have a limited stock of duplicate point of failure hardware components deemed critical in case of a hardware problem. One more approach would be to have an agreement with a vendor to provide immediate replacement hardware.

Individual hardware components are relatively inexpensive in the client/server processing environments. Lower costs notwithstanding, it will likely take some convincing by data center management to sell senior management on the idea of spending money on what may turn out to be redundant hardware. There is a way to approach the issue. If that approach is done correctly, the data center stands an excellent chance of success.

Developing a Scenario for Senior Management: An Example. The way to begin is to develop a case for additional funds to support the idea of managing the points of failure within the client/server processing environment. That case should and easily can be built as a business rather than a technology support issue. One way to develop a business case is to calculate the payroll expense tied to a particular local area network operation.

For example, assume the LAN supports 60 professional employees and that the fully loaded personnel cost for those employees comes to $2,400 an hour. Using that figure, if the LAN is unavailable for four hours, the organization will suffer a loss of $9,600 of productive time. The lost productive time is itself a serious issue, but the negative effect on customer service might be a more serious one to the business.

Two other issues should be mentioned, however. First is that having a critical piece of LAN hardware out of service for four hours is not unheard of. The second is that, given the low cost of microcomputers, $9,600 can buy a great deal of security and peace of mind.

CONTROLLING OPERATING AND APPLICATIONS SOFTWARE

Data center operating procedures for the introduction and change of operating or applications software in the mainframe environment apply equally as well in the client/server environment. Personnel within the data center should be kept fully apprised of changes made to the software environment. In the mainframe world, the data center staff could exert some influence on the testing and introduction of new or changed software. In the client/server environment, such a level of control is not always available, given the many different physical locations of the hardware.

Client/server products for control of software are not yet as robust as people would like them to be. But as appropriate tools are introduced, the sooner they are selected, installed, and worked into data center control procedures, the better.

The management of operating and applications software in client/server processing is within the purview of IS management and must be addressed. It is a mistake to wait until client/server tools have matured to the point of the available mainframe control tools. The rate of change and growth of client/server processing will not wait for the maturity of the required tools. Any delay in doing whatever is possible to gain control of the software environment is going to make the task of control that much more difficult in the future.

Of course, the choice of improper operating or applications software may represent as much a point of failure issue as do hardware issues or change control. It is therefore all the more important that IS management or staff be advised about the software (operating or applications) being introduced into the client/server processing environment and that they be given the chance to object and recommend an alternative, where appropriate. If an application is introduced that will overtax the processing components, and as a result, the desired work cannot be accomplished, another aspect of the point of failure issue will have surfaced.

CHANGE CONTROL

The introduction of changes into the processing environment is no less important with client/server processing than it was in the mainframe world. Because of the greater number of opportunities for difficulty in the client/server processing environment, change control becomes even more important. The key to success is to control changes and appropriately manage them. Whether they are new items or revisions of existing items they must be as clean as possible. Within the context of the topic of change control, "clean" means that the items moved into the processing environment have been carefully tested. It also means that the movement of those items to the production environment has been well planned.

One of the lessons learned in the mainframe environment has been to limit the number of changes introduced to the processing environment at one time. That number should be as few as possible (the ideal number is one). In addition to limiting the number of changes introduced at one time, it helps if there is a period between changes during which there is an opportunity to determine what negative effect (if any) the changes bring in the production environment.

As a practical matter, controlling the number of changes, or the length of time between changes, may not be possible, given the demands of client/server processing. Although it is probably going to be difficult, it is prudent to manage the client/server change process as aggressively as possible.

Moving many changes at a rapid pace into the client/server processing environment almost guarantees difficulty, which only increases the point of failure risk. Because the central idea of a well-managed client/server processing environment should be to limit and manage the points of failure, whatever has to be done to make that happen has to be done.

CONCLUSION

Increasingly, organizations have the goal of what is sometimes described as bullet-proof IT systems. This goal of uninterrupted (i.e., average system downtime of less than one hour per month) IT processing availability is actually being met by a few well-run installations. Organizations that intend to compete in the future are going to have to develop the discipline to ensure that nothing disrupts the IT processing environment.

There is nothing esoteric about moving to a client/server IT processing environment that virtually never fails. The issues involved have more to do with management than with technology. The ability to anticipate problems before they occur and to be able to move aggressively to correct problems if they arise is critical. The key is an understanding of the client/server points of failure and the establishment of a process to manage those areas.

V-2

Adding Multimedia to the Corporate Network

Gilbert Held

THE USE OF IMAGES has recently moved off the individual PC workstation, where the images were most likely incorporated into word processing or desktop publishing applications, and onto network servers and mainframes. Thus images are now available for retrieval by virtually any employee with a PC connected to a local area network or to the corporate network. In addition, the standardi zation of multimedia data storage has increased the ability of organizations to purchase or develop applications that merge audio, video, and data. There is therefore a growing trend of organizations adding images, as well as multimedia data, to applications. This chapter discusses methods of restructuring an existing network to accommodate the transportation of images and multimedia cost-effectively.

MULTIMEDIA

The term *multimedia* is a catchall phrase that refers to the use of two or more methods for conveying information. Thus, multimedia can include voice or sound (both collectively referred to as audio), still images, moving images, and fax images, as well as text documents. This means that multimedia can be considered an extension of image storage. To understand how multimedia data storage requirements differ from conventional data storage requirements, this chapter first focuses on the storage requirements of images.

Image Storage Requirements

Images are converted into a series of pixels or picture elements by a scanner. Software used to control the scanner will place the resulting pixels into a particular order based on the file format selected from the scanning software menu. Some file storage formats require the use of compression before the image can be stored. Compression typically reduces data storage requirements by 50% or more.

Type of Document/Image	Data Storage (Bytes)
Text document containing 300 words	2,000
3" x 5" B&W photograph scanned at 150 pixels/inch	42,188
3" x 5" B&W photograph scanned at 300 pixels/inch	84,375
3" x 5" B&W photograph scanned at 450 pixels/inch	126,563
3" x 5" B&W photograph scanned at 600 pixels/inch	168,750

Exhibit V-2-1. Document Versus Image Storage Requirements

Text and image data storage requirements differ greatly. A full page of text, such as a one-page letter, might contain approximately 300 words, with an average of five characters per word. Thus, a typical one-page text document would require 1,500 characters of data storage. Adding formatting characters used by a word processor, a one-page text document might require up to 2,000 characters, or 16,000 bits of data storage.

When an image is scanned, the data storage requirements of the resulting file depend on four factors. Those factors include the size of the image, the scan resolution used during the scanning process, the type of image being scanned—color or black and white—and whether the selected file format results in the compression of pixels before their storage.

To illustrate the data storage requirements of different types of images, one example focuses on a 3×5 photograph. That photograph contains a total of 15 square inches that must be scanned.

A low-resolution black-and-white scan normally occurs using 150 lines per inch and 150 pixels per line per inch, where a pixel with a zero value represents white and a pixel whose value is one represents black. Thus, the total number of bits required to store a 3×5 black-and-white photograph using a low-resolution scan without first compressing the data would be 337,500 bits, which would result in a requirement to store 42.188 bytes of data. Thus, a 3×5 black-and-white photograph would require 42,188/2000, or approximately 21 times the amount of storage required by a one-page document.

Most scanners now consider 300 lines per inch with 300 pixels per line per inch, to represent a high-resolution scan. However, some newly introduced scanning products now consider 300 lines per inch with 300 pixels per line to represent a medium- or high-resolution scan. Regardless of the pixel density considered to represent a medium- or high-resolution scan, the computation of the resulting data storage requirement is performed in the same manner. That is, storing the photograph would entail multiplying the number of square inches of the document—in this example, 15—by the pixel density squared. Exhibit V-2-1 compares the data storage requirements of a one-page text document to the data storage required to store a 3×5 black-and-white photograph at different scan resolutions.

To store an image in color, data storage requirements would increase significantly. For example, if a scanner supports color, each pixel would require one byte to represent each possible color of the pixel. Thus, a color image would require eight times the data storage of a black-and-white image when a scanner supports up to 256 colors per pixel. This means that the 3×5 photograph scanned at 300 pixels per inch would require 675,000 bytes of storage. Similarly, a 3×5 color photograph scanned at a resolution of 600 pixels per inch would require 1.35M bytes of storage, or 675 times the amount of storage required for a 300 word one-page document.

Without considering the effect of data compression, the transmission of images on a network can require from 20 to more than 600 times the amount of time required to transmit a one-page standard text document. Obviously, the transmission of images by themselves or as a part of a multimedia application can adversely affect the capability of a network to support other users in an efficient manner unless proper planning precedes the support of the multimedia data transfer.

Audio Storage Requirements

The most popular method of voice digitization is known as pulse code modulation (PCM), in which analog speech is digitized at a rate of 64K bps. Thus, one minute of speech would require 480,000 bytes of data storage. At this digitization rate, data storage of digitized speech can easily expand to require a significant portion of a hard disk for just 10 to 20 minutes of audio.

Multimedia applications developers do not store audio using PCM. Instead, they store audio using a standardized audio compression technique that results in a lower level of audio fidelity but significantly lowers the data storage requirement of digitized audio.

Today, several competing multimedia voice digitization standards permit speech to be digitized at 8K bps. Although this is a significant improvement over PCM used by telephone companies to digitize voice, it still requires a substantial amount of disk space to store a meaningful amount of voice. For example, one hour of voice would require 2.8M bytes of data storage. Thus, data storage of audio is similar to video, in that a meaningful data base of images and sound must either be placed on a CD-ROM or on the hard disk of a network server or mainframe computer that usually has a larger data storage capacity than individual personal computers.

Image Utilization

In spite of the vast increase in the amount of data that must be transported to support image applications, the use of imaging is rapidly increasing. The old adage "a picture is worth a thousand words" is especially true when considering many computer applications. Today, several network-compliant data base programs support the attachment of image files to data base records. Using a Canon digital camera or similar product, real estate agents can photograph the exterior and interior of homes and transfer the digitized images to the network server upon their return to the office. When a potential client comes into the office, an agent can enter the client's home criteria, such as the number of bedrooms, baths, price range, school district, and similar information, and have both textual information as well as photographs of the suitable homes meeting the client's criteria displayed on the screen. This capability significantly reduces the time required to develop a list of homes that the client may wish to view firsthand.

Audio Utilization

The primary use of audio is to supplement images and text with sound. Unlike a conventional PC, which can display any image supported by the resolution of the computer's monitor, the use of audio requires specialized equipment. First, the computer must have a sound board or specialized adapter card that supports the method used to digitize audio. Second, each computer must have one or more speakers connected to the sound board or speech adapter card to broadcast the resulting reconverted analog signal.

STORING IMAGES ON A LAN SERVER OR MAINFRAME

There are three methods for storing images on a LAN server or mainframe. First, images can be transferred to a computer's hard disk using either a personal computer and scanner, or, by connecting the PC to a digital camera. Another method for storing images involves forwarding each image after it is scanned or transferred from a digital camera or similar device. A third method for placing images on a file server or mainframe is based on premastering a CD-ROM or another type of optical disk.

Transferring a large number of images at one time can adversely affect network users. To minimize the effect, images can be transferred from a computer to a server or mainframe after normal work hours. As an alternative, a removable hard disk can be used, permitting movement of the disk to a similarly equipped network server to transfer images without affecting network users.

Forwarding Images After Scanning

This method of storing images on the LAN has the greatest potential for negative impact on network users. Some document scanners are capable of scanning several pages per minute. If a large number of images were scanned, transferring the digitized images through a local or wide area network connection could saturate a network during the scanning and transferring process. This happens because, as other network users are transferring a few thousand bytes, transferring images containing 20 to 600 times more data would consume most of the network bandwidth for relatively long periods of time. Thus, the effect of image transfer can be compared to the addition of 20 to 600 network users transferring one-page documents, with the actual addition based on the resolution of the images, and whether they are in black and white or color.

Premastering

Premastering a CD-ROM or other type of optical disk permits images to become accessible by other network users without adversely affecting network operations. However, cost and ease of image modification or replacement must be weighed against the advantage of this method.

From a cost perspective, equipment required to master images on a CD-ROM will cost between $3,000 and $5,000. In comparison, the use of conventional magnetic storage on the server or mainframe can avoid that equipment cost as well as the cost of a CD-ROM drive connected to a file server.

Concerning ease of image modification or replacement, CD-ROM data cannot be modified once a disk is mastered. This means that a new CD-ROM disk must be mastered each time previously stored images or data must be modified or replaced.

If real-time or daily updates are not required, this method of image placement on a network server or mainframe should be considered. The time required to master a CD-ROM disk has been reduced to a few hours, when mastering occurs on a 486-based personal computer. Also, write-once CD-ROM disks now cost under $20. Thus, a weekly update of an image data base could be performed for a one-time cost of between $3,000 and $5,000, and $20 per week for each write-once CD-ROM disk used. Because this method would have no negative impact on network operations, its cost would be minor in comparison to the cost of modifying a network.

The next section focuses on methods used to provide access to images stored in a central repository. Use of both LAN and WAN transmission facilities are examined, with several strategies for minimizing the effect of image transfers on network users.

ACCESSING IMAGES

Once a decision is made to add images to a data base or other application, the potential effect of the retrieval of images by network users against the current organizational network infrastructure must be examined. Doing so provides the information necessary to determine if an existing network should be modified to support the transfer of images, as well as data.

To illustrate the factors that must be considered, this example assumes that images are to be added to a 50-node LAN server. The network server is attached to a 10M-bps Ethernet network as illustrated in Exhibit V-2-2a, with images placed on a CD-ROM jukebox connected to the server.

Based on an analysis of the expected use of the LAN, 15 stations were identified that are expected to primarily use the images stored on the CD-ROM jukebox. The other 35 network users are expected to casually use the CD-ROM jukebox, primarily using the LAN to access other applications on the server, such as workgroup software and other application programs, including a conventional text-based data base and electronic mail.

One method of minimizing the contention for network resources between network users is obtained by segmenting the network. Exhibit V-2-2b illustrates the use of a local bridge to link separate networks. In this illustration the 35

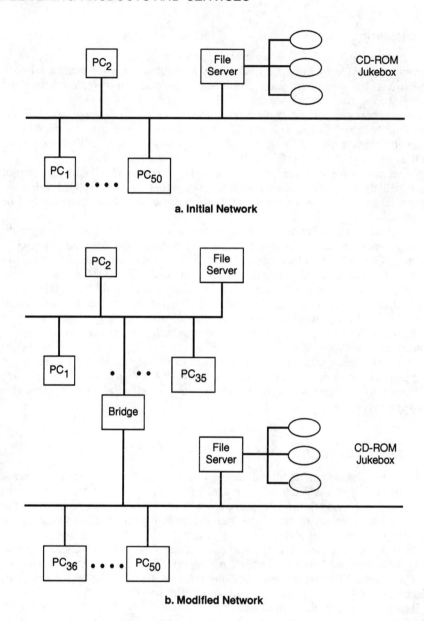

a. Initial Network

b. Modified Network

Exhibit V-2-2. Modifying an Ethernet Network

network users expected to have a minimal requirement for image transfers are located on one network, and the remaining 15 network users who have a significant requirement to transfer images are placed on a second network. The use of the bridge permits users of each network to access applications stored on the file server on the other network. However, this new network structure segments network stations by their expected usage, minimizing the adverse effect of heavy image transfer by 15 users on what was a total network of 50 users.

INTERNETWORKING

The segmentation of an Ethernet LAN into two networks linked together by a local bridge created an internetwork. Although the network structure was created to minimize the effect of transporting images on a larger network, this method of increasing the volume of image traffic through bridges that directly interconnect separate LANs can produce a bottleneck and inhibit the flow of other traffic, such as client/server queues, E-mail, and other network applications.

Placing Images on Image Servers

When constructing a local internetwork consisting of several linked LANs within a building, one method to minimize the effect of image traffic on other network applications is to place image applications on image servers located on a separate high-speed network.

Exhibit V-2-3 illustrates the use of an FDDI backbone ring consisting of two image servers whose access is obtainable from workstations located on several Ethernet and token ring networks through local bridges linking those networks to the FDDI ring. By using the FDDI ring for image applications, the 100M-bps operating rate of FDDI provides a delivery mechanism that enables workstation users on multiple lower operating rate LANs to simultaneously access image applications without experiencing network delays.

For example, one network user on each LAN illustrated in Exhibit V-2-3 accesses the same image application on an image server connected to the FDDI backbone LAN. If each token ring network operates at 16M bps and each Ethernet operates at 10M bps, the composite transfer rate from the FDDI network to each of the lower operating rate LANs bridged to that network is 52M bps. Since the FDDI network operates at 100M bps, it can simultaneously present images to network users on each of the four LANs without any internetwork bottlenecks occurring.

Another advantage associated with using an FDDI backbone restricted to supporting image servers and bridges is economics. This configuration minimizes the requirement for using more expensive FDDI adapter cards to one card per image server and one card per bridge. In comparison, upgrading an existing network to FDDI would require replacing each workstation's existing network adapter card with a more expensive FDDI adapter card.

To illustrate the potential cost savings, assume each Ethernet and token ring network has 100 workstations, resulting in a total of 400 adapter cards, including

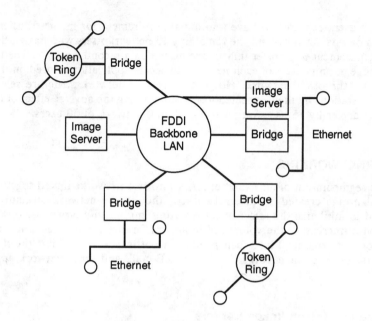

Exhibit V-2-3. Using a High-Speed FDDI Backbone

two image servers that would require replacement if each existing LAN was replaced by a common FDDI network. Since FDDI adapter cards cost approximately $800, this replacement would result in the expenditure of $320,000. In comparison, the acquisition of four bridges and six FDDI adapter cards would cost less than $20,000.

TRANSFERRING IMAGES THROUGH WIDE AREA NETWORKS

In the next example, a group of PC users requires the use of a WAN to access images on a data base at a remote location. Images are placed on a CD-ROM jukebox connected to a server on LAN A, which in turn is connected to LAN B through a pair of remote bridges operating at 64K bps. This network configuration is illustrated in Exhibit V-2-4.

If users on network A access several applications on network B and vice versa, in addition to accessing the images stored on the CD-ROM jukebox on network A, what happens when a user on network B attempts to access text data on network A during an image transfer? If another network B user requested an image transfer, the user requesting a text transfer is now contending for network resources with the user performing the image transfer. This means that alternate

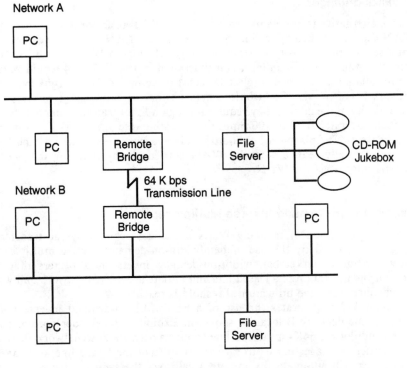

Exhibit V-2-4. Image Transfers Using a WAN Link

frames of data flow over the 64K-bps transmission facility—first a frame containing a portion of an image, then a frame containing a portion of the text transfer. This alternate frame transmission continues until one transfer is completed, prior to all network resources becoming devoted to the remaining transfer.

Thus, not only is the 64K-bps transmission rate a significant bottleneck to the transfer of images, but WAN users must contend for access to that resource. A 640K-byte image would require 80 seconds to transfer between remotely located LANs on a digital circuit operating at 64K bps and devoted to a single remote user. If that remote user had to share the use of the WAN link with another user performing another image transfer, each transfer would require 160 seconds. Thus, transferring images through a WAN connection can result in a relatively long waiting time. Although the WAN connection could be upgraded to a T1 or a fractional T1 circuit, the monthly incremental cost of a 500 mile 64K-bps digital circuit is approximately $600. In comparison, the monthly cost of a 500 mile 1.544M-bps digital circuit would exceed $4,200.

Localizing Images

One alternative to problems associated with the transfer of images through a WAN can be obtained by localizing images to each LAN to remove or substantially reduce the necessity to transfer images through a WAN. To do so with respect to the network configuration illustrated in Exhibit V-2-4 would require the installation of either a single CD-ROM drive or a CD-ROM jukebox onto network B's file server. This would enable network users on each LAN to obtain the majority of the images they require through a LAN transmission facility that normally operates at 10 to 100 times the operating rate of most WAN transmission facilities. The placement of additional image storage facilities on each LAN can substantially reduce potential WAN bottlenecks by reducing the need to transfer images via the WAN.

Bandwidth-on-Demand Inverse Multiplexers

A second method of reducing WAN bottlenecks caused by the transfer of images is obtained by the use of bandwidth-on-demand inverse multiplexers. Several vendors market bandwidth-on-demand inverse multiplexers that can monitor the utilization of a leased line and initiate a switched network call when a predefined lease line utilization threshold is reached.

Exhibit V-2-5 illustrates the use of a bandwidth-on-demand inverse multiplexer at the network B location shown in Exhibit V-2-4. Under normal operating conditions, a 64K-bps leased line connects network A to network B. When the transfer of images begins to saturate the use of the leased line, one inverse multiplexer will automatically initiate a call over the switched network to the other multiplexer. That call can be a switched digital call at 56/64K bps or a call over the public switched telephone network, in which the data transfer operating rate depends on the type of modems used with each inverse multiplexer. Because a switched digital or analog call costs between 10 and 25 cents per minute, the use of inverse multiplexers can represent an economical alternative to the use of additional or higher-speed leased lines when image transfers only occur periodically during the workday.

CONCLUSION

Since multimedia includes either digitized images, digitized speech, or both, the methods and techniques described in this chapter for handling images are applicable for multimedia. Thus, the segmentation of a local area network, the use of a high-speed backbone network for providing access to image servers, or the addition of multimedia storage facilities on individual LANs to reduce WAN traffic are all applicable to the transfer of multimedia information.

Placing images and multimedia on the corporate network can be considered equivalent to the addition of a very large number of network users. When planning to add access to image and multimedia data bases, IS managers should use the same planning process required to support conventional access to file servers and mainframe data bases. When data transfer requirements begin to adversely

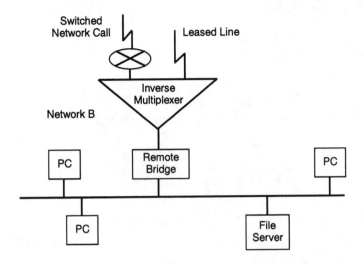

Exhibit V-2-5. Using a Bandwidth-on-Demand Inverse Multiplexer

affect network performance, managers should consider transferring multimedia data to storage repositories and accessing it through the methods suggested in this chapter. The goal at all times is to avoid burdening network users while remaining able to support an organization's image and multimedia data base access requirements in an efficient and cost-effective manner.

V-3

Multiple Protocols

Joe Pruskowski

TODAY'S BUSINESS EMPHASIS on rightsizing is best achieved by moving information closer to the individual workers within the organization, especially through client/server computing. By their very nature, networks are the logical structure to make this happen.

Many corporations have a mix of both departmental and corporate LAN systems combined with legacy systems, all with disparate methods of communicating in a network. Today's networks are very open, but often very chaotic. Managing such complex networks has become a real challenge for IS managers.

For connectivity, IS managers often rely on one of two common methods: stacking multiple protocols, or "multistacking," and using gateway technology. For IS managers facing integration decisions, information on all of the options is critical.

LAN CLIENT SUPPORT

The dominant LAN network operating system is NetWare, and therefore the standard for LAN protocols is IPX/SPX. Parallel to the LAN, legacy systems are still using their proprietary protocols to support access to mission-critical applications and data. Typically IBM's SNA, DEC's LAT and DECnet, together with a variety of applications running on TCP/IP, have become the most prominent protocols running on the host. Exhibit V-3-1 shows the interactions between clients and hosts within the network.

Because the networks in most organizations are made up of a variety of protocols, users in various places on the network cannot access the resources they need. A company attempting to solve this problem must deal with some significant issues:

- Initial setup cost, including purchase and installation cost, for each workstation on the network.
- Ongoing administrative support costs, which include the purchase and installation of software upgrades and the maintenance of network address management. Each protocol stack has a different naming scheme. For example, a LAT host name is a simple text string (e.g., SYSTEM1), whereas

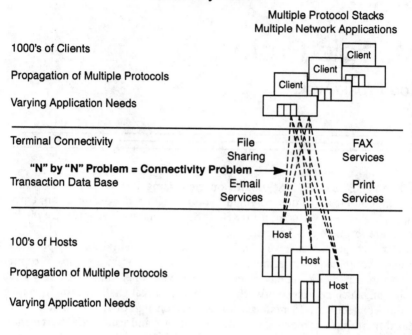

Exhibit V-3-1. Interactions Between Clients and Hosts Within the Network

a TCP/IP node name is tree-structured dot notation (e.g., SYSTEM1.-NORTHWEST.ICXN.COM).

- The limited number of applications supported by any one protocol.
- The burden on the infrastructure when there are too many protocols to support efficiently. This burden is imposed on the network hardware, which now must deal with managing multiple protocols. Support personnel must also know how to deal with these protocols.
- The high administrative costs in large, heterogeneous networks. This is a serious problem because the costs continue to climb.

WHAT IS MULTISTACKING?

Multistacking means that every LAN client would have to run all other legacy protocols (e.g., SNA, LAT, and DECnet) in addition to its native protocol (e.g., IPX) to gain access to all corporate data. The number of LAN clients that must run multiple protocol stacks in most major corporations is very large—typically measured in the thousands. Although in theory multistacking will solve the problem, it comes with an entire set of its own problems, multiplied by the sheer number of LAN clients that are affected.

Some of the major problems that must be dealt with on each DOS/Windows system are:

- Conflicts in memory usage, because many stacks still run in real-mode.
- Conflicts in TSR (terminate and stay resident) programs.
- Conflicts in network address spaces (i.e., differing address schemes).
- Use of network device drivers by multiple protocol stacks, which require complicated setup procedures.

CONNECTIVITY ALTERNATIVES TO MULTISTACKING

Several solutions are available today that minimize protocol stack propagation, each with its advantages and disadvantages.

Proprietary Vendor-Specific Suites. These are typically sold by the major computer vendors. Examples would be Pathworks from Digital Equipment Corp. and IBM's LAN Server products. These usually provide a high level of functionality, but they are mainly account control mechanisms and can be cumbersome to use. In addition, they are usually expensive because a license has to be purchased for every user on the network.

Standardization on One Protocol Stack. In an ideal world, this would be OSI, though TCP/IP seems to be filling this role as a practical solution. However, although TCP/IP is found on the backbones of many corporations, it rarely makes it to the client. TCP/IP can be cumbersome to install on a large number of nodes, but it does provide an excellent "intermediate" protocol. Because TCP/IP can support a wide variety of equipment, there are many parameters that must be set up on each TCP/IP system, not the least of which is the node number, which has to be assigned for each node. This approach can also be expensive, as it is purchased on a per-node basis.

THE SOFTWARE GATEWAY

Another alternative to multistacking is the use of gateway technology. Gateway technology was first introduced as rather expensive hardware. A single vendor had to install and maintain the gateway, typically at a very high cost to the user. New gateway technology is software-only and can be run on virtually any commodity hardware platform. An early example is Novell's NetWare for SAA, which connects LAN clients to IBM mainframes. Another is InterConnections' Leverage Gateway Services, which is based on Novell's NetWare for LAT technology and connects DEC systems with NetWare clients.

The gateway technology emerging today serves as a true gateway—one type of protocol is actually converted to a different protocol type. An example of this would be an inbound terminal session over NetWare IPX that is converted at the gateway to an outbound LAT terminal session. There are several advantages to this new type of gateway:

- It can reside on any Intel 386/486/Pentium hardware platform and provides protocol translation between the LAN client and host environments.
- It is ultimately manageable using the industry-standard SNMP protocol. The management capabilities are based on the translation tables that are inherent within the gateway. This allows for "logical network management" of network resources, building on the physical management capabilities that are currently being deployed by a wide variety of vendors. Logical network management brings meaningful information to the network manager, such as the number of sessions in use and the number of files transferred.
- Concurrent user licensing is cost-effective. Companies only pay for the maximum number of users that are accessing hosts at any point in time. There is no charge for LAN clients that are not actually using the gateway.
- Concurrent host usage is cost-effective. Any supported host can be accessed by the LAN clients. The user company does not have to license each host to allow access from its client systems.
- The number of protocol stacks on the LAN client and host are greatly reduced.
- There is no need for additional kernel-mode protocol stacks on the host machines.

By applying software gateway technology to the multiple protocol situation, IS professionals have a new set of tools that can help them achieve their goals.

A SAMPLE CASE

The next section examines the system at a major airline reservation center. The center has a large collection of NetWare LANs with thousands of IPX/SPX clients. In addition, there are dozens of hosts that are a combination of DEC and UNIX systems. These systems are all physically connected but use very different network protocols to communicate. The LAN clients mainly use IPX, the UNIX systems use TCP/IP, and the DEC systems use a combination of LAT and DECnet.

Personnel at the center take reservations over the phone using a reservation system that runs on UNIX and is connected via TCP/IP. From the same desktop system, they also perform outbound telemarketing (e.g., making customers aware of an upcoming new frequent flyer program) and must access a VAX/VMS system for lead information via the LAT protocol. In terms of connectivity, the company could:

- *Install all protocol stacks (i.e., IPX, TCP, LAT) at each client.* Installing all these protocol stacks at each client would add wear and tear on the network

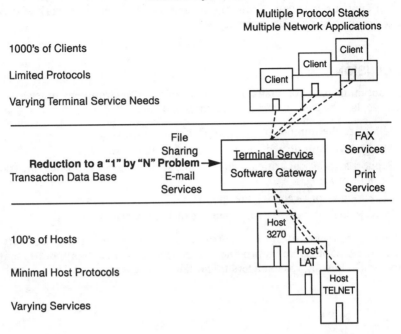

Connectivity Solution

Multiple Protocol Stacks
Multiple Network Applications

1000's of Clients

Limited Protocols

Varying Terminal Service Needs

File Sharing
Reduction to a "1" by "N" Problem →
Transaction Data Base   E-mail Services

Terminal Service
Software Gateway

FAX Services

Print Services

100's of Hosts

Minimal Host Protocols

Varying Services

Host 3270
Host LAT
Host TELNET

Exhibit V-3-2. Applying Gateway Technology—Connectivity Solution

management personnel alone. The stacks have to be loaded and configured on each client and, over time, must be maintained. There is also a charge for each stack-per-client.

- *Install a TCP/IP stack on all hosts and clients.* In most cases this does not support all of the applications required, so it becomes restrictive and might require at least an IPX stack to be coresident. Although the network management personnel have fewer stacks to worry about, they still have to configure and manage two stacks at each client.

- *Install gateways at the edges of the LAN infrastructure to the host systems.* This saves network management personnel wear and tear because the protocol translation gateway is installed at a central point. There are fewer stacks to worry about, and by simply leaving IPX on the LAN clients, the LAN becomes easy to manage on an ongoing basis. Cost is also minimized because money is saved on protocol stacks and their subsequent maintenance.

In the future, more companies will implement strategic protocols such as IPX and TCP/IP across their network backbone while applying software gateway technology to bring legacy systems into the network. Exhibit V-3-2 illustrates the effect of applying gateway technology to simplify the overall network and provide basic functionality for all legacy systems.

CONCLUSION

An optimum plan for managing a multiprotocol environment must achieve certain goals. The minimum set of requirements are:

- Minimize the number of protocol stacks at the client.
- Minimize the number of protocol stacks at the host.
- Support a variety of critical applications, such as terminal service, file transfer, and printing.
- Take a "network-centric" viewpoint.
- Provide logical network management of these services.

With the emergence of software gateways that run on commodity hardware, it has become cost-effective to provide a high level of connectivity and manageability while allowing IS managers to contain their costs.

V-4

Equipment Leasing

Nathan J. Muller

SEVERAL FINANCIAL REASONS warrant that equipment leasing be considered over purchasing, such as when a company cannot secure credit for an installment loan on the system and has no available line of credit, or cannot make the down payment required for an installment loan. Leasing can improve a company's cash position, because costs are spread over a period of years. Leasing can free up capital for other uses, and even cost-justify technology acquisitions that would otherwise be too expensive. Leasing also makes it possible to procure equipment on short notice that has not been planned or budgeted for.

A purchase, on the other hand, increases the debt relative to equity and worsens the company's financial ratios in the eyes of investors, creditors, and potential customers.

An operating lease represents an additional source of capital and preserves credit lines. Beyond that, leasing can help companies comply with the covenants in loan agreements that restrict the amount of new debt that can be incurred during the loan period. The purpose of such provisions is to make sure that the company does not jeopardize its ability to pay back the loan. In providing additional capacity for acquiring equipment without violating loan agreements or hurting debt-to-equity ratios, leasing in effect allows companies to have their cake and eat it too.

LOWER EQUIPMENT COSTS

With major improvements in technology becoming available every 12 to 18 months, leasing can prevent a company from becoming saddled with obsolete equipment. The potential for losses when replacing equipment that has not been fully depreciated can be minimized by leasing rather than purchasing. Furthermore, with rapid advancements in technology and consequently shortened product life cycles, it is becoming more difficult to sell used equipment. Leasing eliminates this problem too, because the leasing company owns the equipment.

For organizations concerned with controlling staff size, leasing also minimizes the amount of time and resources spent in cost-justifying capital expenditures, evaluating new equipment and disposing of old equipment, negotiating trade-ins, comparing the capabilities of vendors, performing reference checks on vendors, and reviewing contractual options. There is also no need for additional administrative staff to keep track of configuration details, spare parts, service records, and equipment warranties. Because the leasing firm is usually responsible for installing and servicing the equipment, there is no need to contract for skilled technicians or outside consulting services. Lease agreements may be structured to include ongoing technical support and even a help hotline for end users.

Because lessors have a stake in keeping the equipment functioning properly, they usually offer on-site repair and the immediate replacement of defective components and subsystems. In extreme cases, the lessor may even swap the entire system for a properly functioning unit. Although contracts vary, maintenance and repair services that are bundled into the lease can eliminate the hidden costs often associated with an outright purchase.

Flexible Contract Terms

Leasing usually allows flexibility in customizing contract terms and conditions. There are no set rates and contracts when leasing. Unlike many purchase agreements, each lease is negotiated on an individual case basis. The items typically negotiated in a lease are the equipment specifications, schedule for upgrades, maintenance and repair services, and training. End-of-lease options are also negotiable. This can include signing another lease for the same equipment, signing another lease for more advanced equipment, or buying the equipment. Many lessors will allow customers to end a lease ahead of schedule without penalty if the customer agrees to a new lease on upgraded equipment.

NONFINANCIAL INCENTIVES

There are also some very compelling nonfinancial reasons for considering leasing over purchasing. In some cases, leasing can make it easier to try new technologies or the offerings of new vendors. After all, leases always expire or can be canceled (a penalty usually applies), but few vendors are willing to take back purchased equipment. Leasing permits users to take full advantage of the most up-to-date products at the least risk and often under very attractive financial terms.

Leasing is particularly attractive for companies that use technology for competitive advantage because it means that they can continually upgrade by renegotiating the lease, often with little or no penalty for terminating the existing lease early. Similarly, if the company grows faster than anticipated, it can swap the leased equipment for an upgrade.

It must be noted, however, that many computer and communications systems are now modular in design, so the fear of early obsolescence may not be as great as it once was. Nevertheless, leasing offers an inducement to try vendor implementations on a limited basis without committing to a particular platform or architecture, and with minimal disruption to mainstream business operations.

Getting Rid of Dated Equipment

Companies that lease equipment can avoid a problem that invariably affects companies that purchase equipment: how to get rid of outdated equipment. Generally, no used equipment is worth more on a price/performance basis than new equipment, even if it is functionally identical. Also, as new equipment is introduced, it erodes the value of older equipment. These by-products of improved technology make it very difficult for users to unload older, purchased equipment.

With equipment that has been leased, the leasing company assumes the responsibility of finding a buyer. Typically, the leasing company is staffed with marketers who know how and where to sell used equipment. They know how to prospect for customers who might consider a secondhand system a step up from the 10-year-old hardware they are currently using.

Convenience and Easier Budget Planning

Leasing offers the lessee the convenience of not having to maintain detailed depreciation schedules for accounting and tax purposes. Budget planning is also made easier, because the lease involves fixed monthly payments. This locks in pricing over the term of the lease, allowing the company to know in advance what its equipment costs will be over a particular planning period.

With leasing, there are also lower overhead costs to contend with. For example, there is no need to stockpile equipment spares, subassemblies, repair parts, and cabling. It is the responsibility of the leasing firm to keep inventories up to date. Their technicians (usually third-party service firms) make on-site visits to swap boards and arrange for overnight shipping of larger components when necessary.

Whereas it may take up to eight weeks or longer to obtain equipment purchased from a manufacturer, it may take from one to 10 working days to obtain the same equipment from a leasing firm. Often, the equipment is immediately available from the leasing firm's lease/rental pool. For customers who need equipment that is not readily available, some leasing firms will make a special procurement and have the equipment in a matter of two or three days, provided the lease term is long enough to make the effort worthwhile.

Many leasing companies offer a master lease, giving the customer a preassigned credit limit. All of the equipment the customer wants goes on the master lease and is automatically covered by its terms and conditions. In essence, the master lease works like a credit card.

DECISION FACTORS

In addition to the traditional financial trade-offs, IS managers must consider such factors as the long-range business plan of the company, the pace of technological change in the industry, and ongoing requirements for equipment maintenance and repair before they can recommend the lease or purchase of equipment. Assuming that internal needs have been properly assessed with input from appropriate departments, the IS manager must take into account the following business issues.

Equipment Title. Equipment purchase results in the transfer of title to the purchaser, but the title remains with the lessor when equipment is leased. A company must have title ownership to be eligible for certain tax considerations, including first-year expensing and depreciation.

First-Year Expensing. First-year expensing is an immediate deduction that applies to property purchased for business or professional use. Under current federal tax laws, self-employed individuals and businesses are allowed to immediately deduct up to $17,500 of the cost of business equipment and software placed into service in one year. Any amount over $17,500 must be depreciated over a five-year period. Software can be depreciated over a three-year period.

Depreciation. Depreciation is a deduction for the obsolescence of equipment or software due to normal wear and tear, as well as technological advances that render such products out of date. An individual or company can deduct for depreciation. The deduction results in a lowered adjusted net income upon which federal income taxes are computed.

The marginal tax rate translates depreciation deductions into actual tax dollars saved. The marginal tax rate is derived from and usually equals an individual's or company's tax bracket. Therefore, a 34% tax bracket has a marginal tax rate of 34% and thus saves $34 in taxes for every $100 of depreciation deductions available per year.

Under current tax laws, depreciation is usually fixed according to property type. Computer and communications equipment usually falls into the five-year property class, as do most types of office equipment, including computers, copiers, facsimiles, and telephone systems. Software, as noted, falls into the three-year property class.

Taxes. Despite changes in the federal tax laws, which eliminated the investment tax credit, the tax benefits of leasing can still be quite substantial. In addition, the lessee is usually exempt from the state and local taxes applicable to owned equipment, including intangible taxes and property taxes; such taxes are the responsibility of the lessor. The monthly payments of an operating lease are fully deductible, because they represent business expenses and not assets, which must be depreciated over time.

Insurance. Depending on the terms of the lease, the lessee may or may not be responsible for insurance, whereas the purchaser is always responsible for insuring purchased equipment. If a loan was used to purchase the equipment, the lender usually requires insurance as a condition of the loan until it is paid in full.

Payment Terms. Under most equipment lease arrangements, the lessee is obligated to pay a fixed amount per time period, usually monthly. Upon expiration of the lease, the equipment may be purchased. On the other hand, purchasing equipment requires a large, one-time expenditure unless all or a portion of the purchase cost is financed. Even so, the terms of the loan may require a down payment, which may be quite substantial—as much as 25%—depending on the total purchase price.

Maintenance. Maintenance is often provided by the lessor and is included in the lease cost. When maintenance is a separate charge, it should be considered an additional lease charge and simply added to the monthly cost of the lease.

Price Protection. Under a leasing arrangement, the lessee is protected against the effects of inflation for the duration of the lease. The monthly charge is locked in for the term of the lease and does not fluctuate as current money market rates do. For this reason, it is advisable to have such things as maintenance, disaster recovery, training, and consulting services bundled into the lease. With many purchase contracts, these support costs may rise during periods of inflation because vendors often tie such costs to the government's consumer price index.

Discount Potential. Because equipment purchase results in an immediate expenditure of a large amount of money, many vendors provide discounts for purchased equipment or offer some support services at a reduced rate. Although some leasing firms will also negotiate discounts on leased equipment, such discounts usually require an extension on the life of the lease.

Replacement. Purchased equipment often represents a large dollar investment; thus, many companies are reluctant to replace such equipment until it has been fully depreciated. Equipment obtained through a leasing arrangement is usually more easily replaced. The lessee simply waits until the lease expires and returns the equipment, or pays an early termination penalty and then returns the equipment. The user can also renegotiate the lease at little or no extra charge, provided that a new lease is signed for upgraded equipment.

PAYMENT ALTERNATIVES

When considering the purchase of equipment, several payment plans are available:

- *Cash.* If the company has the financial reserves, it can simply pay cash for the purchase.
- *Installment purchase.* Some manufacturers offer an installment purchase plan, similar to a mortgage, where the system is used as collateral for the loan offered to cover the price. A down payment is normally required, but may be minimal.

- *Credit line.* The company may borrow the money for the purchase from a bank, or draw it from an available line of credit.

The Cost of Paying Cash

The attraction of paying cash is that it costs nothing. No interest is paid, as with a loan or lease, so the cost of the item is the purchase price. However, there are several reasons why cash payment may not be a good idea, aside from the obvious reason that the company may have no cash available.

One reason to avoid paying cash for a purchase is that the money may be needed to finance other, more urgent activities. Sometimes a major purchase can be made based on a very low interest rate relative to prevailing commercial rates. To pay cash for equipment when it could be financed at 7%, then to pay 11% interest on a loan six months later, is unsound financing. If financing is at an attractive rate, it is probably better to use that rate and finance the system, unless company cash reserves are so high that future borrowing for any reason will not be required.

Another reason for not using reserves to finance a large purchase concerns the issue of credit worthiness. Often a company with little financial history can borrow for a collateralized equipment purchase but cannot borrow readily for such intangibles as ordinary operating expenses. Other times, an unexpected setback will affect the credit standing of the firm. If all or most of the firm's reserves have been depleted by a major purchase, it may be difficult or impossible to secure quick loans to meet operating expenses, and the company may falter.

Deferred Payment Plans

Those who elect to purchase equipment, but who cannot or choose not to pay cash, will require a loan financing arrangement. These arrangements are often difficult to interpret and compare, so users should review the cost of each alternative carefully.

If the company is not able to or willing to pay cash, the alternative is some form of deferred payment. The purpose of these payments is to stagger costs over a longer period and reduce the cash flow in a given year. But a substantial price to be paid is the interest—whether the equipment is leased or installment purchased, interest will be paid.

The question of financial priorities must be answered early in the equipment acquisition process. Provided that the interest premium is not unreasonable, a purchase that is financed over a longer period will have a lower net cost per year, taking tax effects of depreciation into consideration.

Credit Line

Many companies have an open credit line established with one or more banks. When companies need money to finance short-term obligations, they draw from the credit line. Because credit lines for most businesses have a limit, it may not be wise to finance equipment purchases from this source because it may leave less money available for urgent needs that may arise unexpectedly. Requesting an extension of the credit line is always an option, but it may result in closer scrutiny of the company's finances that may hinder future borrowing.

TYPES OF LEASES

Assuming that the decision has been made to lease rather than purchase equipment, it is important to differentiate between the two main types of leases available, because each is treated differently for tax purposes. One type of lease is the operating lease, in which the leasing company retains ownership of the equipment. At the end of the lease, the lessee may purchase the equipment at its fair market value. The other kind of lease is the capital lease, in which the lessee can retain the equipment for a nominal fee, which can be as low as $1.

Operating Leases

With the operating lease (also known as a tax-oriented lease), monthly payments are expensed, which means that they are subtracted from the company's pretax earnings. With a capital lease (also known as a non-tax-oriented lease), the amount of the lease is counted as debt and must appear on the balance sheet. In other words, the capital lease is treated as just another form of purchase financing and, therefore, only the interest is tax deductible.

The Financial Accounting Standards Board (FASB) guidelines help users distinguish an operating lease from a capital lease. A true operating lease must meet the following criteria, some of which effectively limit the maximum term of the lease:

- The term of the lease must not exceed 80% of the projected useful life of the equipment. The equipment's "useful life" begins on the effective date of the lease agreement. The lease term includes any extensions or renewals at a preset fixed rental.
- The equipment's estimated residual value in constant dollars (with no consideration for inflation or deflation) at the expiration of the lease must equal a minimum of 20% of its value at the time the lease was signed.
- Neither the lessee or any related party is allowed to buy the equipment at a price lower than fair market value at the time of purchase.
- The lessee and related party are also prohibited from paying, or guaranteeing, any part of the price of the leased equipment. The lease, therefore, must be 100% financed.
- The leased equipment must not fall into the category of "limited use" property; that is, equipment that would be useless to anyone except the lessee and related parties at the end of the lease.

With the operating lease, the rate of cash outflow is always balanced to a degree by the rate of tax recovery. With a purchase, the depreciation allowed in a given year may have no connection with the amount of money the buyer actually paid in installment payments.

Capital Leases

For an agreement to qualify as a capital lease, it must meet one of the following FASB criteria:

- The lessor transfers ownership to the lessee at the end of the lease term.
- The lease contains an option to buy the equipment at a price below the residual value.
- The lease term is equal to 75% or more of the economic life of the property. (This does not apply to used equipment leased at the end of its economic life.)
- The present value of the minimum lease rental payments is equal to or exceeds 90% of the equipment's fair market value.

From these criteria, it becomes clear that capital leases are not set up for tax purposes. Such leases are given the same treatment as installment loans. In the case of a capital lease, only the interest portion of the fixed monthly payment can be deducted as a business expense. However, the lessee may take deductions for depreciation as if the transaction were an outright purchase. For this reason, the monthly payments are usually higher than they would be for a true operating lease.

Depending on the amount of the lease rental payments and the financial objectives of the lessee, the cost of the equipment may be amortized faster through tax-deductible rentals than through depreciation and after-tax cash flow.

Capital Lease Variations

Two common capital lease variations are lease with option to purchase (LWOP) and lease with ownership. Under a LWOP contract, a portion of each monthly payment is applied toward purchasing the equipment. Typically, 50% or less of the rent applies to the capital. Under a lease with ownership agreement, ownership passes to the lessee upon the last lease payment for a nominal amount. The monthly lease cost of these two variations usually exceeds the payments required under the terms of an operating lease agreement.

LWOP permits the lessee to decide whether to purchase the equipment while equity builds with each payment. The lessee can also hedge on quantity purchased and later return excess equipment. In addition, LWOP can be used as a cash-management tool. The lessee continues lease payments until funds are available to pay the purchase price, less the payment accruals for the equipment.

A lease with option to purchase can be complicated to implement because only a percentage of each monthly payment is applied toward the purchase of the total equipment, only a certain percentage of the total equipment purchase price can be accrued before equity buildup stops, and additionally monthly payments are treated as conventional lease payments.

THE DOWNSIDE OF LEASING

Leasing does have a downside. Although leasing can be used as an alternative source of financing that may not appear on the corporate balance sheet, the cost of a conventional lease arrangement generally exceeds that of outright purchase. Excluding the time value of money and equipment maintenance costs, the simple lease versus purchase break-even point can be determined by a formula:

$$N = \frac{P}{L}$$

where:

P = the purchase cost

L = is the monthly lease cost

N = is the number of months needed to break even.

Thus, if equipment costs $10,000 and the lease costs $250 per month, the break-even point is 40 months. This means that owning equipment is preferable if its use is expected to exceed 40 months.

As in any financial transaction, there may be hidden costs associated with the lease. If a lease rate seems very attractive relative to rates offered by other leasing companies, a red flag should go up. Hidden charges may be embedded in the lease agreement. These hidden charges can include shipping and installation costs, higher-than-usual maintenance charges, consulting fees, or even a balloon payment at the end of the lease term.

The lessee may even be required to provide special insurance on the equipment. Some lessors even require the lessee to buy maintenance services from a third party to keep the equipment in proper working order over the life of the lease agreement. The lessor may also impose restrictions on where the equipment can be moved, who can service it, and what environmental controls must be in place at the installation site.

ROLE OF IS MANAGERS

As noted, IS managers often play a key role in the corporate decision to purchase or lease equipment. In fact, several areas may elude the expertise of financial analysts, so the input of IS managers is needed. The IS manager should therefore be prepared to answer the following types of questions:

- Are there any elements of the new system that have a very short useful life? A special data interface needed for a computer that is to be phased out later might be a candidate for separate rental rather than purchase.
- Is there a chance that the entire system might have to be traded at a later point? This would affect the depreciation period the accounting organization might set on the system.
- Are there likely to be additions to the system that might be covered as addendum to the installment loan if the vendor's own financing were se-

lected, but that might require renegotiations if another financial source is selected?

- Are there any special terms on equipment protection (e.g., right of modification) that might be expensive or difficult to comply with?

CONCLUSION

Every IS manager should understand the fundamentals of equipment leasing. Knowledge of the basics enables the IS manager to work more effectively with the company's financial and legal departments to choose the best equipment procurement method. To make an informed decision about buying versus leasing, IS managers should examine the financial condition of their companies, in addition to the speed at which technology changes in their industry. Those managers who are not supported by financial and legal experts may wish to seek out software packages specifically designed to automate the lease-versus-purchase decision process.

V-5

Operating Standards for LANs

Leo Wrobel

THE FOLLOWING SCENARIO is common in many organizations: There are 200 local area networks (LANs) located across the country, in everything from small sales offices with a handful of people to regional distribution centers. The company does not know if these outlying locations handle mission-critical data. The company does not know with certainty who is running these LANs, because staffing ranges from office managers and clerical employees right up to seasoned IS professionals. A site that once had 10 salespeople now has 9 salespeople and a LAN administrator. The company does not know how these sites are buying equipment, yet it is reasonably sure that they are paying too much, because they are not buying in bulk or enjoying any economies of scale in equipment purchases.

Locations are beginning to lean on IS for help desk support because there is no way they can keep up with the rapid proliferation of hardware platforms, software, and special equipment being installed in the field. The telecommunications department is worried about connecting all of these locations together.

Although some attempts at standardization of these locations may be made, LAN managers in the field invariably consider standards to be an attempt by the IS department to regain control of the LAN administrators' environment. Because LAN managers seldom have had any input into what these standards would be, they were soundly rejected.

Today, there are literally thousands of companies fighting this same battle. This chapter offers some solutions to these problems. First, however, it is important to understand why standards are required and how IS can implement standards without stifling productivity or adversely affecting the organization.

WHY LANS REQUIRE STANDARDS

In an ideal environment, the LAN administrator can select exactly the type of equipment best tailored to do the job. LAN managers are historically close to the core business. For example, if the company is involved in trading stock, the LAN operations department can go out and buy equipment tailored exactly to trading stock. If the organization is engaged in engineering, the LAN administrator can buy equipment exactly tailored to engineering.

From the standpoint of operational characteristics, LANs are far more desirable than mainframes because they are closer to the business, they empower people, and they make people enormously productive by being close to the core business. This is not the whole story, however. It is equally as important to support LANs once they are in place. This is where the trade-offs come in.

Lessons from Mainframe Experience

Because mainframes have been around so long, there is a high degree of support available. When users in the mainframe environment call the help desk with a hardware or a software problem, the help desk knows what they are talking about. Help desk staff are well trained in the hardware and the software packages and can quickly solve the users' problems.

As another example, in an IBM 3070 terminal environment, 100 terminals or more could be supported by a single technician. When those terminals became PCs, the ratio perhaps dropped to 50 PCs per technician. When those PCs became high-end workstations, the ratio dropped even further. The value of a mainframe level of technical support cannot be underestimated.

Mainframe professionals had 20 years to write effective operating and security standards. These standards cover a number of preventive safeguards that should be adopted in the operational environment to ensure smooth operation. These range from:

- How often to change passwords.
- How often to make backups.
- What equipment should be locked up.
- Who is responsible for change control.
- Defining the standards for interconnecting between environments.

In the mainframe world it was also easy to make very large bulk purchases. Because the mainframe has been around for so long, many advanced network management systems exist that provide a high degree of support and fault isolation.

Balancing Productivity and Support Requirements for LANs

Because LAN platforms are relatively new, in comparison to mainframes, there has not been as much time to develop operating and security standards. This is especially irritating to auditors when mission-critical applications move from the traditional mainframe environment onto LANs and the protective safeguards around them do not follow. Something as simple as transporting a tape backup copy of a file between LAN departments can be extremely complicated without standards. What if everyone buys a different type of tape backup unit? Without standards on what type of equipment to use, bulk purchases of equipment become difficult or impossible.

Even though major improvements have been made in network management systems over the past five years, the management systems associated with LANs often lag behind those associated with mainframe computers. Again, this causes the company to pay penalties in the area of maintenance and ease of use.

One answer, of course, is to force users into rigid standards. Although this pays a handsome dividend in the area of support, it stifles the users' productivity. They need equipment well suited to their core business purpose.

An alternative is to let users install whatever they want. This may increase productivity greatly, though it is doubtful that a company could ever hire and support enough people to maintain this type of configuration. Worse, mission-critical applications could be damaged or lost altogether if users are not expected to take reasonable and prudent safeguards for their protection.

It is the responsibility of both users and technical staff to find the middle ground between the regimented mainframe environment and the seat-of-the-pants LAN environment. Through careful planning, it is possible to configure a set of standards that offers the advantage of greater productivity that is afforded by LANs, but also the advantages learned through 20 years of mainframe operations in the areas of support, bulk purchases, and network management.

The remainder of this chapter concentrates on exactly what constitutes reasonable operating and security procedures for both LANs and telecommunications.

STANDARDS COMMITTEES

One method for establishing LAN standards is through the formation of a communications and LAN operating and security standards committee. An ideal size for a standards committee would be 10 to 12 people, with representatives from sales, marketing, engineering, support, technical services (including LANs), IS and telecommunications, and other departments. It is important to broaden this committee to include not only technical staff, but also people engaged in the core business, since enhancement of productivity will be a key concern.

The actual standards document that this committee produces must deal with issues for both the operation and protection of a company's automated platforms (Exhibit V-5-1 provides a working table of contents from which to begin to write a document). Subjects include:

- Basic physical standards, including access to equipment rooms, where PBX equipment is kept, what type of fire protection should be employed, standards for new construction, standards for housekeeping, and standards for electrical power.
- Software security, change control, which people are authorized to make changes, and how these changes are documented.
- The security of information, such as identifying who is allowed to dial into a system, determining how to dispose of confidential materials, determining

At a minimum, an operating and security standards document should incorporate the following areas:

I. Objective: Defining Mission Critical
    1. For Non-Mission-Critical Support Systems
    2. For Mission-Critical Support Systems

II. Physical Security
    1. For Non-Mission-Critical
    2. For Mission-Critical

III. Operational Support Issues
    1. Standards for All LAN and Telecommunications Installations
    2. Documentation Standards for Software and Application
    3. Server and PBX Class-of-Service Indicator Backups

IV. Access Control
    1. Procedures for Passwords

V. Change Control Policy and Procedures

VI. Virus Protection Procedures

VII. Disaster Recovery Procedures
    1. For Non-Mission-Critical Equipment
    2. For Mission-Critical Equipment

Exhibit V-5-1. Sample Operating and Security Standards Document Table of Contents

---

which telephone conversations should be considered private, and the company's policy on telecommunications privacy.

- Weighing options with regard to technical support of equipment.
- Resolving issues regarding interconnection standards for the telecommunications network.
- Disaster backup and recovery for both LANs and telecommunications, including defining what users must do to ensure protection of mission-critical company applications.

Defining "Mission Critical"

Before all of this, however, the committee is expected to define and understand what a mission-critical application is. Standards are designed to cover both operational and security issues, so the business processes themselves must be defined to avoid imposing a heavy burden of security on users who are not engaged in mission-critical applications, or not imposing a high enough level of security on users who are.

Standards for equipment that is not mission critical are relatively easy. In practice, this means securing the area in which the equipment resides from unauthorized access by outside persons when there is danger of tampering or theft. It also includes avoiding needless exposures to factors that could damage the equipment, such as water and combustibles, and controlling food items around the equipment, such as soft drinks and coffee.

Mission-critical equipment, however, has a value to the company that far exceeds the value of the equipment itself, because of the type of functions it supports. Determination of what constitutes a mission-critical system should be made at a senior management level.

LAN and telecommunications equipment that supports an in-bound call center for companies such as the Home Shopping Club, would definitely be mission-critical equipment, because disruption of the equipment, for whatever cause, would cause a financial hit to the company that far exceeds the value of the equipment. Therefore, mission-critical equipment should be defined as equipment that, if lost, would result in significant loss to the organization, measured in terms of lost sales, lost market share, lost customer confidence, or lost employee productivity.

Monetary cost is not the only measurement concerning mission-critical. If an organization supports a poison-control line, for example, and loss of equipment means a parent cannot get through when a child is in danger, it has other implications. Because financial cost is a meaningful criteria to probably 90% of the companies, it is the measurement used for purposes of this discussion.

There is not necessarily a correlation between physical size and mission criticality. It is easy to look at a LAN of 100 people and say that it is more mission-critical than another LAN that has only 4 people. However, the LAN with 100 people on it may provide purely an administrative function. The LAN with four people on it may have an important financial function.

WRITING THE OPERATING AND SECURITY STANDARDS DOCUMENT

The following approach recommends that two distinct sets of standards be created for mission-critical versus non-mission-critical equipment.

Network Software Security and Change Control Management

One item that should be considered in this section is, Who is authorized to make major changes to LAN or telecommunications equipment?

There is a good reason to consider this question. If everyone is making major changes to a system, a company is inviting disaster, because there is little communication concerning who changed what and whether these changes are compatible with changes made by another person. Standards should therefore include a list of persons authorized to make major changes to a mission-critical technical system. It should also have procedures for changing passwords on a regular basis, both for the maintenance and operation functions of LANs and telecommunications. Procedures should be defined that mandate a back-up before major changes in order to have something to fall back on in case something goes wrong.

Procedures should be established to include DISA (direct inward system access). Unauthorized use of DISA lines is a major cause of telecommunications fraud or theft of long-distance services. Automated attendants, for example, should also be secured and telephone credit cards properly managed. As a minimum, establish a procedure that cancels remote access and telephone credit to employees who leave the company.

Physical and Environmental Security

There should be a set of basic, physical standards for all installations, regardless of their mission-critical status. These might include use of a UPS (uninterruptible power supply) on any LAN server. A UPS not only guards against loss of productivity when the lights flicker, but also cleans up the power somewhat and protects the equipment itself.

There should be standards for physically protecting the equipment, because LAN equipment is frequently stolen and because there is a black market for PBX cards as well. There should be general housekeeping standards as far as prohibitions against eating and drinking in equipment areas and properly disposing of confidential materials through shredding or other means. No-smoking policies should be included. Standards for control of combustibles or flammables in the vicinity of equipment should also be written.

Physical standards for mission-critical applications are more intensive. These might include sign-in logs for visitors requiring access to equipment rooms. They may require additional physical protection, such as sprinkler systems or fire extinguishers. They may require general improvements to the building, such as building fire-resistant walls. They should also include protection against water, since this a frequent cause of disruption, either from drains, building plumbing, sprinklers, roof leaks, or other sources.

Technical Support

The standards committee ideally should provide a forum for users to display new technologies and subject them to a technical evaluation. For example, LAN managers or end users may find a new, innovative use of technology that promises to greatly enhance productivity in their department. They can present this new technology to the standards committee for both productivity and technical evaluations. The technologist on the committee can then advise users of the feasibility of this technology; whether it will create an undue maintenance burden, for example, or whether it is difficult to support.

If it is found that this equipment does indeed increase productivity and that it does not create an undue maintenance burden, it could be accepted by the committee and added to a list of supported services and vendors that is underwritten by the committee. Other issues include what level of support users are required to provide for themselves, what the support level of the help desk should be, and more global issues, such as interconnection standards for a corporate backbone network and policies on virus protection.

CONCLUSION

The LAN operating and securities standards document is designed to be an organization's system of government regarding the conduct and operation of technical platforms supporting the business. A properly written standards document includes input from departments throughout the organization, both to enhance productivity and to keep expenses for procurement, maintenance, and support under control. Standards also ensure that appropriate preventive safeguards are undertaken, especially for mission-critical equipment, to avoid undue loss of productivity, profitability, or equity to the company in the event something goes wrong. In other words, they are designed to prevent disruptions.

Use of a LAN operating and security standards committee is advised to ensure that critical issues are decided by a group of people with wide exposure within the company and to increase ownership of the final document throughout the organization. If properly defined, the standards document will accommodate the advantages of the mainframe environment and needs of LAN administrators by finding the middle ground between these operating environments. By writing and adopting effective standards, an organization can enjoy the productivity afforded by modern LAN environments while at the same time enjoying a high level of support afforded through more traditional environments.

Exhibit V-5-1 lists examples of typical standards for these types of installations. Readers are recommended to use them as a baseline in developing standards.

Section VI
Quality and Control

ENSURING QUALITY AND CONTROL remains one of the primary tasks of the IS management team. Even when IS services are outsourced, internal staff members must ensure the quality of the service being provided and satisfy top management that the business's information resources are properly controlled.

One step in this process is knowing where the IT department stands and how IT adds value to a business. This becomes doubly important when IS services are outsourced. Benchmarking—a technique companies use to compare themselves against other companies and identify best practices—can uncover ways to show how information technology contributes to business value. Chapter VI-1, "Benchmarking the IT Function," discusses six key components for baselining the IS organization. The chapter's worksheets and graphs can be used by IS management to create a baseline snapshot of the organization and to measure the performance of outsourced services.

Outsourcing is an evolving trend in IS. However, the decision to outsource is usually not made by the IS manager, who is often not even involved in the deliberations that lead to the consideration of the outsourcing option. Although it may not be the IS manager's job to make the outsourcing decision, the IS manager is responsible for ensuring that the proper safeguards provide the organization with long-term protection of its assets. Chapter VI-2 reviews why the outsourcing decision is often controversial and presents steps to ensure "Control of Information Systems Outsourcing."

Today's business organizations make every attempt to streamline operations to their most cost-effective level and still compete in a global market in which the high quality of a product or service is the measure of its success. Proving that the IS function is producing at an optimal quality level makes the difference in the perception of the group's ongoing value to the organization. One highly visible product that most IS organizations offer is technical training. Although the measurement of training success is often subjective, IS managers can help ensure quality learning by applying adult learning theory to computer training design and delivery. Chapter VI-3, "Ensuring Quality in Computer Learning," discusses curricula and delivery methods, managing the expectations of management, and setting a climate for learning—all areas that contribute to learning success.

Viruses and hackers are a blight on the IT industry—they can strike at any time and any place. The proliferation of dispersed computing systems and of the use of computing technology in the workplace makes it incumbent on IS managers to be aware of the threats and safeguards related to the viral and hacker syndrome. The need for viruses to be dealt with in the same way as any other security threat mandates the development of "An Advanced Strategy for Combatting Viruses" (Chapter VI-4). Because users can no longer rely solely on software solutions to provide effective antivirus protection, the strategy presented in the chapter is based on a multilevel and diversified combination of hardware and software techniques.

To protect their computer and communications systems against hacker attacks, IS managers need to understand the motives and modes of operation of external intruders. By learning how hackers gather and share information and how they break into systems, IS practitioners can ensure that systems safeguards remain able to detect and thwart attempts at unauthorized access. Chapter VI-5, "Countering Hacker Attacks," presents a profile of hackers and hacker clubs, their methods of communication, and specific methods of information gathering and attack. The chapter also reviews recommended procedures and controls for countering hacker attacks.

VI-1

Benchmarking the IT Function

Howard A. Rubin

EFFORTS TO IMPROVE QUALITY and increase efficiency are often based on benchmarking, a technique that companies use to compare themselves against other companies and identify best practices. In IT organizations, the use of benchmarking as a proactive tool for performance assessment and goal setting is rare but on the rise.

There are two fundamental reasons why this technique has not been widely applied in IT. First, benchmarking requires measurement, and few IT organizations have mature measurement programs. Second, there is a limited understanding of the key aspects of IT performance to be benchmarked.

One source of the problem is that measures in the world of IT are thought to be overhead and are not evaluated in terms of the value they add. In addition, those who have attempted to measure usually get caught up in trying to find the best measure instead of a suitable one. Finally, IT is under tremendous pressure to reduce expenses while producing more work. Most IT executives believe that to establish a baseline they have to impede progress before moving on again. If they slow down, they are unemployed. In short, baselining and benchmarking in IT are generally resisted for all of the wrong reasons.

USING BENCHMARKING TO SET PERFORMANCE TARGETS

There are some documented cases of IT organizations that have invested the time and energy to focus their benchmark efforts by identifying key areas of performance, measuring them, and then comparing themselves against others using the same rigorous measurement criteria. Here are two examples that illustrate the results of properly applying benchmarking to the IT organization.

Case 1. A bank's IT organization seeking to lower costs while strengthening the business alignment of IT. Bank X focused its internal measurement efforts on characterizing the yield of the support costs of its work prioritization process, the support process cycle time, the application quality, organizational structure, and new development productivity. By applying the same measures to a broad-based group of organizations with exemplary IT workflow management and support, the following findings became evident:

- Approximately 60% of the application enhancement requests being approved in the process had no business value.
- It was taking longer to approve work to be done than to actually do it.
- The organization had a hierarchical structure with seven levels; peer companies only had three layers.
- Support costs were 40% higher than would be expected and applications were almost twice as defect-prone compared to equivalents at other companies.
- Almost three times more staff was allocated to support the applications portfolio than was the average in the benchmark group.

Using the insights and observations obtained from the benchmarking project as a basis for setting IT performance targets, Bank X redeployed approximately 55% of its IT staff from support to new development while decreasing support cycle time by approximately 40%. The time frame for this radical change: 10 months.

Case 2. A multinational chemical company wanting to become more responsiveto environmental regulations while improving the quality of its applications portfolio. Company Y focused on its applications maintenance process complexity, productivity, and cycle time. Simultaneously, it assessed its entire portfolio from the vantage points of technical quality and functional quality. It also determined its current return-on-investment for its extensive suite of support and quality assurance tools. By doing a benchmark analysis with peer companies and vendors of packages in its industry, Company Y discovered that:

- Its maintenance processes were more serial in nature and had more bottlenecks than those in the comparison group.
- Technical quality of its applications was about 22% better than others, but functional quality was 35% worse. Customers were not benefiting from these technically high-quality systems.
- Tool penetration was low. The high technical quality of the applications could be attained with roughly 67% of the current level of effort if the toolsets were used as intended.

Within three months, Company Y had a program in place that reduced the cycle time of enacting a regulatory change from an average of four months to three weeks. In addition, specific functional quality targets were being set for each application. Skills upgrading and retraining of the staff was under way, with a target of increasing support productivity by 25%.

These two examples illustrate how benchmarking can be effective when the results are used for target setting and action. Benchmarking is not a passive activity, but one in which quantifiable findings must be turned into measurable gains. Benchmarking is also a continuous process.

BASELINING: THE LINK TO BUSINESS VALUE

Perhaps the biggest challenge facing IT organizations is to establish the link between their work efforts and business value. The starting point for making this happen is obtaining a total picture of the IT organization and relating it to the production of value for the business.

The key element in making the connection is the creation of an IT baseline—a quantitative view of where the IT organization is today—focusing on six basic factors that are the drivers of IT business value:

- The applications and project inventory.
- The management practices portfolio.
- The delivery process methodology.
- The technology infrastructure.
- The business-IT interface.

Once complete, the baseline provides a framework for comparing an organization against competitive benchmarks and a context for improvement and innovation.

Among the criticisms of baselining is that it is costly, time-consuming, and involves too much introspection. Resistance to measurement is quite widespread. Less than 10% of software-producing organizations worldwide have any kind of ongoing measurements program. Only one out of six organizations that start measurement programs is successful.

To be a success, a measurement program must be perceived by all to add value to the organization's processes and products, must supply information used for decision making and organizational learning (e.g., continuous process improvement), and must serve as a common basis for communication both within the IT organization and throughout the business itself. This definition of success fits with analyses undertaken by the Software Engineering Institute (SEI) of Carnegie Mellon University in Pittsburgh.

The SEI methodology classifies an organization's software process maturity into one of 5 levels. Level 1 is the Initial level, where there is no formalization of the software process; Level 5, by contrast, is the Optimizing level, where methods, procedures, and metrics are in place with a focus on continuous improvement. According to SEI studies, 80% to 86% of organizations in the US are at Level 1.

GETTING READY TO BENCHMARK

The ability and capability to measure is a prerequisite for benchmarking. The first step is to carefully assess the IT organization's "measurement readiness." Answers to the following questions can be a basis for setting the direction for the IT organization's measurement strategy; each answer is scaled from 0 to 5:

1. How intense is the organization's desire to improve its performance? 0—No desire; 5—Intense desire.
2. Is the enterprise willing to invest time and money to improve systems

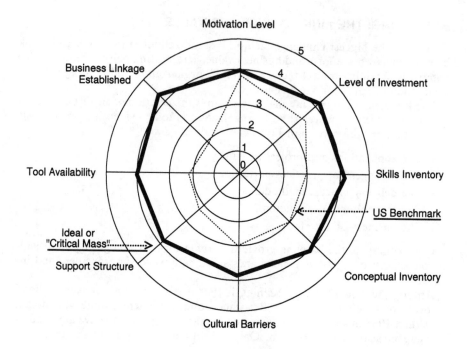

Exhibit VI-1-1. Measurement Readiness Profile

performance with measurement? 0—No; 5—The organization already allocates funds and people.

3. What is the level of the systems skill inventory for using metrics? 0—None; 5—Already in widespread use.

4. To what extent are measurement concepts known and understood by the systems staff? 0—No staff members have this knowledge; 5—Staff is 100% trained.

5. Is the systems culture opposed to using measurements at the organizational and individual level? 0—100% opposed; 5—Eager to implement.

6. To what extent is a support structure in place to foster measurement practices and perform metrics technology transfer? 0—No infrastructure; 5—An in-place team exists.

7. Are tools and repositories for acquiring and analyzing metrics data in place? 0—No; 5—A full suite and warehouse are available.

8. Does the systems organization understand its role in business processes? 0—No; 5—Yes, and it is documented and tracked through metrics.

Readers can chart their answers to these questions on Exhibit VI-1-1.

Actions for Beginners

If the answer to these questions is at the low end of the scale, the IT organization's measurement readiness is quite low. A good starting point is to contact professional societies so that experiences in measurement can be shared and exchanged. Readers can make contacts through the International Function Point User Group, the IEEE Computer Society, the Quality Assurance Institute, the Gartner Group, and at seminars offered by Digital Consulting and Software Quality Engineering.

Actions for Improving Readiness

If the IT organization's readiness is somewhat higher according to the readiness profile in Exhibit V-1-1, several actions should be taken in parallel.

First, IS management should reinforce the measurement infrastructure by acquiring automated tools to help with collection and analysis, then build a rapid baseline using the structure outlined in this chapter and produce a measurement program design. Next, it should embark on a 30-day mission to collect and analyze information using the 80/20 rule as a guide. The metrics findings for the baseline should be consolidated into a single page and should paint a picture of the six driver areas.

The baseline then has to be related to published benchmarks, translating the opportunities uncovered into business terms that will provide value from the efforts. This step brings focus to all the work and provides a platform for transformation and the ongoing use of measurement.

BUILDING A COMPLETE INFORMATION TECHNOLOGY BASELINE

IT productivity and quality measures do not in themselves provide a complete picture of IT performance. Establishing a baseline as a prelude to benchmarking goes beyond just productivity and quality. A complete baseline involves assessing an IT organization's current portfolio of projects and applications, its human resources and organizational structure, its management practices and processes, the technology infrastructure, and most important, business factors that drive the computing function.

The typical time it should take to construct such a baseline is approximately 30 to 60 days with a dedicated team of no more than three individuals (including consultants). The goal is to create a workable and useful organization profile rather than accomplish 100% complete data acquisition—the 80/20 rule applies here.

Six Baseline Components

A divide-and-conquer approach is needed for assessing the baseline performance of an organization; this means viewing the baseline as containing six key segments that can be combined into a single comprehensive picture.

Applications and Project Portfolio Baseline. The work performed by the software side of a typical IT organization takes the form of creating new software applications or modifications to existing applications. This baseline segment creates an inventory of the applications and current projects as they exist today "as is." Key descriptive information and metrics for each existing system and project underway includes:

- Demographics (e.g., age, language, implementation date, technology platform, and tools and techniques used).
- Financial history (e.g., cost to build, cost to maintain, cost to use, and cost to operate).
- Size (e.g., lines of code or function points counts).
- Support information (e.g., number of people on staff, number of requests, and average request size).
- Quality attributes, such as:
  - Rating of functional quality by the user (i.e., the ability to support user requirements in terms of functionality, accuracy, reliability, and data quality).
  - Rating of technical quality by systems staff (i.e., design strength, complexity, architecture, maintainability, portability, and interoperability).
  - Problem history.
  - Defects found per line of code or function point.
- Productivity attributes, such as:
  - Support ratios (e.g., lines of code or function points per support staff member).
  - Original delivery rate (e.g., lines of code or functions points per team member per month).

Systems Organization and Human Resources Baseline. This baseline segment provides a profile of the people side of the IT equation and the current organizational structure, including:

- Organizational chart (functional).
- Average managerial span of control.
- Human resources profile (e.g., skills inventory, educational inventory, training history, team and individual profiles such as Meyers-Briggs).
- Work distribution (i.e., percentage of people and dollars expended on development versus support).

Ultimately, this effort attempts to answer one question: Does the IT organization have the right resources to support the business today and into the future?

The production of an "organizational readiness" footprint, to determine the ability to assimilate new technology, is a major baseline output. This parallels the measurement readiness footprint used earlier (and shown in Exhibit VI-1-1) but concentrates on software technology instead of measurement. Assessment questions include:

1. How intense is the organization's desire to improve its performance? 0—No desire; 5—Intense desire.

2. How much is the organization willing to invest to improve its performance? 0—No investment; 5—Up to $100,000/professional.

3. What is the current level of the systems skills inventory in software engineering? 0—Abstractions and models not used at all; 5—Formalization and models used by all.

4. To what extent are basic software engineering concepts known and understood by the systems staff? 0—No staff members have been exposed to software engineering principles; 5—Staff is 100% trained.

5. Is the systems culture averse to using new tools, techniques, or innovations? 0—100% opposed; 5—Eager to implement.

6. To what extent is a support structure in place to foster measurement software engineering technology transfer? 0—Not in place; 5—An in-place team of critical mass exists.

7. What is the current software engineering platform? 0—Dumb terminals; 5—Client/server workstations.

8. What is the development and support split? 0—0% versus 100%; 5—100% versus 0%.

The results should be plotted on a circular scale similar to the measurement assessment. This time, however, it is necessary to plot where the IT organization should be in regard to either a particular technology (e.g., client/server) or the overall software process (e.g., SEI Level 1 through 5). The gaps that become apparent are those that need to be filled to transform an organization to where it should be.

Management Practices Baseline. The focus of this baseline segment is on how the existing resources perform work. It means gathering and summarizing answers to basic questions about management practices:

- How are planning and prioritizing done?
- How does the organization translate requests into systems?
- How well defined is the systems development life cycle?
- What is in the organization's tool inventory and what is actually used (i.e., tool penetration)?
- What is the organization's current software process maturity level? (This entails performing a formal or informal SEI assessment.)

This information is typically gathered through interviews and workshops conducted to assess the rigor, actual end use, and effectiveness of these practices themselves.

Delivery Process Baseline. This is the baseline segment in which specific representative development and maintenance projects are examined in detail to assess schedule and effort productivity and quality. However, it is often necessary to go beyond these issues and assess other factors likely to affect productivity and quality.

By determining delivery and support rates at the project level and comparing them to external benchmarks, an organization can create a framework to quantitatively assess the impact of potential changes and identify opportunities. Furthermore, the framework provides a clear basis for understanding the impact that tools potentially have on the overall delivery rate and product/process quality.

Typical metrics collected at the project level include:

- Lines of code or function points per professional by project size.
- Lines of code or function points per work month by project size.
- Defects per line of code or function discovered before and after implementation.
- Percentage of defects originating from each life cycle phase.
- Point in life cycle where defects were found.
- Percentage of defects removed by phase.

Technology Infrastructure Baseline. This segment of the baseline identifies current and proposed delivery and production environments. If a company is, for example, wrestling with the possibility of shifting from mainframe to workstation-based development to reduce cost while increasing productivity, the practical steps that must be taken to accomplish this transition are evaluated.

Business Factors Baseline. Perhaps the most important component of any baseline is mapping the link between the software engineering function and the business's performance itself. Executive interviews with major systems customers have to be undertaken to develop an understanding of the mix of internal and external factors that may be changing the business. Understanding the volatility of the customers' environment sets the stage for examining how the systems organization is aligned to support the business. In addition, interviews with key end users should be used to identify projects not currently being worked on that could provide a measurable difference in the way the business is run.

The essence of this baseline segment is to discover how business value is created by the systems area from the vantage point of the business. This step also sets the stage for defining business-value-level metrics.

The results of this baseline segment should be used to create a table that separates all the people interviewed into peer group audiences. For each audience the cross-reference table shows which performance assessment areas are essential. Another table can then be constructed to link each performance area to the measurements that support it. The resulting set of tables is essentially the IT organization's measurement program design document.

Making the Connection to Business Value

The baseline process illustrates a metrics dashboard. With proper instrumentation, it can be used to monitor and manage organizational performance as well as to clearly identify the system's contribution to business value.

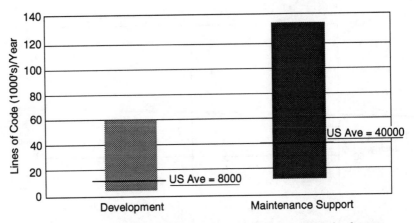

a. Using Lines of Code—Max/Min Observed Against the Average

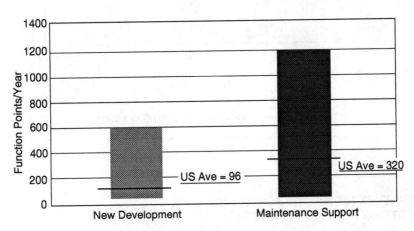

b. Using Function Points—Max/Min Observed Against the Average

Exhibit VI-1-2. Rating Development and Support Productivity

The exact business measures can be derived by extending the business factors baseline segment. If external business customers and internal business customers are included in addition to the IT audiences, a complete dashboard framework will be the result, showing what performance improvement looks like to each constituency and what the suitable indicators (metrics) are. Using this as a framework, two types of dashboards should be constructed—one containing the navigation gauges, the other containing the destination gauges used to declare success.

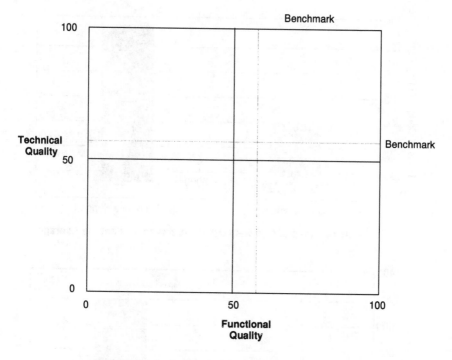

Exhibit VI-1-3. Application Portfolio Characteristics

USING EXTERNAL BENCHMARKS:
A STEP-BY-STEP APPROACH

If the IT baseline is constructed following the guidelines given, it then becomes possible to assess IT performance against best-in-class benchmarks. Exhibits VI-1-2 to VI-1-11 are tools to help readers create a baseline/benchmark snapshot. The steps to construct a snapshot of an IT organization are detailed next.

Applications Portfolio. Using Exhibit VI-1-2a (lines of code) or VI-1-2b (function points), mark a point for each application for which a support ratio is computed per support professional. Using Exhibit VI-1-3, fill in the percentage of the total portfolio that is in each of the following categories:

- Low functional quality (FQ) and low technical quality (TQ).
- High FQ and low TQ.
- Low FQ and high TQ.
- High FQ and high TQ.

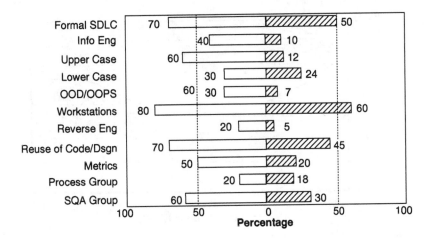

KEY:
⬜ % Using
▨ % Penetration

Exhibit VI-1-4. Tool/Technique Inventory: US Data

Technology Infrastructure. Using the inventory of tools and techniques in Exhibit VI-1-4, indicate what percentage of the target audience is properly employing each tool and technique in the intended manner at least 80% of the time.

Delivery Process. Mark a point on Exhibit VI-1-5a (lines of code) or VI-1-5b (function points) for each project that has been assessed in terms of delivered lines of code or function points per person month. Then, mark a point on Exhibit VI-1-6 that represents either the average number of postimplementation defects detected per function points or lines of code.

Management Practices. Using Exhibit VI-1-7, place an X in the segment that most clearly relates the IT organization's SEI process maturity rating.

Organization and Human Resources. On Exhibit VI-1-8, mark the point that shows the average span of control, then answer the organizational readiness assessment questions and plot the results on Exhibit VI-1-9. Using Exhibit VI-1-10, indicate the percentage of resources allocated to maintenance and development. At a more detailed level use Exhibit VI-1-11 to categorize the work as corrective, adaptive, and perfective maintenance.

When used together, Exhibits VI-1-2 through VI-1-11 provide a snapshot of conditions in the IT department. Though this picture does not take into account

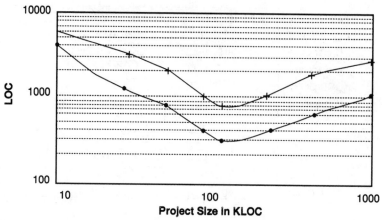

KEY:
+ Efficient
● Average

**a. Productivity in Thousands Lines of Code
(KLOC) per Staff Month**

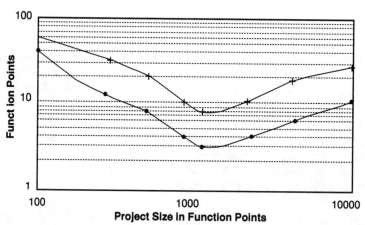

KEY:
+ Efficient
● Average

b. Productivity in Function Points per Staff Month

Exhibit VI-1-5. Rating Effort Productivity

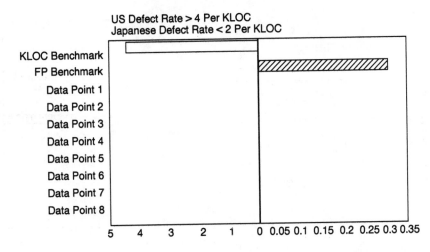

Exhibit VI-1-6. Defect Density

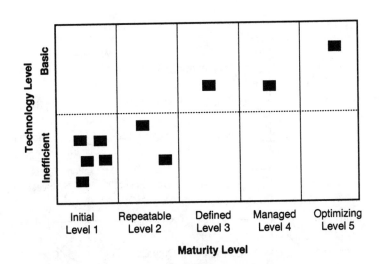

Note: *With the exception of the Level 5 point, each square represents 10 companies*

Exhibit VI-1-7. Software Process Maturity (US)

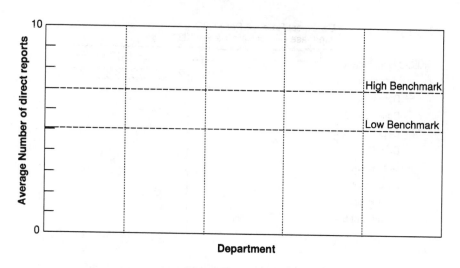

Exhibit VI-1-8. Span of Control

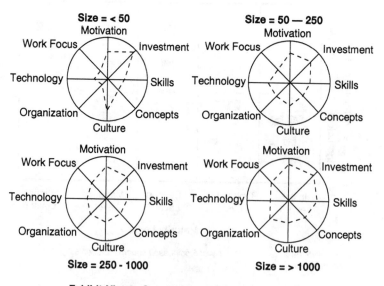

Exhibit VI-1-9. Organizational Readiness Profits

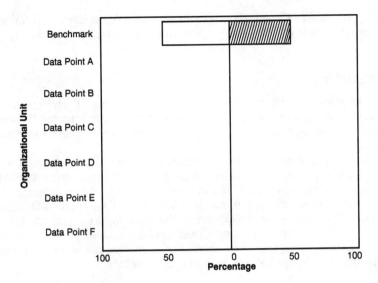

Exhibit VI-1-10. Development Versus Maintenance

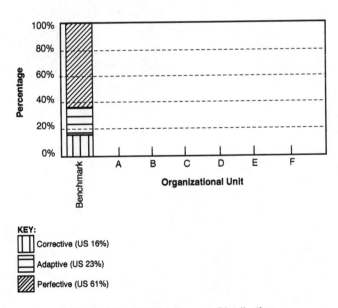

Exhibit VI-1-11. Maintenance Distribution

industry specifics, IT managers can still use the worksheets to get value from their baseline through comparisons with the benchmarks provided.

CONCLUSION

Benchmarking clearly provides a context for assessing IT performance, business contribution, and competitive positioning. The real issue for IT organizations is how to transform performance and produce business value through computing.

In the context of benchmarking, metrics are a core competency that an organization must develop to promote learning and continuous improvement. The road to a learning organization is a difficult and complex one. It starts with the basics—knowing where the business is, where it is going, and how it is going to get there. These issues are the essence of the benchmarking process.

IT organizations must transform their performance as business transforms. The benchmarking steps and worksheets in this chapter can be a tool and catalyst for making this change happen in the IT department.

VI-2

Control of Information Systems Outsourcing

S. Yvonne Scott

OUTSOURCING IS A REALITY. As an industry force that causes significant change in the established environment, it raises several issues that warrant the IS manager's attention. One of these issues stems from the fact that information—and the systems used to generate it—can differentiate a company from its competitors; therefore, information is a valuable asset worthy of protection. Increasing organizational reliance on outsourcing has thus created a new area of audit responsibility.

A MATURE CONCEPT

Outsourcing IS is not a new trend. The use of service bureaus, contract programmers, disaster recovery sites, data storage vendors, and value-added networks are all examples of outsourcing. There are even examples of entire large IS organizations being outsourced 25 years ago. Orange County CA did this in the mid-1970s.

Functions such as time-sharing, network management, software maintenance, applications processing, limited facilities management, full facility management, and EDI services are now considered potentially outsourced functions. In 1989, Eastman Kodak entered into a ten-year agreement to outsource its entire IF function, a deal worth an estimated $100 million.

Outsourcing is not a transfer of responsibility. Tasks and duties can be delegated, but responsibility remains with the organization's management. Therefore, outsourcing does not relieve the organization or management of the responsibility to provide IS services for internal operations and, in some cases, for customers.

Outsourcing is not an excuse for substandard customer service, regardless of whether the customers are internal or external to the organization. Customers do not care how or by whom services are provided. Their concern is that they receive the quality services they need, when they are needed.

The most successful outsourcing deals are tailored relationships that are built around specific business needs and strategies. There has been a definite shift from an all-or-nothing approach to a more selective application of outsourcing. In many cases, deals have been structured to more closely resemble partnerships or alliances rather than service agreements. For example, some of these deals include agreements to share in the profits and products that result from the alliance.

Outsourcing does not eliminate the need to audit the outsourced services. It is the auditor's responsibility to safeguard all of the assets of an organization. Because information is clearly an asset, the organization must ensure that information confidentiality, integrity, and availability are preserved.

OUTSOURCING SERVICES

Any agreement to obtain services from an outside vendor rather than to provide them internally meets the definition of outsourcing. The following list includes the types of IS outsourcing service contracts that the IS community is being required to address:

- Time-sharing and applications processing.
- Contract programming.
- Software and hardware maintenance.
- Contingency planning and disaster recovery planning and services.
- Systems development and project management.
- Electronic data interchange services.
- Network management.
- Reengineering services.
- Transitional services.
- Limited facilities management.
- Full facility management.
- Remote LAN management.

It should be noted that the first six services in this list have been outsourced for at least 20 years. The remainder of the list represents expansions of the other services. For example, facilities management is the use of time-sharing on a broader basis, and remote LAN management is hardware maintenance on a distributed basis.

WHY OUTSOURCE?

Outsourcing should be specifically tailored to the business needs of an organization. It appears to be most feasible for those organizations with the following characteristics:

- *Organizations in which IS is not a competitive tool.* If there is little opportunity for an organization to distinguish itself from its competition through systems applications or operations, there is less concern over entrusting the execution of these services to a third party.

- *Organizations in which short-term IS interruptions do not diminish the organization's ability to compete or remain in business.* An outsourcing vendor should be able to recover operations in one to two days. It is probably not reasonable to rely on a third party to recover complex systems within one to two hours. Contracts can be structured to specify that the outsourcer must recover within a one- to two-hour time frame or incur severe penalties. However, if the outsourcer fails to comply with the contract, it is unlikely that the penalty adequately compensates the organization for the long-term effects of losing customers. Therefore, the shorter the tolerable window of exposure, the less viable outsourcing becomes.

- *Organizations in which outsourcing does not eliminate critical internal knowledge.* If outsourcing eliminates internal resources that are key to the future innovations or products of the organization, the risk may be too great to assume.

- *Organizations in which existing IS capabilities are limited or ineffective.* If this is the case and the organization is considering outsourcing, management has probably determined that additional investments must be made in the area of IS. In this situation, it may make more sense to buy the required expertise than to build it.

- *Organizations in which there is a low reward for IS excellence.* In this case, even if the organization developed and operated the most effective and efficient information systems the payback would be minimal. Because every organization must capitalize on its assets to survive, the effort that would be expended could probably be spent more wisely in other areas.

MOTIVATING FACTORS

Companies have various reasons for outsourcing. Just as the outsourcing agreement itself should be tailored to the individual circumstances, the factors that cause an organization to achieve its objectives through outsourcing are unique.

It is important to understand these motivating factors when evaluating whether a particular solution meets an organization's objectives. In addition, as in all cases in which the IS manager has an opportunity to participate in the solution of a business problem (e.g., systems development audits), it is important to understand the overall objectives. To add value to the process, these objectives and their potential shortcomings should be considered when evaluating whether the outsourcing agreement maximizes asset use and maintains the control environment. For this reason, the motivating factors often cited by management, as well as some of the reasons why these objectives may not be readily met, are discussed in the following sections.

Cost Savings. As the global economy grows, management faces increased competition on reduced budgets. The savings are generally believed to be achievable through outsourcing by increasing efficiency (e.g., staff reductions, shared resources). However, several factors may preclude cost savings. Comparable reductions in service levels and product quality may occur, and comparable staff reductions may not be reflected in decreased fees to outsourcers. In addition, vendors may not achieve the economies of scale previously gained through shared hardware because many software vendors have changed licensing agreements to vary with the size of the hardware.

Fixed Cost versus Variable Cost. In some cases, management has been driven to a fixed-cost contract for its predictability. However, service levels may decrease as the cost of providing those services increases. In addition, should business needs dictate a reduction in information systems, the company may be committed to contracted fees.

Flexible IS Costs. Management may have indicated that outsourcing is preferred because it allows management to adjust its IS costs as business circumstances change. However, necessary revisions in service levels and offerings may not be readily available through the vendor at prices comparable to those agreed on for existing services.

Dissatisfaction with Internal Performance. Dissatisfaction is often cited by senior management because it has not seen the increases in revenue and market share nor the increased productivity and cost reductions used to justify projects. Many outsourcing agreements, however, include provisions to transfer employees to the outsourcer. The net result may be that the personnel resources do not change significantly.

Competitive Climate. Speed, flexibility, and efficiency are often considered the keys to competitive advantage. By outsourcing the IS function, personnel resources can be quickly adjusted to respond to business peaks and valleys. However, the personnel assigned to respond to the business needs that determine the organization's competitive position may not be well acquainted with the company's business and its objectives. In addition, short-term cost savings achieved through reactive systems development may lead to long-term deficiencies in the anticipation of the information systems needs of both internal and external customers.

Focus on Core Business. Outsourcing support functions such as IS allows management to focus on its primary business. If IS is integral to the product offering or the competitive advantage of the organization, however, a shift in focus away from this component of the core business may lead to long-term competitive disadvantage.

Capital Availability and Emerging Technologies. Senior management does not want to increase debt or use available capital to improve or maintain the IS function. If IS is proactive and necessary to support the strategic direction of the organization, however, delaying such investments may result in a competitive disadvantage. In addition, precautions must be taken to ensure that the outsourcing vendor continues to provide state-of-the-art technology.

Staff Management and Training. Outsourcing eliminates the need to recruit, retain, and train IS personnel. This becomes the responsibility of the vendor. But regardless of who these individuals report to, IS personnel need to receive training on the latest technologies in order to remain effective. After control over this process is turned over to a vendor, provisions should be made to ensure that training continues. In addition, the cost of this training is not actually eliminated. Because the vendor is in business to turn a profit, the cost of training is included in the price proposal. In addition, this cost is likely to be inflated by the vendor's desired profit margin.

Transition Management. As mergers and acquisitions take place, senior management views outsourcing as a means to facilitate the integration of several different hardware platforms and application programs. In addition, some managers are using outsourcing as a means to facilitate the organization's move to a new processing environment (e.g., client/server). However, knowledge of strategic information systems should not be allowed to shift to an outside vendor if the long-term intention is to retain this expertise within the organization. In such cases, the maintenance of existing systems should be transferred to the outsourcer during the transition period.

Reduction of Risk. Outsourcing can shift some of the business risks associated with capital investment, technological change, and staffing to the vendor. Because of decreased hands-on control, however, security risks may increase.

Accounting Treatment. Outsourcing allows the organization to remove IS assets from the balance sheet and begin to report these resources as a nondepreciable line item (e.g., rent). The organization should ensure that outsourcing is not being used as a means of obtaining a capital infusion that does not appear as balance sheet debt. This can be achieved if the outsource vendor buys the organization's IS assets at book (rather than market) value. The difference is paid back through the contract and, therefore, represents a creative means of borrowing funds.

All of these driving forces can be valid reasons for senior management to enter into an outsourcing arrangement. It should be noted that the cautions discussed in the previous sections are not intended to imply that outsourcing is undesirable. Rather, they are highlighted here to allow the reader to enter into the most advantageous outsourcing agreement possible. As a result, these cautions should be kept in mind when control measures are considered.

CONTROL MEASURES

Although it is desirable to build a business partnership with the outsource vendor, it is incumbent on the organization to ensure that the outsourcer is legally bound to take care of the company's needs. Standard contracts are generally written to protect the originator (i.e., the vendor). Therefore, it is important to critically review these agreements and ensure that they are modified to include provisions that adequately address the following issues.

Retention of Adequate Audit Rights. It is not sufficient to generically specify that the client has the right to audit the vendor. If the specific rights are not detailed in the contract, the scope of a review may be subject to debate. To avoid this confusion and the time delays that it may cause, it is suggested that, at a minimum, the following specific rights be detailed in the contract:

- Who can audit the outsourcer (i.e., client internal auditors, outsourcer internal auditors, independent auditors, user-controlled audit authority).
- What is subject to audit (e.g., vendor invoices, physical security, operating system security, communications costs, and disaster recovery tests).
- When the outsourcer can or cannot be audited.
- Where the audit is to be conducted (e.g., at the outsourcer's facility, remotely by communications).
- How the audit is conducted (i.e., what tools and facilities are available).
- Guaranteed access to the vendor's records, including those that substantiate billing.
- Read-only access to all of the client company's data.
- Assurance that audit software can be executed.
- Access to documentation.
- Long-term retention of vendor records to prevent destruction.

Continuity of Operations and Timely Recovery. The time frames within which specified operations must be recovered, as well as each party's responsibilities to facilitate the recovery, should be specified in the contract. In addition, the contract should specify the recourse that is available to the client, as well as who is responsible for the cost of carrying out any alternative action, should the outsourcer fail to comply with the contract requirements. Special consideration should be given to whether these requirements are reasonable and likely to be carried out successfully.

Cost and Billing Verification. Only those costs applicable to the client's processing should be included in invoices. This issue is particularly important for those entering into outsourcing agreements that are not on a fixed-charge basis. Adequate documentation should be made available to allow the billed client to determine the appropriateness and accuracy of invoices. However, documentation is also important to those clients who enter into a fixed invoice arrangement. In such cases, knowing the actual cost incurred by the outsourcer allows the client to effectively negotiate a fair price when prices are open for renegotiation.

It should also be noted that, although long-term fixed costs are beneficial in those cases in which costs and use continue to increase, they are equally detrimental in those situations in which costs and use are declining. Therefore, it is beneficial to include a contract clause that allows rates to be reviewed at specified intervals throughout the life of the contract.

Security Administration. Outsourcing may be used as an agent for change and, therefore, may represent an opportunity to enhance the security environment. In any case, decisions must be made regarding whether the administration (i.e., granting access to data) and the monitoring (i.e., violation reporting and follow-up) should be retained internally or delegated to the outsourcer. In making this decision, it is imperative that the company have confidence that it can maintain control over the determination of who should be granted access and in what capacity (e.g., read, write, delete, execute) to both its data and that of its customers.

Confidentiality, Integrity, and Availability. Care must be taken to ensure that both data and programs are kept confidential, retain their integrity, and are available when needed. These requirements are complicated when the systems are no longer under the physical control of the owning entity. In addition, the concerns that this situation poses are further compounded when applications are stored and executed on systems that are shared with other customers of the outsourcer. Of particular concern is the possibility that proprietary data and programs may be resident on the same physical devices as those of a competitor. Fortunately, technology has provided us with the ability to logically control and separate these environments with virtual machines (e.g., IBM's Processor Resource/System Management). It should also be noted that the importance of confidentiality does not necessarily terminate with the vendor relationship. Therefore, it is important to obtain nondisclosure and noncompete agreements from the vendor as a means of protecting the company after the contract expires. Similarly, adequate data retention and destruction requirements must be specified.

Program Change Control and Testing. The policies and standards surrounding these functions should not be relaxed in the outsourced environment. These controls determine whether confidence can be placed in the integrity of the organization's computer applications.

Vendor Controls. The physical security of the data center should meet the requirements set by the American Society for Industrial Security. In addition, there should be close compatibility between the vendor and the customer with regard to control standards.

Network Controls. Because the network is only as secure as its weakest link, care must be taken to ensure that the network is adequately secured. It should be noted that dial-up capabilities and network monitors can be used to circumvent established controls. Therefore, even if the company's operating data is not proprietary, measures should be taken to ensure that unauthorized users cannot gain access to the system. This should minimize the risks associated with unauthorized data, program modifications, and unauthorized use of company resources (e.g., computer time, phone lines).

Personnel. Measures should be taken to ensure that personnel standards are not relaxed after the function is turned over to a vendor. As was noted earlier, in many cases the same individuals who were employed by the company are hired by the vendor to service that contract. Provided that these individuals are competent, this should not pose any concern. If, however, a reason cited for outsourcing is to improve the quality of personnel, this situation may not be acceptable. In addition, care should be taken to ensure that the client company is notified of any significant personnel changes, security awareness training is continued, and the client company is not held responsible should the vendor make promises (e.g., benefits, salary levels, job security) to the transitional employees that it does not subsequently keep.

Vendor Stability. To protect itself from the possibility that the vendor may withdraw from the business or the contract, it is imperative that the company maintain ownership of its programs and data. Otherwise, the client may experience an unexpected interruption in its ability to service its customers or the loss of proprietary information.

Strategic Planning. Because planning is integral to the success of any organization, this function should be performed by company employees. Although it may be necessary to include vendor representatives in these discussions, it is important to ensure that the company retains control over the use of IS in achieving it objectives. Because many of these contracts are long-term and business climates often change, this requires that some flexibility be built into the agreement to allow for the expansion or contraction of IS resources.

In addition to these specific areas, the following areas should also be addressed in the contract language:

- Definition and assignment of responsibilities.
- Performance requirements and the means by which compliance is measured.
- Recourse for nonperformance.
- Contract termination provisions and vendor support during any related migration to another vendor or in-house party.
- Warranties and limitations of liability.
- Vendor reporting requirements.

PROTECTIVE MEASURES DURING TRANSITION

After it has been determined that the contractual agreement is in order, a third-party review should be performed to verify vendor representations. After the contract has been signed and as functions are being moved from internal departments to the vendor, an organization can enhance the process by performing the following:

- Meeting frequently with the vendor and employees.
- Involving users in the implementation.
- Developing transition teams and providing them with well-defined responsibilities, objectives, and target dates.
- Increasing security awareness programs for both management and employees.
- Considering a phased implementation that includes employee bonuses for phase completion.
- Providing outplacement services and severance pay to displaced employees.

CONTINUING PROTECTIVE MEASURES

As the outsourcing relationship continues, the client should continue to take proactive measures to protect its interests. These measures may include continued security administration involvement, budget reviews, ongoing reviews and testing of environment changes, periodic audits and security reviews, and letters of agreement and supplements to the contract. Each of these client rights should be specified in the contract. In addition, a continuing review and control effort typically includes the following types of audit objectives:

- Establishing the validity of billings (IBM's Systems Management Facility type-30 records can be used).
- Evaluating system effectiveness and performance. (IBM's Resource Management Facility indicates the percentage of time the central processing unit is busy. As use increases, costs may rise because of higher paging requirements.)
- Reviewing the integrity, confidentiality, and availability of programs and data.
- Verifying that adequate measures have been made to ensure continuity of operations.
- Reviewing the adequacy of the overall security environment.
- Determining the accuracy of program functionality.

AUDIT ALTERNATIVES

It should be noted that resource sharing (i.e., the sharing of common resources with other customers of the vendor) may lead to the vendor's insistence that the audit rights of individual clients be limited. This is reasonable. However, performance review by the internal audit group of the client is only one means of approaching the control requirement. The following alternative measures can be taken to ensure that adequate control can be maintained.

Internal Reviews by the Vendor. In this case, the outsourcing vendor's own internal audit staff would perform the reviews and report their results to the customer base. Auditing costs are included in the price, the auditor is familiar with the operations, and it is less disruptive to the outsourcer's operations. However, auditors are employees of the audited entity; this may limit independence and objectivity, and clients may not be able to dictate audit areas, scope, or timing.

External Auditor or Third-Party Review. These types of audits are normally performed by an independent accounting firm. This firm may or may not be the same firm that performs the annual audit of the vendor's financial statements. In addition, the third-party reviewer may be hired by the client or the vendor. External auditors may be more independent than employees of the vendor. In addition, the client can negotiate for the ability to exercise some control over the selection of the third-party auditors and the audit areas, scope, and timing, and the cost can be shared among participating clients. The scope of external reviews, however, tends to be more general in nature than those performed by internal auditors. In addition, if the auditor is hired by the vendor, the perceived level of independence of the auditor may be impaired. If the auditor is hired by each individual client, the costs may be duplicated by each client and the duplicate effort may disrupt vendor operations.

User-Controlled Audit Authority. The audit authority typically consists of a supervisory board comprising representatives from each participating client company, the vendor, and the vendor's independent accounting firm and a staff comprising some permanent and temporary members who are assigned from each of the participating organizations. The staff then performs audits at the direction of the supervisory board. In addition, a charter, detailing the rights and responsibilities of the user controlled audit authority, should be developed and accepted by the participants before commissioning the first review.

This approach to auditing the outsourcing vendor appears to combine the advantages and minimize the disadvantages previously discussed. In addition, this approach can benefit the vendor by providing a marketing advantage, supporting its internal audit needs, and minimizing operational disruptions.

CONCLUSION

Outsourcing arrangements are as unique as those companies seeking outsourcing services. Although outsourcing implies that some control must be turned over to the vendor, many measures can be taken to maintain an acceptable control environment and adequate review. Some basic rules can be followed to ensure a successful arrangement. These measures include:

- Segmenting the organization's IS activities into potential outsource modules (e.g., by technology, types of processing, or businesses served).
- Using analysis techniques to identify those modules that should be outsourced.
- Controlling technology direction setting.

- Treating outsourcing as a partnership, but remembering that the partner's objective is to maximize its own profits.
- Matching the organization's business needs with the outsource partner's current and prospective capabilities (e.g., long-term viability, corporate culture, management philosophy, business and industry knowledge, flexibility, technology leadership, and global presence).
- Ensuring that all agreements are in writing.
- Providing for continuing review and control.

The guidelines discussed in this chapter should be combined with the client's own objectives to develop individualized and effective control.

VI-3

Ensuring Quality in Computer Learning

Ann Shelton Angel

OVER THE PAST 20 YEARS, leaders in the field of adult education have developed a clearer understanding of the methods and motivational factors that create a positive learning environment for adults. This work has been coined *andragogy* to compare with *pedagogy*, which has for years been the model for childhood education theory. We understand through the work of Dr. Malcom Knowles and others that there are critical differences between the learning patterns of adults and those of children. Exhibit VI-3-1 outlines Knowles's assumptions about the adult learner and processes that take place in adult learning.

In the corporate world, training focuses on the skills required to accomplish a job. The essential ingredients to remember in developing programs to teach computer skills are getting the right person in the right class at the right time. Quality training is ensured through careful planning.

AUDIENCE ANALYSIS

The first step in planning is to determine the user's current level of knowledge and the expectation of application requirements through a questionnaire or interview. This need not be extremely time-consuming, though the more that is known about the learner, the better the chances for successful planning. This information provides a clearer idea of how many classes to plan and what levels of training to provide.

Research on adult learning styles had shown that people vary greatly in the way they approach the learning process. Some people do very well in a tutorial or video-based self-study program. Others insist that a classroom environment in which an instructor is available is the only way they can learn. Trainers should provide both delivery methods so that the adult learner can choose the delivery method that works best for his or her particular learning style. Exhibit VI-3-2 outlines sample questions trainers can use to help identify particular learning preferences.

ASSUMPTIONS ABOUT THE LEARNER

View of Student or Trainee	Self-directed
Experience	Rich experience
	Incomplete, unfinished tasks
Readiness	Self-achievement
	Responsibilities
Time View	It is needed now!
Orientation to Learning	Problem-centered training
Acceptance or Need	Personal pressure, need satisfaction

PROCESSES IN LEARNING

Diagnosis of Needs	Mutual diagnosis
Setting of Objectives	Mutual negotiation through learning contracts
Planning and Timing	Joint planning; timing is critical
Design	Sequences in terms of readiness and usefulness Varied resources Problem units with practice or simulation
Climate	Mutual respect, participatory, open Students are encouraged to make judgments Informal and collaborative Teacher is facilitator Student competes only with himself or herself
Activities	Discussion Discovery, hands-on Simulations Experience Transfer of learning
Evaluation	Mutual evaluation Job and life performance

Exhibit VI-3-1. Knowles's View of Adult Learning (Andragogy)

1. When faced with learning a new skill, which circumstance seems to work best:
One on one with the teacher _____
Small class in which the group shares experiences _____
Large class in which there is autonomy, but still an instructor is present _____
Computer-based tutorial _____
Reading a manual and figuring it out alone _____

This question asks whether the end user is a dependent or independent learner. (Experience with other computer systems is often a strong part of this confidence level.)

2. Do you understand new ideas better when:
There are lots of graphics and pictures demonstrating the idea or concept_____
Someone reads about or explains the concept before you try it _____
You can read the instructions without any interference from anyone_____

This question asks whether the end user is a visual or auditory learner and if the trainer needs to prepare intricate visual aids.

3. Which statement fits you the best:
I like to get the feel of something by talking about it before I try to do it_____
Once I get the big picture in my mind I am more apt to tackle the task _____
I like to take lots of notes and I hate it when someone rushes me_____
I jump right in and see if I can figure it out before the teacher finishes the presentation _____

This question asks whether the end user needs to interact with the instructor and other peers to learn.

SOURCE: David Kolb, McBer & Co, Boston

Exhibit VI-3-2. Identifying Learning Preferences

CURRICULA AND DELIVERY METHOD

Because training should target the level of the learner, a curriculum must allow for progression of learning and skill development. Establishing prerequisites for each level or class is critical; many trainers and learners have suffered when novices and intermediate learners participate in the same class. Adults want to feel at ease in a learning environment, and the single most important factor in accomplishing that is for them to know that everyone in the class is at a similar skill level. Trainers often hear end users say, "I don't want to be the only stupid one in the class." Of course, the person is not stupid—only inexperienced in working with computers, but to the adult ego that translates as stupid.

Another way to group learners is by work group or by peer status. For example, a word processing curriculum for professionals should include different functions than one for secretaries. A class exclusively for executives is often appropriate because executives have a strong need to preserve their image or credibility with subordinates and are typically ill-at-ease with subordinates in the class. It may even be worthwhile to use an outside trainer for executive-level students to remove the status barrier for internal trainers.

A common division of class levels is introductory, intermediate, and advanced, but these designations can often be arbitrary and unclear. A useful rule of thumb is to cover the basic skills required to construct and print a simple letter or spreadsheet in an introductory class. The intermediate level should address skills that will expand the capability of the end user to perform such tasks as using business graphics within spreadsheets or merging elements in word processing. Advanced-level courses can push into the bells and whistles of more sophisticated software.

Dividing training into smaller, more specific components lets end users sign up for the element that meets their need and therefore helps ensure that all attendees are at the appropriate level for the class. Exhibit VI-3-3 shows how a spreadsheet curriculum might be so divided. Setting a maximum number of people in a classroom enables the instructor to provide quality of learning. Six to eight students is ideal.

TIMING

Statistics show that timing is a critical part of the learning process. Because of the need to practice new skills without delay, classes should be scheduled when the hardware and software are available immediately after class. A training class can only accelerate the learning; most learning occurs as those skills are applied in the work environment. Ideally, trainers should work with the supervisors of the trainees before the class to create applications that will use the new skills when the trainee returns to the job.

Training must also take place early enough for the skills to be developed before productivity is critical. That is, if a project begins in six weeks, training on a new tool that is to be used as part of the project should occur far enough ahead to allow the end user to develop the skill and become productive by the time the project starts. A high level of productivity rarely occurs immediately.

Whenever possible, the trainer should address the application requirements directly in the class through exercises or case studies that are specific to the particular group of learners. An excellent technique is to require that a project be completed and turned in before a training certificate is received.

MANAGING THE EXPECTATIONS OF MANAGEMENT

Too often, the managers of employees sent to a computer training class have no knowledge of the software. These managers can benefit from having at least an overview of applications that could be produced by the employees as well as other more advanced capabilities of the software. This helps the manager make intelligent assignments for the employees and develop realistic expectations (e.g., not expecting a person who has just completed an introductory course to be able to produce a published newsletter).

INTRODUCTION TO SPREADSHEETS (7 hours, 2 sessions)

Objectives:
- Learn to create spreadsheets and formulas and to format data.
- Learn to print spreadsheets.

Prerequisite courses: Introduction to microcomputers, DOS and disk management

INTRODUCTION FOR MANAGERS (7 hours, 2 sessions)

Objective:
- Learn to use Lotus to build a budget and track monthly expenditures by using a preconstructed template.

Prerequisite courses: Introduction to microcomputers, DOS and disk management

GRAPHICS (3 hours, 1 session)

Objectives:
- Learn to create graphs and charts based on the data in a spreadsheet.
- Learn which type of graph to use to accurately portray data.
- Learn how to print graphs.

Prerequisite course: Introduction to spreadsheets

DATA BASE FUNCTIONS IN A SPREADSHEET (7 hours, 2 sessions)

Objectives:
- Learn the basics of data base management concepts.
- Learn to sort, find, and extract data.
- Learn to design reports.

Prerequisite course: Introduction to spreadsheets

ADVANCED FEATURES (3½ hours, 1 session)

Objectives:
- Learn advanced formula construction and various @ Functions.
- Learn about data ranges and how to use them.
- Master linking files.
- Learn to import and export files.

Prerequisite course: Introduction to spreadsheets

MACRO PROGRAMMING (7 hours, 2 sessions)

Objectives:
- Learn the concepts of macro programming and how they apply to spreadsheets.
- Learn to create and keyboard macros.
- Create interactive macros.
- Learn to test and debug macros.

Prerequisite courses: Introduction to spreadsheets, spreadsheet data base, and advanced functions

SPREADSHEET PUBLISHING (3½ hours, 1 session)

Objectives:
- Learn to understand WYSIWYG.
- Learn to use the formatting features such as fonts and shading.

Prerequisite course: Introduction to Spreadsheets

Exhibit VI-3-3. Sample Spreadsheet Curriculum

The manager can encourage management buy-in to training by discussing applications and the training required to accomplish these applications with managers and involving them in planning application exercises whenever possible. This interaction with the project may inspire managers to become more productive with their own computers.

For managers who are reluctant to spend time or money on providing training for their employees, the IS managers can easily develop statistics that show the cost in lost productivity when no training occurs compared to the cost of the training program. Securing senior management support for training is well worth the effort. In fact, when rolling out a corporatewide or departmentwide system, IS managers should start the program with senior management. Any system has better results when management uses it and pushes use downward.

Often the biggest battle with management is over the length of training. IS managers must work to convince management that effective training cannot be done quickly. If management is set on having only four hours of training, the trainer should plan a four-hour course that will address only the bare essentials but from which trainees can set out on their own or ask for more training. It is almost impossible to train someone to use a software product even at the basic level in such a short time. Seven to eight hours is a minimum. Trainers who promise to deliver training to 14 people in 3 hours are setting themselves up for failure.

COURSE MATERIAL

Once the right person is in the right class at the right time, details about course material must be decided. The risk with using training programs produced by third-party vendors is that they may not be perfectly applicable to the individual company. In addition, many trainers have found that careful examination of training materials from even the most reputable company has revealed poor editing and error-ridden examples. If such an examination does not occur far enough in advance, instructors must prepare at a frantic pace.

Courseware modules that are available in electronic form can be extremely beneficial for providing customized training. Several vendors offer their courses this way, and with them the trainer can build manuals in the exact content preferred. Customization can be done for any group without extra expense.

As previously mentioned, trainers should plan to have a variety of media available for different types of learners. Computer-based training (CBT) tutorials can be used as a preview for classroom training or standalone training for advanced learners. Interactive video or video concepts with hands-on modules and exercises are great tools, but they are confining for larger groups.

Reference materials must be available for ongoing support. Too often in LAN environments, end users do not have access to their own set of manuals. In such a case, the trainer should at least provide some job aids and quick reference guides for end users. It is less expensive to provide these than to staff help desks.

INSTRUCTION GUIDELINES

Effective instructors are made, not born, though some traits make a person a better candidate to be a trainer than others. Excellent communication skills and patience are two of the most important skills. Too many potential trainers suffer from the delusion that if someone knows computers and the software, they can train. In fact, it is often preferable for the IS manager to hire trainers with proven classroom skills and teach them the software.

The following tips can help trainers excel in the classroom:

- *Use humor.* Put the computer magic in its place and encourage the student to have fun.
- *Use props.* Have a Nerf bat for the student to hit the pesky microcomputer with.
- *Assign seats.* Put slow learners in front and fast learners in the back. It may also help to set up teams.
- *Give positive feedback only.* Never criticize either the question asked or the asker.
- *Identify potential problems.* For example, a self-taught technocrat in a class of novices can be quite disruptive. To prevent problems, have the person demonstrate applications to the group during the break. This adds to that person's self-esteem and is likely to keep him or her out of everyone's hair during class.
- *Be honest.* Trainers should offer to find out the answers to any questions they cannot answer and to get back to the students.
- *Check for feedback.* Ask questions about topics previously covered and get the students involved.
- *Let the class dictate the speed of the learning.* Just making sure all the material has been covered is not effective training.
- *Teach to the course level.* Do not get lured into more advanced discussion by more advanced students.

SETTING A CLIMATE FOR LEARNING

The chart in Exhibit VI-3-4 resembles Maslow's hierarchy of needs; it is the hierarchy of conditions that must be met before optimum learning conditions are achieved. The physical needs of temperature and space are on the bottom rung. The next rung requires the instructor to set up parameters of behavior—housekeeping rules as they are sometimes called. For example, the trainer should make it clear that telephone calls should be made only during breaks. Expectations about learning outcomes or project requirements should be explained so the students know what is coming. The trainer should also plan creative ways to give individual recognition during the learning process; a fun way is to give inexpensive gifts or treats to those who participate in discussion, answer questions, or finish their project first.

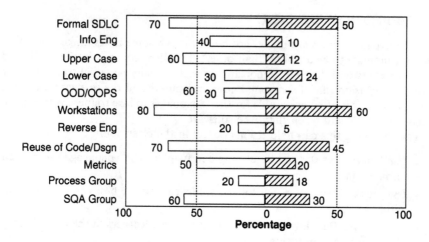

Exhibit VI-3-4. Hierarchy of Conditions for Learning to Occur

TESTING

People who have actively participated in the learning process have been known to freeze when confronted with an open book test. Testing, especially a multiple-choice written test, is not the way to measure learning. The real test is whether end users can apply what they have learned back on the job. Requiring a project or case study to be completed before the course is finished is a useful first step, but many end users still want some kind of evaluation form to show their managers.

One way is to use a form that asks the students to review the learning objectives before the class begins and to rate their knowledge of those objectives. At the end of the class they go back to the form and evaluate their acquired skills on each objective. Although this is a subjective way of measuring learning, it provides immediate feedback on how the trainee perceived the information. An internal training department can use effective long-term techniques. For example, the trainer can ask end users to submit their on-the-job applications and then evaluate the trainee's technique and use of software.

CONCLUSION

The following techniques can help trainers evaluate learning and motivate students to learn:

- Set up a library of innovative or commonly used applications to be available as templates.
- Let users submit ideas and articles for the support group newsletter to give them recognition.
- Have a creative application of the month award.
- Report to management regarding the training evaluations.
- Set up a certification program that will give end users a certificate of proficiency after completion of a curriculum.
- Establish in-house user groups. These can:
  — Increase user productivity by providing a forum for sharing tips and tricks.
  — Reach new computer users.
  — Boost user self-sufficiency.
  — Encourage the development of reference materials.

VI-4

An Advanced Strategy for Combatting Viruses

Joseph Piazza

IN 1988 there were a grand total of three DOS-based computer viruses, which at that time were considered a nuisance for the most part. Their signature strings were obvious as was their method of attack and their target. As such, they were easily detected, and their eradication was simple.

Eight years later, more than 3,000 viruses are threatening the very core of our data integrity. Viruses have evolved into sophisticated, devastatingly destructive forms of malicious code that are just as astonishing in their capabilities as the most advanced legitimate applications. Viruses can change identities every time they execute. They can intercept the video signal so that the user cannot see the warning given by antivirus software. They can remove themselves from any infected file that is being checked by antivirus software. Viruses know the search strings of specific brands of antivirus software and will target them or use them as a trigger. Viruses can tunnel under antivirus software to avoid detection.

Not only are viruses more advanced, but so too is the computing environment in which they operate. Migration from mainframe to distributed processing amplifies the potential harm that can be caused by any single virus. In combination, these developments have created the perfect formula for catastrophe.

Despite the dangers, many IS professionals continue to deny the seriousness of the problem posed by computer viruses. At best, they are content to rely on scanners. Unfortunately, the reputation of scanners is based solely on their early successes. Blind reliance on scanners is comparable to dependence on door locks to protect valuables. Such a single strategy approach will deter only the most primitive of attackers.

Technologists are searching for a silver bullet cure that does not exist for this or any other security problem. Viruses must be dealt with in the same manner as any problem. What is needed is a diversified combination of techniques that offer multiple layers of defenses that compensate for weaknesses in each other. Any asset protection model requires such a multifaceted approach, yet in the area of LAN security, practitioners continue to naively rely on one technique.

This chapter presents a discussion of the strengths and weaknesses of various antivirus strategies and suggests a diversified approach to virus control. Before discussing these strategies, however, some basic terms and concepts regarding virus targets, attack mechanisms, and tools should be discussed.

DEFINING TERMS

The hard disk drive provides information about its physical parameters and logical partition setup through the use of several records. The first is called the *master boot record*. The master boot record provides information on the number of heads, sectors, and cylinders available on the drive. It also defines the number of logical partitions, size and location within a drive. A hard disk drive can have several logical partitions (i.e., logical drives) within one physical drive.

Additional information about the data contained on the hard disk drive resides within each partition. The additional data information includes the DOS boot records, file allocation tables (FATs), the root directory, and the actual data sectors. Each of these areas may be subject to attack by malicious code or a virus. The DOS boot record contains information about the operating system, the size of the FAT, and the logical makeup of the partition. The FAT is a "look-up" table that points to where the data sectors reside throughout the logical partition for a specific file. The root directory stores the file names and additional subdirectories, if any. The data sectors contain the actual data of the file. Each sector is usually of a fixed size (e.g., 512 bytes per sector).

AVENUES OF ATTACK

Generally, there are two main objectives for a virus attack, and a virus can have one or both of these objectives. The first objective is to propagate or replicate and attach itself to other files. The second is to cause some type of unexpected action to happen. This action can be as deadly as destroying a target area or as benign as displaying a message on the monitor.

Two avenues of attack are currently used by viruses and malicious code to gain unauthorized access to microcomputers. They can be categorized as *disk-resident*, and *memory-resident attacks*, on the basis of the location of the targets of each type of attack. *Disk-resident* targets are targets that reside on the hard disk drive. Because such key information sectors as the master boot record, the DOS boot record, and file allocation tables reside in specific locations on a hard drive, viruses can be easily programmed to locate these sectors. For example, in DOS systems the master boot record is always found on cylinder 0, track 0, head 0 on a hard disk drive. These sectors become targets for modification and destruction by virtue of their standardization. Attacks to these key areas can render all information on the hard disk drives useless.

Memory-resident targets reside in system memory. These targets are the DOS, Basic Input/Output Services (BIOS) and hardware registers. When input-output (I/O) operations are performed, such as reading or writing a file to the hard disk drive, the application program usually calls a routine from the MS-DOS operating system. Use of the DOS routines relieves the application of having to specify the actual mechanics of storing and retrieving data from the application program. This application I/O function is accomplished by generating a software interrupt to call the DOS-level routine. The DOS routine then generates an interrupt that calls a lower-level software routine at the BIOS level. The BIOS routine then executes the necessary reads and writes to the actual hardware registers that control the hard disk drive. Unauthorized attacks can occur when the virus or a Trojan horse calls any of these memory-resident targets.

At the DOS level, the attack can occur by a call to Interrupt 21 (Int21). The call to Int21 gives a program access to a host of general services such as disk read/write operations.

Because some antivirus programs monitor the use of DOS interrupts, an attack can occur below the DOS level by calling a BIOS-level routine directly. A call to BIOS Interrupt 13 for example, gives the program access to a host of specific disk services routines. Other BIOS-level interrupts can also be used for surreptitious system manipulations.

The virus can even bypass both the DOS- and BIOS-level routines and attack the hardware register ports directly. For example, the hardware address 300(h) is commonly used for many add-on boards. Attacks at this level will escape all software monitors that are looking for DOS- and BIOS-level routine calls.

Scrutinizing the relationship between antivirus software, viruses, and microcomputer resources makes the weaknesses of any type of protective software techniques readily apparent. All antivirus software depends on DOS and BIOS services to function. This dependency ranges from reading from the hard drive to displaying a warning of virus activity on the monitor. (Some antivirus software, such as activity monitors, monitor DOS and BIOS services for illicit system activity.)

Viruses are able to exert as much control over DOS and BIOS services as do the most sophisticated applications or users with keyboard access. Because a virus must remain covert to maximize damage, it usually depends on subversion of services and attempts to avoid user awareness of its activities. Viruses incorporate increasingly sophisticated capabilities designed to avoid detection by antivirus software. The dependency of antivirus software on DOS and BIOS services will always constrain its ability to detect and prevent viruses.

Most antivirus hardware, on the other hand, is not controlled by any code when in protective mode. The protection exists completely in hardware and cannot be manipulated by software. The protection or interception of commands and services exists at the lowest point in the data stream to the hard drive (after the hard drive controller). Because the antivirus hardware sits logically between the controller and the hard drive and is controlled by a physical switch, it is immune to software-initiated circumvention.

Having identified areas of vulnerability on the microcomputer, the next step is to incorporate protection mechanisms. The techniques being used to protect the microcomputer environment from these various exposures can be broken into two categories—software techniques and hardware techniques. It must be noted, however, that without addressing needed changes in corporate policies and procedures, the technological tolls will fall short of the required level of protection.

Established rules and guidelines for daily operations can dramatically enhance or severely degrade the degree of protection provided by any technology. For example, if an organization provided virus scanning software for all workstations but provided no guidelines for its use, the effectiveness of the scanning software would be significantly degraded.

Virus symptom recognition and user reaction is another area that should be addressed by clear policies and procedures. Without such procedures, users who detect erratic system behavior might only call for technical support after they are no longer able to operate the computer. By this point, they may have spread the infection to others and increased damage to their own systems.

SOFTWARE TECHNIQUES

The main software techniques used in commercial antivirus products are the antitamper integrity check, signature scanning, heuristic scanning, and activity monitoring. Some products on the market may use a combination of these techniques to provide a layered approach with diversified strategies. The latest of these also enforces basic policy so that all foreign media or reintroduced media must be scanned before it can be read by any microcomputer within the protected environment. This is accomplished through the use of an administrator or quarantine machine that writes an encrypted signature to the diskette after the diskette is scanned. This encrypted signature allows all computers in the protected environment to read and write to that diskette. Each time a diskette is written to by a computer outside the protected environment, the encrypted signature is erased. This forces virus scanning to occur the next time the diskette is read by a protected computer. This same process applies to all new diskettes and software applications.

Products using a combination of techniques in addition to forced scanning fall into a class of advanced software solutions that are called policy enforcement or clean system maintenance solutions.

Antitamper Integrity Check

The antitamper integrity check operates by creating a checksum or key for every file and directory. The checksum is then used to detect if a change has occurred to any of the files or directories. The methods for generating the checksum can range from such simple methods as a straight additive checksum to such exotic methods as a cyclic redundancy check or even a cryptographic checksum. (A cryptographic checksum prevents a virus from changing the file and the corresponding checksum file.)

The advantages of antitamper integrity checks are that program and data files can be protected without the need for prior knowledge of the assailant to detect changes to files and programs. Any change will be flagged.

The disadvantages of the antitamper integrity check include that the program must go through every program and directory to generate and evaluate the checksums, which can be time-consuming. In addition, the checksum files themselves can become targets of attack.

Checksum files can be defeated because checksums for commonly used fields (e.g., command.com) are known. A virus that initiates this type of attack is trying to surreptitiously infect a file. Attacks can be made rendering a valid but altered checksum or the checksum files can be deleted or replaced with new checksum files that hide the file corruption. Many antivirus programs generate checksum files with a known file extension that makes them easy to detect. Also, a checksum does not protect against a file that has already been infected; it will simply generate a valid checksum of the file with the virus in place. Despite these drawbacks, checksums can be useful as part of an overall software defense.

Signature Scanning

The signature scan technique scans for specific code combinations that may indicate that a virus is present. The software uses a list of known virus signatures that it then compares with all the files on the hard disk drive. Scanning software can only recognize the virus if the signature is known and programmed into the scanning software. (Therefore, such software must be regularly updated to be useful.) If a match is found, the user is notified that a virus may be present in the file.

The advantages of this technique are that a virus can be detected prior to execution of the program. The signature identifies the type of infection, which may make it possible for the user to reverse the damage of the infection or remove the virus.

The disadvantages of signature scanning are that it must be run in a clean DOS operating system and must itself be uninfected. The software must go through every file looking for all known signatures, which can be time-consuming. As the number of signatures increases, the possibility of false alarms also increases. In addition, constant software updates are required to keep up with new viruses.

Heuristic Scanning

Heuristic scanning is a technique used to increase the effectiveness of signature scanning. Heuristic scanning is employed as an integrated function performed during the signature scan. Heuristic scanning functions much the same as signature scanning in that it searches for strings of code. However, heuristics search for code strings historically prevalent in viruses. This allows them to detect polymorphic viruses that would be overlooked by a signature scan because of these viruses' ability to change or encrypt their signature when they execute.

Activity Monitoring

The activity monitor (also referred to as a behavior blocker) differs from the previously mentioned techniques in that the software is loaded in the background and monitors systems activity. If the application software executes an operation that the monitor considers suspicious, the monitor alerts the user of a possible virus attack. The advantage of this technique is that is can sometimes detect viruses that get by the scanners. The disadvantage of this technique is that it can be bypassed. The search criteria of the monitor may not be broad enough to catch all virus activity. If the monitor criteria is widened, the search would increase the number of false alarms. (Calls to technical support to investigate false alarms are a drag on productivity, which ultimately only encourages users to ignore such warnings altogether.) Because the monitor program resides in memory itself, it may also be subject to attack.

Policy Enforcement Software

This is the latest type of antivirus product to be developed. Policy enforcement (also referred to as clean system maintenance) software combines two techniques to provide a multilevel diversification of controls. At the first layer of protection, the user is forced to scan any diskette entering the environment, including diskettes that have been written to by a computer outside the environment. This is accomplished through the insertion of an encrypted authorization signature (as previously explained); the lack of this signature would prevent any computer in the protected environment from reading or writing to the alien diskette. If a user attempts to read an unscanned diskette, the computer will disallow the action until the user takes the diskette to a quarantine computer and performs a virus scan. This first layer of protection eliminates a large percentage of easily recognized viruses.

The second layer of protection is in the form of an activity monitor (behavior blocker) that is designed to stop some of the more sophisticated viruses that may elude the scanners.

Although the most secure of the software strategies, this combination of techniques also has weaknesses. The perimeter detection relies on a scanner running form the hard drive. This assumes a clean boot, a secure DOS operating system, and an uninfected antivirus scanner. Because this scan takes place on a quarantine or administrative computer that scans all incoming media, it is highly probable that infection will occur in this environment and therefore jeopardize the integrity of the scan.

The second layer of detection relies on the integrity of behavior blocking software that once again must be free of subversion and operate in a clean environment. Even if the behavior blocker is not infected, it always allows the user to disregard its warning and continue processing.

In summary, policy enforcement software provides a layered, diversified approach and enforces the scanning of all incoming diskettes. To be effective, DOS and the attendant antivirus software must be clean; even then these controls can still be subverted and circumvented.

HARDWARE TECHNIQUES

Four types of hardware techniques are currently available. They are boot-up protection, command monitoring, fencing, and sector-by-sector protection. The first two techniques do not involve protecting the actual physical drive. They sit logically on the microcomputer bus and perform the same operation that software does except in a hardware-protected state. The last two techniques are physical drive protection techniques. They sit logically between the hard disk controller card and the actual physical hard drive.

Command Monitoring and Boot-Up Protection

Command monitoring and boot-up protection are implemented in hardware. Depending on the vendor, these techniques may be incorporated into a single antivirus product.

Boot-Up Protection. Boot-up protection is implemented using a hardware board that plugs into a microcomputer bus slot and operates logically on the microcomputer bus. This board prevents a boot from the floppy disk drive, thereby eliminating a major source of infections. The advantage of this technique is that the board operates before the DOS bootstrap. The firmware on the board is executed before any floppy or hard disk drive access occurs.

The disadvantage of boot-up protection is that it only protects against a single avenue of attack. It offers no protection after the boot is complete.

Command Monitoring. This technique is implemented on a board that plugs into the microcomputer bus. This technique is basically a hardware implementation of the software activity monitor. The board monitors the microcomputer bus for suspicious activity. Because the implementation is in hardware, the monitor firmware routines do not reside in main memory, making them more difficult for viruses to attack. The disadvantages are the same as for the software activity monitor. The search criteria may be too narrow, causing viruses to be missed, or too wide, causing false alarms. Updates to the firmware are also more costly than its software counterpart.

Fencing and Sector-by-Sector Protection

The next two techniques involve protection of the actual hard disk drive. They are boards that sit logically between the hard disk controller card and the actual physical drive. The boards monitor all commands going out to the hard disk drive and physically intercept the commands that are not allowed (referred to as the command intercept technique). There is no way a command can bypass the board and no countermeasure to this physical command intercept. This protection is analogous to write protection using a write-protect tab on a diskette.

Fencing. The fence technique uses the physical protection offered by the command intercept function and divides a physical drive into two logical sections. One section is designated as read only. The other section remains read/write-enabled. The user defines the area under this fence and loads all files that need to be read only. The fence is lowered and from then on the files are only readable; all write operations are stopped.

The advantages of this technique include that it provides absolute hardware write protection. It is a proactive protection technique as opposed to a solely detective technique. Fencing is able to protect against new, stealth, and polymorphic viruses, and it can protect antivirus software from infection. Last, it ensures a clean boot of the operating system.

Its disadvantages are that the fence area is not easily reconfigured, and installation is complex and time-consuming. Raising the fence to update files can expose the entire partition to attack.

Sector-by-Sector Protection. Sector-by-sector protection enhances the fence technique by using a feature called independent random sector lock to write protect sectors individually. This capability allows for greater flexibility in file protection. Each sector is protected independent of all other sectors. This eliminates the primary weakness of fencing—the complex and time-consuming reconfiguration of the hard drive. There is no need to relocate files to a protected logical drive.

This type of protection has several advantages. It is proactive rather than reactive, and protects against new, stealth, and polymorphic viruses. It is "drop-in" compatible with existing partition configurations. Other advantages include:

- The protection is hardware-based.
- The independent random sector lock locks files in their existing address.
- A clean boot of the master boot record, DOS boot record, and file allocation tables is guaranteed.
- Antivirus software is protected from infection by specific antiviral-software-targeting viruses.

The disadvantages include that sector-by-sector protection does not prevent the "sneakernet" spread of infection to unprotected microcomputers. (Sneakernet—a shortened form of sneaker network—describes the manual transportation of diskettes from one computer to another.) It is also unable to determine if protected files are virus free or contaminated before they are protected. Sector-by-sector products are also relatively expensive.

Some sector-by-sector hardware products are offered with a feature called total write lock. With the turn of a keyswitch, total write lock will designate the unit's entire hard drive as read only. This feature may also be used to prevent modification to files when the units are left unattended.

COMBINING SOFTWARE AND HARDWARE TECHNIQUES

As noted, the software and hardware techniques presented in this chapter each contain distinct and unique advantages and disadvantages. To overcome the limitations of the various techniques, and to achieve the most effective protection from viruses and Trojan horse attacks, it is advisable to implement a solution that encompasses both types of techniques.

In a combined approach, software techniques should be used to achieve these objectives:

- Scan new applications for known and detectable viruses before they can be introduced in the system.

- Scan files before they are protected by hardware.
- Continually flag suspicious activity.
- Detect and prevent propagation of known and detectable viruses.

Hardware solutions, on the other hand, should be used to provide these services:

- Ensure a clean boot of the master boot record, DOS boot record, and file allocation tables.
- Protect sensitive files by means of physical intercepts.
- Stop unauthorized alterations to files or to the operating system.
- Protect against attacks that target hardware registers.
- Protect antivirus software from antiviral-software-specific viruses.

Antivirus countermeasures, as with any form of security, must be continuously measured by their effectiveness against changing threats. As malicious code changes, so too must the protective controls.

CONCLUSION

In summary, a diversified virus protection program should include:

- An ongoing awareness program for motivating participation and cooperation.
- Policies and procedures to guide behavior.
- A perimeter detection system consisting of at least two of the most effective scanners.
- An interior detection system consisting of a reliable activity monitor.
- Antivirus hardware to protect the operating system, antivirus software, security software, and other applications.

Ideally, policy enforcement software would be used to maximize the effectiveness of the antivirus program.

As this approach makes clear, users can no longer rely solely on software solutions to provide effective antivirus protection. Sole reliance on antiviral software exposes the organization to an unacceptable level of exposure. The only effective solution is continuous scrutiny by security professionals using a diversified set of antivirus controls.

VI-5

Countering Hacker Attacks

Ed Norris

===

THE TERM *hacker* means different things to different people. The author of the book *Prevention and Prosecution of Computer and High Technology Crime* defines hackers as computer criminals and trespassers who view illegal computer access as an intellectual challenge and a demonstration of technical prowess. *The New Hacker's Dictionary* offers a more benign definition: "A person who enjoys learning the details of computer systems and how to stretch their capabilities—as opposed to most users of computers who prefer to learn only the minimum amount necessary." Indeed, many people who consider themselves hackers would never attempt to gain unauthorized access to a computer or telephone system.

Regardless of their nomenclature, the problem of people breaking into computer and telephone systems is not new. Such activities have occurred since the first introduction of these technologies. As new technologies become available, it can be expected that new methods of obtaining unauthorized access to these technologies will be developed.

To protect their systems against unauthorized intrusion, IS managers need to understand hackers: who they are, what motivates them to break into systems, and how they operate. This chapter examines these issues, describes specific hacking techniques, and recommends actions that should be taken to reduce exposure to hacker attacks.

WHAT IS A HACKER?

Additional terms have come into use that define hackers by their area of expertise. For example, phreaks are hackers that target telephone systems. The terms *computer intruder* and *cracker* are also commonly used for computer hackers. This chapter modifies the definition from *The New Hacker's Dictionary*, adding that some hackers may attempt to gain unauthorized access to computer and telephone systems to achieve their goals.

A Hacker Profile

In the early 1980s, the hacker profile was of a highly intelligent, introverted teenager or young adult male who viewed hacking as a game; most were thought to be from middle- and upper-class families. Like most stereotypes, this profile has proved to be wrong. In reality, hackers can be very smart or of average intelligence, male or female, young or old, and rich or poor. And recent hacker arrests and convictions have taught hackers that, whatever they may have thought in the past, hacking is not a game.

To succeed, hackers need three things: motive, opportunity, and means. The motive may be increased knowledge, a joy ride, or profit. Many IS practitioners have the opportunity and means to hack systems but lack the motive.

The opportunity to hack systems has increased greatly over the years. Today, computer systems can be found everywhere. Hackers do not need state-of-the-art equipment to hack systems—used equipment is inexpensive and adequate to the task. Most companies allow some type of remote access by means of either dial-up lines or connections to external networks. For a relatively small monthly fee, anyone can have access to the Internet. Unfortunately many corporations provide opportunities to access their systems by failing to provide adequate security controls. And many hackers believe that the potential for success outweighs the possible penalties of being caught.

The means of attack is limited only by the imagination and determination of the hacker. A basic law of hacking can be summarized as "delete nothing, move nothing, change nothing, learn everything."

Some hackers target such entities as corporations, security and law enforcement personnel, and other hackers. Kevin Mitnick allegedly electronically harassed a probation officer and FBI agent who got in his way. Some hackers target organizations for political reasons. For example, the Chaos Computer Club supports Germany's Green Party. And others target any machine that runs an operating system capable of executing a particular virus, worm, or Trojan horse.

The estimates of the number of people involved in hacking vary greatly. Estimates range from about one hundred serious hackers to hundreds of thousands. No one really knows the number of people involved. Suffice it to say there are enough hackers to warrant taking precautions to prevent unauthorized access.

Hackers often use aliases, such as Shadow Hawk 1, Phiber Optik, Knight Lightning, Silent Switchman, Dark Avenger, and Rock Steady. These aliases allow hackers to remain anonymous while retaining a recognizable identity. And they can change that identity at any time simply by choosing another handle. For example, Shadow Hawk 1 is known to have also used the handles Feyd Rautha, Captain Beyond, and Mental Cancer. Changing handles is intended to confuse security personnel as to the identity of the hacker, which makes it more difficult to monitor hacker activity. A hacker may also want the targeted organization to think that several people are attacking the target. IS managers need to be aware of these methods of operation to understand the identity and the true number of hackers involved in an attack.

Hacker Clubs

Some hackers and phreaks belong to such hacker clubs as Legion of Doom, Chaos Computer Club, NuKE, The Posse, and Outlaw Telecommandos. These clubs give a sense of companionship, although most members never physically meet. More importantly, they help members work as a team toward common goals. By bringing together unique technical skills of individual hackers (e.g., specialties in UNIX or TCP/IP), these teams can achieve goals that might be out of reach for an individual hacker. Some hackers may also view membership in hacker clubs as demonstrating to the hacker and security communities that they are skilled members of an elite.

Hacker clubs come and go. The more willing the members are to contribute to club activities, the longer such clubs remain active. Hack-Tic and the Chaos Computer Club have been in existence for a relatively long time, whereas such groups as MAGIK (Master Anarchists Giving Illicit Knowledge) and RRG (Rebels' Riting Guild) lasted only a very short time.

Hacker Publications

Some hacker and phreak clubs produce publications. For example, the Legion of Doom produces *Phrack*, Phalcon/Skism produces *40Hex*, and the Chaos Computer Club produces *Chaos Digest*. In addition to providing technical information, the publications serve a social function. Some hacker publications can be received by means of electronic mail over the Internet; others are sent through the postal system. Some book stores and magazine stands sell *2600 The Hacker Quarterly*, which has been published for ten years. This publication periodically publishes a list of addresses of other hacker publications.

IS managers with access to the Internet should subscribe to the nonhacker publication *Computer underground Digest*. This electronic digest covers general issues related to information systems, as well as hacker- and security-related topics. It often provides pointers to other sources of hacker information. Searching these sources can help the security administrator learn about the ways hackers obtain knowledge. *Computer underground Digest* can be subscribed to by sending an electronic mail message to listservvmd.cso.uiuc.edu; the message should be sub cudigest your-name.

Hacker Conventions

Some hacker groups sponsor hacker conventions. For example, the Chaos Computer Club sponsors the Chaos Congress, Hack-Tic sponsors Hacking at the End of The Universe, and Phrack and the Cult of the Dead Cow sponsor Ho-HoCon. These conventions are held in the US and Europe. Hackers and phreaks, as well as security and law enforcement personnel, are featured speakers. The conventions are open to all interested parties.

Most of these conventions serve primarily as venues for hackers to brag, swap stories, and exchange information. They tend not to be highly organized; most substantive information is exchanged in hotel rooms and lobbies. There have been a few raids and some arrests at some conventions.

Bulletin Boards and Newsgroups

Hackers and hacker clubs primarily communicate by means of bulletin board systems. It is estimated that there are about 1,300 underground bulletin boards in the US. The information found on bulletin board systems is usually current and state-of-the-art. Timeliness of this information is important; hacker techniques described in print publications are usually already well known by the time they appear in print, and these published methods may no longer work.

Even old information can be valuable, however. The LOD (Legion of Doom) Communications is selling old bulletin-board system archives. Even though these message bases are from the mid-1980s, many organizations are still being successfully attacked using methods described in those files.

It can be difficult to gain access to an underground bulletin board. A hacker has to have been active for some time and shared valid information in the hacker community. Some bulletin boards even require background checks and references. As new members become more trusted among their peers, their level of access to sensitive information increases. Above-ground hacker bulletin boards usually grant access to anyone, and they may even invite security professionals to join the communications exchange. The telephone numbers for this type of bulletin board are sometimes published in the Internet newsgroup alt.bbs. Internet newsgroups are similar to bulletin board systems in that they allow people a vast forum for communication. Currently there are three active hacker newsgroups: alt.2600, de.org.ee, and zer.t-netz.blueboxing. The *Computer underground Digest* is also posted in the newsgroup comp.society.cu digest. The alt.2600 newsgroup is very active. Two other newsgroups that sometimes have information relevant in this arena are alt.wired and the Electronic Freedom Foundation's comp.org.eff.talk.

METHODS OF ATTACK

As technology has changed, so too have the challenges facing security professionals and IS managers. It is important to keep informed of the many methods of attack used by hackers. The following sections of this chapter describe some of the most popular techniques.

Social Engineering

Social engineering is used to describe techniques for getting someone to do something for an unauthorized individual. Hackers and phreaks are usually very adept at the art of social engineering. For example, a hacker may simply ask someone for help. He or she may not get the intended information, but the person asked will often provide at least some useful information. In one case, for example, an intruder told a guard that he needed access to an office because he had a report due on Monday; he went on to complain about having to work in the weekend. The guard accepted these facts and let him in without asking for his company identification or any other job-related information. The more sincere and knowledgeable the hacker sounds to the person being targeted, the more likely the hacker will get what he or she wants.

Knowledge can also be gained by many other methods: for example, by reading newspapers, magazines, and annual reports. An annual report might disclose the projects a corporation is pursuing and the people who are working on those projects. Reading Internet newsgroups may provide the hacker with a good idea of certain corporate projects; it may also let the hacker know which computer system is being used on which projects. Postings in newsgroups usually contain much useful information; telephone books or information can provide the hacker with a telephone number for the company. By assembling these various pieces of information, the hacker can appear as if he or she were an employee of the targeted company.

One hacker publication recommended that hackers write out a script before calling a target. The script should include the initial explanation, plus answers to questions that they might be asked.

Exhibit VI-5-1 illustrates how Internet newsgroups can reveal information useful to hackers. The newsgroup article in the exhibit tells the reader that John Smith is a geologist in the MIS department of Eastern Mining Corporation and that the company is located in New York. The phone number to reach John is 212-555-1234. John is using the computer system emcmis and his user ID is jds. Eastern Mining has access to the Internet and has (at least) outgoing file transfer protocol (FTP) service as well as news and incoming mail access. Last, John's current project involves geological surveys. There is enough information in this one message for someone to start a social engineering attack.

To help limit disclosure of at least some of this information, the IS manager might implement an application-level firewall to standardize the mail addresses to the corporation and other key access information.

Employees should also be made aware of social engineering and the ways to combat it. Because anyone can be the subject of such attacks, awareness programs should be directed to general employees as well as to systems operators and help desk personnel.

Employees should also be informed as to whom to notify if they believe someone is asking for information or requesting them to perform a task that is suspect. External requests for corporate information should be passed to a trained public relations department staffperson. Requests to perform a task should not be carried out until that person can verify who the caller is and if the caller is authorized to request that the task be performed. If the verification cannot be completed successfully, someone in the organization should be notified of the attempted intrusion. Often, what appears to be an isolated attempt at unauthorized access is part of a larger social engineering attack. If such an attack is detected, advisories should be sent to employees warning them to be on guard.

```
Newsgroups:   comp.programming
From:         jds@emcmis.emc.com (John Smith (Geologist - MIS))
Subject:      USGS Code ????
Reply-To:     jds@emcmis.emc.com
Organization: Eastern Mining Corporation
Date:         Fri, 6 May 1996 01:23:41 GMT
```

Does anyone out there know if it is possible to gain access to
the USGS (US Geological Survey) source code that I have seen
mentioned in journal, using the net.
If it is available on the net, can anyone provide me with a
site (or even better a list of sites) that I can access using ftp.

Thanks in advance ....

       John

John D. Smith   Eastern Mining Corporation
jds@emcmis.emc.com   Phone: 212-555-1234
                            New York, NY

Exhibit VI-5-1. Gathering Information from a Newsgroup Message

---

Dumpster Diving

Dumpster diving is a term used to describe the searching of garbage for information. Hackers frequently search dumpsters located outside of buildings for such information sources as operator logs, technical manuals, policies, standards, company phone books, credit card numbers, and dial-in telephone numbers, all of which might aid the hacker in gaining access to the organization.

IS managers should make employees aware that confidential material should be disposed of in accordance with the organization's security standards. After material is destroyed, it may be recycled as part of the regular recycling program.

Hardware and Software Tools

Hackers also rely on hardware and software tools for carrying out attacks. For example, phreaks use hardware devices to generate tones that allow them to navigate the various telephone switches and gain free phone access. These devices, referred to as boxes, are known by their color. For example, the red box is used to generate the coin tones used by pay phones. The newest type of red box makes use of Hallmark greeting cards that allow users to record a message; the phreaks use them to record coin tones. This is not the first time an innocent device has been used for illicit purposes; a whistle given away in Captain Crunch cereal boxes was used to generate the 2600 tone.

Many software tools are available on the Internet or on bulletin board systems. The most infamous is the war dialer. War dialers scan a telephone exchange

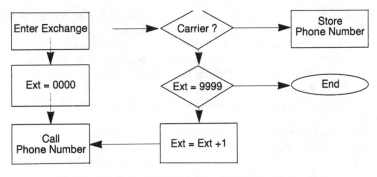

Exhibit VI-5-2. Logic of Simple War Dialer Program

looking for modem tones. When one is found, the modem phone number is saved. Software tools need not be complicated to be of use to hackers. Exhibit VI-5-2 illustrates the logic for a simple war dialer that requires only a few lines of code.

Although it is not possible to stop attempts to connect to a modem, unauthorized successful connections are very easy to stop. Modem access can be protected by means of strong passwords, tokens, or other mechanisms. The protection mechanism should have the ability to log access attempts. If the organization is experiencing many unsuccessful access attempts, it may be the target of a hacker or hacker group.

A war dialer expects a quick answer to its call. Some war dialers can be thwarted by increasing the number of rings before the modem answers the call.

One problem that has become widespread is use of unauthorized modems. Internal models can be purchased for under $30, well within the price range of an average employee. They are very easy to install in a PC workstation and can be used with the office phone line. The IS manager should conduct a periodic check of telephone numbers that belong to the corporation. A check against the list of authorized modems will detect use of any unauthorized modems.

Password crackers are another popular tool. With this approach, a hacker downloads a targeted password file (e.g., UNIX's /etc/passwd or Open VMS's SYS$SYSTEM:SYSUAF.DAT) to his or her computer and then attempts to crack the passwords locally. The hacker can do this without triggering any alarms or having to run through the log-in sequence. Six-character UNIX-based passwords have been cracked in less than an hour. If only lower-case letters are used in the password, the password can be cracked in less than one minute. It should be recognized that what is considered a strong password with today's technology may not be adequate a year from now.

Many intrusions succeed because of weak passwords. A security administrator can run a password cracker program against system authorization data bases to find vulnerable passwords. The IS manager should schedule and conduct such checks periodically. Anyone whose password is cracked should be instructed on how to select effective passwords. These persons should also be reminded that their failure to do so may jeopardize corporate assets.

Network sniffer software has also been used on the Internet to capture user IDs and passwords; TCP/IP packets were scanned as the packets passed through a node that a hacker already had under his control. (Some security professionals argue that use of Kerberos on the network cures the network sniffer problem, but this only protects the password when it travels between the Kerberos daemon and slave.)

The underlying problem presented by this hacker attack has to do with how the hacker was able to get control of one or more of the network nodes. Many corporations that have connected to the Internet fail to implement any security measures to counter the additional risk of public access. Any organization that plans to connect to the Internet should first install a firewall.

Firewalls are a collection of components placed between two networks. They have the following properties:

- All traffic in both directions must pass through the firewall.
- Only authorized traffic, as defined by the local security policy, is allowed to pass.
- The firewall itself is immune to penetration.

A firewall allows the organization to block or pass access to the internal and external networks based on application, circuit, or packet filtering.

In summary, the IS manager should be familiar with the types of hardware and software tools used to attack computer and communications systems. By searching the Internet, he or she should be able to find the same tools that hackers are using. These tools can be used to verify that the organization is adequately protected against them.

Reverse Intent

Reverse intent refers to a phenomenon in which an object that is intended to perform an action is used to perform the opposite action. For example, a deliberate reverse intent message might state: "This product is not to be used to increase the octane in gasoline." The message is intended to warn us that the use of the product is prohibited for the purpose of increasing octane levels, but it also discloses that the product is capable of boosting the octane rating.

Hackers and phreaks can use this to their advantage. Computer Emergency Response Team (CERT) advisories and Computer Incident Advisory Capability (CIAC) information bulletins are intended to notify people of security problems. They contain information about a given product, the damage that can occur from use or misuse of the product, the solution, and additional information. As illustrated by Exhibit VI-5-3, this information can be useful to hackers. In this exhibit, it is reported that Sun Solaris V2.x and SunOS V5.x have a security problem that gives local users the ability to gain root (full privilege) access. The local user can execute the expreserve utility that gives access to system files. If the computer system does not have expreserve disabled or the system administrator has not installed the patch solution provided by the vendor, the security of the

The Computer Incident Advisory Capability
INFORMATION BULLETIN
Solaris 2.x expreserve patches available

Number D-18
PROBLEM: The expreserve utility allows unauthorized access to system files.
PLATFORM: Sun workstations running Solaris 2.0, 2.1, and 2.2
           (SunOS 5.0, 5.1, and 5.2).

DAMAGE: Local users can gain root access.
SOLUTION: Disable expreserve immediately, then install patch from Sun.

Exhibit VI-5-3. Example of Reverse Intent

---

system may be compromised. If a hacker has access to a Sun workstation, the hacker can find out how to exploit this security exposure, either on his or her own or with the help of others.

It is important that the appropriate department within the organization receive security problem notification from software vendors. (Such notification should not be made to the purchasing department simply because it signed the check for the software.) CERT and CIAC information can be received by means of electronic mail over the Internet. Some vendors have their own advisory mailings over the Internet (e.g., *Hewlett-Packard Security Bulletin*).

IS managers should develop an action plan for installing security patches. The IS manager should also conduct a postmortem after the installation of security patches, noting which actions completed without problems and which actions did not. The action plan can then be adjusted to fix deficiencies and to reflect changes to the business environment.

In addition to obtaining information from advisories, hackers also seek out such sources of information as the system security manuals (or sections of other manuals) provided by software vendors with their products. These books are intended to instruct the system administrator on how to secure the product. Supplemental computer manuals found in almost every book store are another source for the hacker. A security manual might state: "Do not disable high-water marking on disk volumes." This statement tells a hacker that if one or more disks have disabled high-water marking, there is a potential problem to be exploited. In this case, the hacker may discover the art of disk scavenging and access the information contained in unallocated blocks.

Some professional organizations advocate sharing published security standards among their members. But it can be difficult to control the distribution of these standards, and they can also be used with reverse intent. The standards tell how a corporation secures its business. Many standards contain such sensitive information as group names, employee names and titles, phone numbers, electronic mailing address, and escalation procedures. A standard in the hands of a hacker becomes a powerful tool for social engineering.

It is impossible to stop reverse intent. Security practitioners must be aware of information that is available to hackers and ensure that they act appropriately according to the intent of the information. When an advisory or other piece of information reaches the security administrator, he or she should try to gauge how a hacker might use this information and modify his or her actions accordingly.

SECURITY MONITORING AND REVIEW

To stop a hacker, the IS managers must know when the hacker is knocking at the door or has already entered the system. Waiting until something has gone wrong may be too late. Auditing a system is more than turning on every auditable event, however. Security staff must monitor enough events to be able to detect an attack, but not so many that the audit information becomes unmanageable. Too much data tends not to be analyzed properly, and exceptions to normal behavior become more difficult to detect.

One of the first things a hacker attempts to do is delete the audit trail. Novice hackers may stop the audit processes and delete the entire audit data base; experienced hackers remove only their records from the data bases. If warranted, audit information should be printed directly to a hardcopy device or to a write-once storage device. The data should be analyzed on a regular basis with follow-up done on any suspect activity. Most hacker intrusions produce a few knocks on the door before a successful penetration takes place. It is easier to keep a hacker out than to recover after a successful intrusion.

CONCLUSION

It is important to understand how hackers navigate throughout the electronic world and how they attack systems. IS managers also need to understand the threats hackers pose to the organization and implement appropriate controls to counter those risks. The existing security program should also be monitored to ensure that it continues to be able to counter the risks created by hackers.

About the Editor

ROBERT E. UMBAUGH is principal consultant and head of Carlisle Consulting Group, an affiliated consulting firm specializing in productivity improvement in IS and the strategic application of technology. He is a consulting editor for Auerbach Publications and served for many years as chief information officer for Southern California Edison. As an adjunct professor of information systems at Claremont Graduate School (Claremont CA) and visiting lecturer at other schools, Umbaugh has helped educate many of today's IS managers. He can be reached at (717) 245-0825 or by mail at 700 West Old York Rd., Carlisle PA 17013.

Index